ALL THE POEMS OF STEVIE SMITH

by the same author
** available from New Directions*

poetry

A GOOD TIME WAS HAD BY ALL

TENDER ONLY TO ONE

MOTHER, WHAT IS MAN?

HAROLD'S LEAP

NOT WAVING BUT DROWNING

SELECTED POEMS

THE FROG PRINCE AND OTHER POEMS

TWO IN ONE

SCORPION AND OTHER POEMS

BEST POEMS *

fiction

NOVEL ON YELLOW PAPER *

OVER THE FRONTIER

THE HOLIDAY

drawings

SOME ARE MORE HUMAN THAN OTHERS *

editions

CATS IN COLOUR

THE BATSFORD BOOK OF CHILDREN'S VERSE

collections

ME AGAIN: UNCOLLECTED WRITINGS OF STEVIE SMITH

A VERY PLEASANT EVENING (SELECTED SHORTER PROSE) *

All the Poems of
STEVIE SMITH

edited and introduced by
WILL MAY

A New Directions Book

Published by arrangement with Faber & Faber
Manufactured in the United States of America
First published by New Directions in 2016
New Directions Books are printed on acid-free paper

Library of Congress Cataloging-in-Publication Data
Names: Smith, Stevie, 1902–1971, author. | May, William, 1982– editor.
Title: All the poems of Stevie Smith / [Stevie Smith] ;
edited, and introduced by Will May.
Other titles: Poems
Description: New York : New Directions, [2016]
Identifiers: LCCN 2015045653 | ISBN 9780811223805 (alk. paper)
Classification: LCC PR6037 .M43 2016 | DDC 821/.912—dc23
LC record available at http://lccn.loc.gov/2015045653

2 4 6 8 10 9 7 5 3 1

New Directions Books are published for James Laughlin
by New Directions Publishing Corporation
80 Eighth Avenue. New York 10011

for Rufus and Andrew

Contents

Acknowledgments xxiv

Introduction xxv

A Note on the Text xxxvii

Chronology xxxviii

A GOOD TIME WAS HAD BY ALL (1937)
The Hound of Ulster 3
On the Death of a German Philosopher 4
Papa Love Baby 5
Bandol (Var) 6
Egocentric 7
Alfred the Great 8
Heber 9
Mrs Simpkins 10
How far can you Press a Poet? 12
Forgive me, forgive me 13
Progression 14
To the Tune of the Coventry Carol 15
The Suburban Classes 16
Spanish School 17
Night-Time in the Cemetery 19
The Songster 20
Up and Down 21
From the Greek 22
Alone in the Woods 23
Intimation of Immortality 24
Infant 25
God and the Devil 26
Es war einmal 27
Dream 29
Numbers 31

From the County Lunatic Asylum 32
Barlow 33
Lament of a Slug-a-bed's Wife 34
The Bereaved Swan 35
Correspondence between Mr Harrison in Newcastle and
 Mr Sholto Peach Harrison in Hull 36
Nature and Free Animals 37
The Parklands 38
Eng. 40
Death Bereaves our Common Mother Nature Grieves for
 my Dead Brother 41
Aubade 42
Bag-Snatching in Dublin 43
The River Deben 44
Death Came to Me 46
No Respect 48
The Reason 49
I Like to Play with Him 50
Analysand 51
All Things Pass 53
Sunt Leones 54
I do not Speak 55
Lord Mope 56
Feminine Charm 57
To the Dog Belvoir 58
Never Again 59
Little Boy Lost 60
Does No Love Last? 62
Death of the Dog Belvoir 63
Angel of Grace 64
Freddy 65
Appetite 67
From My Notes for a Series of Lectures on Murder 68
Is it Wise? 69
This Englishwoman 70
Lord Barrenstock 71
Maximilian Esterhazy 73

What is the Time? *or* St Hugh of Lincoln 74
Major Macroo 75
Private Means is Dead 77
Bereavement 78
Death of Mr Mounsel 79
Who Killed Lawless Lean? 80
Road Up 82
Mrs Osmosis 83
The Fugitive's Ride 84
Suburb 87
Beware the Man 89
Breughel 90
The Blood Flows Back 91
Now Pine-Needles 92
Portrait (1) 93
Louise 94

TENDER ONLY TO ONE (1938)

Tender Only to One 99
O Happy Dogs of England 100
Darling Daughters 101
The Bishops of the Church of England 102
The Toll of the Roads 103
Eulenspiegelei 104
The Abominable Lake 106
One of Many 107
Death's Ostracism 108
The Boat 110
Parrot 111
The Doctor 112
I Hate this Girl 113
Infelice 114
Come, Death (1) 115
The Cock and the Hen 116
Silence and Tears 117
A Father for a Fool 119
Siesta 120

Brickenden, Hertfordshire 121
The Cousin 123
The Murderer 124
Mother, among the Dustbins 125
Le Désert de l'Amour 127
Portrait (2) 128
To a Dead Vole 129
Arabella 130
The Deathly Child 131
Reversionary 132
Dear Karl 133
In Canaan's Happy Land 135
Proud Death with Swelling Port 136
My Soul 138
In My Dreams 139
Noble and Ethereal 140
Dear Female Heart 141
How Slowly Time Lengthens 142
The Man Saul 143
The River Humber 145
La Gretchen de Nos Jours (1) 147
Nourish Me on an Egg 148
Dear Muse 149
Souvenir de Monsieur Poop 150
Vater Unser 152
Gnädiges Fräulein 153
The Friend 154
The Lads of the Village 156
Upon a Grave 157
Bye Baby Bother 158
The Photograph 159
'. . . and the clouds return after the rain' 160
Out of Time 161
'I'll have your heart' 163
Flow, Flow, Flow 164
The Children of the Cross 165
Fallen, Fallen 166
Rothebât 167

Look, Look 168
Tableau de l'Inconstance des Mauvais Anges 169
Will Ever? 170
Ceux qui luttent . . . 171
Suicide's Epitaph 172
Come 173
Little Boy Sick 174
The Violent Hand 175
Fuite d'Enfance 176

MOTHER, WHAT IS MAN? (1942)

Human Affection 181
A King in Funeral Procession 182
La Gretchen de Nos Jours (2) 184
Murder 186
Girls! 187
Where are you going? 188
Autumn 189
Poet! 190
Bog-Face 191
The Zoo 192
Advice to Young Children 194
The Face 195
If I lie down 196
The Sad Mother 196
Ah, will the Saviour . . . ? 197
Conviction (I) 198
Conviction (II) 198
Conviction (III) 199
Conviction (IV) 199
The Virtuoso 200
Villains 201
Le Majeur Ydow 201
The Little Daughters of America 202
She said . . . 203
Quand on n'a pas ce que l'on aime, il faut aimer ce
 que l'on a – 204

The Sad Heart 205
The Conventionalist 206
Study to Deserve Death 207
Dirge 208
La Speakerine de Putney 209
Distractions and the Human Crowd 210
Be off! 212
Love Me! 213
The Wild Dog 214
The Heavenly City 215
Lady 'Rogue' Singleton 216
Mother 217
My Heart was Full 218
Croft 218
Rencontres Funestes 219
The Film Star 220
The Bottle of Aspirins 221
The Governess 222
The Actress 223
The Devil-my-Wife 224
The Repentance of Lady T 225
The Smile 226
Forgot! 227
A Man I Am 228
The Broken Heart 229
The White Thought 230
In the Night 231
The Magic Morning 232
Après la Politique, la Haine des Bourbons 235
The Poets are Silent 236
The Pleasures of Friendship 237
Happiness 238
Lot's Wife 239
The Fool 240
Old Ghosts 241
Death in the Rose Garden 242
No More People 243

Hast Du dich verirrt? 244
Satin-Clad 245
Unpopular, lonely and loving 246
'Ceci est digne de gens sans Dieu' 247
When the Sparrow Flies 248
Voices against England in the Night 249
'N'est-ce pas assez de ne me point haïr?' 250
The Failed Spirit 251
The Sliding Mountain 252
The Recluse 253
'I could let Tom go – but what about the children?' 254
Christmas 255

HAROLD'S LEAP (1950)

The Roman Road 261
The Castle 262
To Dean Inge Lecturing on Origen 264
Behind the Knight 265
The Warden 266
Harold's Leap 267
A Mother's Hearse 268
Touch and Go 269
Man is a Spirit 271
Thought is Superior 272
The River God of the River Mimram in Hertfordshire 273
Cool as a Cucumber 275
The Orphan Reformed 276
A Shooting Incident 277
'Oh stubborn race of Cadmus' seed . . .' 281
The Ambassador 282
Persephone 283
Do Take Muriel Out 285
The Weak Monk 286
Le Singe Qui Swing 287
Pad, pad 288
The Broken Friendship 289
'Duty was his Lodestar' 290

The After-thought 291
The Wanderer 292
No Categories! 293
The Deserter 295
I rode with my darling . . . 296
God and Man 298
Mr Over 299
My Cats 300
Drugs Made Pauline Vague 301
Our Bog is Dood 302
Wretched Woman 304
Lightly Bound 305
Le Revenant 306
Friskers *or* Gods and Men 307
Cool and Plain 308
To School! 309
To an American Publisher 310
The Rehearsal 311
Death-bed of a Financier 312
The Hat 313
Thank You 314
The Ride 315
I Am 316
The Crown of Bays 317
Homage to John Cowper Powys 319
Little Child of Brightest Face 320
Our Office Cat 321
A Jew is Angry with his Friend who does not Believe in
 Circumcision 322
From the Coptic 323
A Humane Materialist at the Burning of a Heretic 325
In Protocreation 326
Do Not! 327
The Death Sentence 328
The Commuted Sentence 329
The Celtic Fringe 330
The Leader 332

Oh, If Only . . . 333
Who Shot Eugenie? 334
Full Well I Know 337
Voices about the Princess Anemone 338
Deeply Morbid 340
The Ghost of Ware 343

NOT WAVING BUT DROWNING (1957)

Not Waving but Drowning 347
The English Visitor 348
'What is she writing? Perhaps it will be good' 350
The Fairy Bell 351
The New Age 353
The Blue from Heaven 354
The Lady of the Well-Spring 357
The Queen and the Young Princess 359
A Dream of Comparison 360
My Hat 362
The Engine Drain 364
Saint Anthony and the Rose of Life 367
Anger's Freeing Power 369
Fafnir and the Knights 371
Songe d'Athalie 373
The Hostage 374
Away, Melancholy 377
Dido's Farewell to Aeneas 379
Childe Rolandine 380
The Jungle Husband 382
'Come on, Come back' 383
Why are the Clergy . . .? 385
I Remember 386
But Murderous 388
This is Disgraceful and Abominable 389
God the Eater 390
God the Drinker 391
Will Man Ever Face Fact and not Feel Flat? 392

Every Lovely Limb's a Desolation 393
A Dream of Nourishment 395
The Airy Christ 396
It Filled my Heart with Love 398
I. An Agnostic 399
II. A Religious Man 399
Dear Little Sirmio 400
'Great Unaffected Vampires and the Moon' 401
The Celts 402
The Passing Cloud 403
Loin de l'Être 405
Nipping Pussy's Feet in Fun 406
Cat Asks Mouse Out 406
My Cat Major 407
Parents 408
To a Lady in a Train 409
Adelaide Abner 410
The English 411
King Hamlet's Ghost 412
At School 413
Can it Be? 416
The Old Sweet Dove of Wiveton 417
The Past 419
The Singing Cat 420
Longing for Death because of Feebleness 421
My Heart Goes Out 422
Look! 423
Who is this Who Howls and Mutters? 425
Oh What is the Thing He Done? 426
Magna est Veritas 427
The Light of Life 428
In the Park 429
Evangelie, or The Figure of Literary Corruption, seeking
 Glory not Truth 432
Jumbo 433
The Choosers 434
The Occasional Yarrow 435
The Sorrowful Girl 437

The Starling 439
Die Lorelei 441
Farewell 442

SELECTED POEMS (1962)

Thoughts about the Person from Porlock 445
Thoughts about the Christian Doctrine of Eternal Hell 448
Recognition not Enough 450
Was He Married? 451
Was it not curious? 454
The Frozen Lake 455
Poor Soul, poor Girl! 458
From the French (1) 459
Admire Cranmer! 460
Votaries of Both Sexes Cry First to Venus 461
From the French (2) 463
I Was so Full . . . 464
From the Italian 465
God Speaks 466
Edmonton, thy cemetery . . . 467
My Muse 468

THE FROG PRINCE AND OTHER POEMS (1966)

The Frog Prince 471
Tenuous and Precarious 474
A House of Mercy 476
The Best Beast of the Fat-Stock Show at Earls Court 479
Exeat 481
Easy 482
Oh Christianity, Christianity 484
Why do you rage? 486
The True Tyrant *or* The Spirit of Duty Rebuked 487
Under Wrong Trees . . . *or* Freeing the Colonial Peoples 488
I had a dream . . . 489
Dear Child of God 492
The Wedding Photograph 494
Phèdre 495

Everything is Swimming 498
'The Persian' 499
Emily writes such a good letter 500
November 502
Monsieur Pussy-Cat, blackmailer 503
Si peu séduisante 504
To Carry the Child 505
Mutchmore and Not-So 507
The Last Turn of the Screw 509
Company 513
Saffron 514
Avondale 516
Avondall 517
Valuable 518
I Wish 520
The Listener 522
Hymn to the Seal 523
Fish Fish 524
Venus When Young Choosing Death 526
Lord Say-and-Seal 528
The Days of Yore 529
Pearl 530
Yes, I know 531
Widowhood or The Home-Coming of Lady Ross 532
Voice from the Tomb (1) 534
Voice from the Tomb (2) 535
Voice from the Tomb (3) 536
Voice from the Tomb (4) 536
Voice from the Tomb (5) 536
The Dedicated Dancing Bull and the Water Maid 537
Night Thoughts 539
Piggy to Joey 541
Pretty 542
The Small Lady 544
Animula, vagula, blandula 545
Friends of the River Trent 546
Is it Happy? 548

Watchful 551
How Cruel is the Story of Eve 556
The Story I Have Told 559
Fairy Story 562
Angel Face 563
The Grange 564
Mrs Arbuthnot 567
Magnificent Words 568
So can anger . . . 570
On Walking Slowly After an Accident 571
I am a girl who loves to shoot 572
I love . . . 574
Cœur Simple 575
Nodding 576
v. 578
A British Song 579
When the wind . . . 580
Northumberland House 582
The Crown of Gold 584
Why do I . . . 587
Some Are Born 588

SCORPION AND OTHER POEMS (1972)

Scorpion 593
Seymour and Chantelle *or* Un peu de vice 594
How do you see? 596
The Ass 602
A Soldier Dear to Us 605
The Forlorn Sea 608
Angel Boley 610
The Donkey 616
Cock-A-Doo 617
Francesca in Winter 618
So to fatness come 620
The Sallow Bird 621
When Walking 622
Her-zie 623

The Word 624
Nor We of Her to Him 625
Mrs Blow and Her Animals 626
Oh grateful colours, bright looks! 629
O Pug! 630
Archie and Tina 632
The Poet Hin 634
The House of Over-Dew 637
Oblivion 646
The Galloping Cat 647
Hippy-Mo 650
Hendecasyllables 652
Black March 653
Grave by a Holm-Oak 655
The Sea-widow 656
The Stroke 657
Come, Death (2) 658

APPENDICES
I UNCOLLECTED POEMS

'Casmilus' 661
'As falls the gravelled grouse' 661
Henry Wilberforce 661
From the Latin 662
Portrait of a Fool 662
Souvenir de Jacky Vandenbroeck 662
'The grief of an unquiet mind is a thing accursed' 663
Marriage I Think 663
Lulu 664
Death of Cold 664
Via Media Via Dolorosa 664
Sigh No More 665
Salon d'Automne 665
Sterilization 666
The Word 667
Landrecie 668
This Baronet 668

Swift to Depart 669
The Horror of the Midnight 669
The Angel 670
Revenge 670
Lift Thy Sad Heart 670
Flounder 671
The Pupil 671
Portrait 672
Left, Right 672
Ichabod 672
On Coming Late to Parnassus 673
A Portrait 673
The Horrible Man 673
The Octopus 674
As Sways 674
Portrait 675
Two Friends 675
'When I Awake' 676
'O Silent Visitation' 676
I Forgive You 677
'The Midwife' 677
'The Royal Dane' 678
O Lord! 678
The English 678
Beautiful 679
Why d'You Believe? 679
The Vision 682
Heartless 683
Silence 684
The Old Poet 685
I walked in the graveyard . . . 685
La Robe Chemise 686
From the French 687
The Holiday 687
When One 688
Miss Snooks, Poetess 689
Saint Foam and the Holy Child 689
B.B.C. Feature Programme on Prostitution 691

Pretty Baby 693
Our Doggy 693
My Tortoise 694
Have Done, Gudrun 695
William the Dog 695
Sapphic 696
The Hound Puss 697

II UNPUBLISHED POEMS

Northumberland Park (c.1936) 701
Fussy (c.1937) 701
Goodnight (1938) 702
Porgy Georgie (1938) 702
Father Damien Doshing (1938) 703
Bed (1938) 703
My Earliest Love (c.1938) 704
The Ballet of the Twelve Dancing Princesses (c.1939) 705
Song in Time of War (c.1947) 706
Mrs Midnight (1952) 707
They Killed (c.1953) 707
Professor Snooks Does His Worst with a Grecian
 Fragment (1957) 708
The Lesson (1957) 709
On the Dressing gown lent me by my Hostess the
 Brazilian Consul in Milan, 1958 (1958) 708
A Fiend (1962) 711
Le Paquebot (1962) 712
Voice from the Tomb (1966) 712
To the Brownes' Cat (1966) 713
To the Brownes' Hamster (1966) 713
Mort's Cry (1967) 714
Friend and Neighbour (1968) 714
The Publisher (1968) 715
Lord Henry de Bohon (1969) 715
The Stream with Two Faces (1969) 716
I thank thee, Lord (1969) 716
Soupir d'Angleterre (1969) 717

He preferred . . . (c.1970) 717
Like This (1) (c.1970) 717
Like This (2) (c.1970) 718
Telly-me-Do (c.1970) 718
Accented 719
Cars 719
César 720
Childhood and Interruption 721
Death 722
Mabel 723
'Mother Love' 723
None of the Other Birds 723
Oh Thou Pale Intellectual Brow 724
Roaming 724
Ruory and Edith 726
She got up and went away 726
The Easter Rose 727
The Little Birdies 728
The Old Soul 730
The Pearl 730
There is an Old Man 730
Tom Snooks the Pundit 731
Wife's Lament at Hereford 732

III TABLE OF CONTENTS FOR SELECTED POEMS, THE FROG
PRINCE AND OTHER POEMS, AND PENGUIN MODERN
POETS 8 733

IV LIST OF ALTERNATIVE TITLES 741

Notes 743

Index by Title 791

Index by First Line 798

Acknowledgments

The editor wishes to thank Jack Barbera and William McBrien, whose magisterial Smith bibliography made a challenging task possible; Hermione Lee, whose critical selection of Smith's work set an exceptional standard; and Frances Spalding, whose rich biography offered connections the archive could not reveal alone. James MacGibbon and Linda Stearns produced a fine edition in their original *Collected Poems*, and it proved a wise guide throughout the editing process. Smith's executor Hamish MacGibbon has been a supportive and judicious presence throughout.

Monika Class and George May both provided expert translations, and Kristen Marangoni kindly assisted me on a number of archival queries. The editor also wishes to thank the University of Southampton, which provided a grant to support archival work for the project, and staff at the McFarlin Library, University of Tulsa, for their unfailing generosity and good humour.

This project would not have been possible without the knowledge, guidance, and commitment of Matthew Hollis and Martha Sprackland at Faber, to whom I owe an immense debt. I am also grateful for the proofreading expertise of Laura Ashby, George May and Silvia Crompton. Any errors or inaccuracies are acknowledged here as the editor's.

Introduction

Rather a fishy thing to do –
And yet this is not wholly true.

<div align="right">'Flounder (Part of an Acrostic)'</div>

Like all great poets, Stevie Smith invites contradictions. Several poems play with the word 'easy', but are neither straightforward nor comfortable: 'easy in feeling' is 'easily excessive', we are reminded in 'To Carry the Child'. Smith is refreshingly no-nonsense, but her poetry sometimes flirts with it, as in the miniature above, which is designed to leave readers not wondering but floundering. She takes poetry seriously enough to risk not being taken seriously: it's no accident her poems are interested in those with more courage than is good for them, from the superfluous acrobatics of the cat in 'Can it Be?' to the stoic war veterans in 'A Soldier Dear to Us' who are too brave to ask 'if there was any hope'. She is often dogmatic, even indignant, and few modern poets make such use of imperatives and exhortations: we're asked to admire newspaper editors in 'Magnificent Words', honour penny-pinched fathers in 'Alfred the Great', or disparage the recent work of a French actress in 'Phèdre', sometimes with little room for disagreement. Yet Smith is compelled by the protean nature of truth, which is often made up of two opposing views, 'the one meanly begot, the other nobly' (p. 635), or couched in French euphemism, as in 'Loin de l'Être' and 'Si peu séduisante'. Philip Larkin borrowed the French term '*fausse-naïve*'[1] to equivocate about Smith's poetry in a 1962 review, but helped himself to her equivocations for *The Whitsun Weddings* (1964): the words 'not true' and 'unkind' in 'I Was so Full . . .'

[1] Philip Larkin, 'Frivolous and Vulnerable', *Required Writing: Miscellaneous Pieces 1955–1982* (London: Faber, 1983), p. 153.

become Larkin's 'words not untrue and not unkind'.[2] In Smith's autobiographical allegory poem 'A House of Mercy', the speaker conflates 'True' with some surprising adjectives:

> Now I am old I tend my mother's sister
> The noble aunt who so long tended us,
> Faithful and True her name is. Tranquil.
> Also Sardonic. And I tend the house.

If true tends towards the sardonic, we might begin to wonder if what we know about Smith is 'wholly true' or a good deal more 'fishy'.

Stevie Smith was born in Hull in 1902, moved to Palmers Green aged three, and lived there for the rest of her life. After school, she spent thirty years working at Newnes Publishing as a secretary to Sir Neville Pearson, and produced three semi-autobiographical novels and eight collections of poetry. The apparently narrow canvas of her life is, for many, part of her appeal: singer-songwriter Morrissey rhapsodises on a writer who 'appeared to live like a never-opened window',[3] while poet Amy Clampitt imagines 'a routine so settled that the tiniest subverting of the expected comes as a betrayal'.[4] While most dramatic representations of writers give us the misleading impression their life is more interesting than their work, Hugh Whitemore's play *Stevie* (1978) goes out of its way to suggest the opposite. We hear, through interrupted anecdotes, tales of an absconding father, a childhood battle with TB, and a failed suicide, yet much of this happens off-stage or before the play begins. Tales from school-days are recounted with Beckettian compulsion, as if memory might take the place of event. Potential lovers are undone by their

[2] Philip Larkin, 'Talking in Bed', *The Whitsun Weddings* (London: Faber, 1964), p. 29.
[3] Morrissey, *Autobiography* (London: Penguin, 2013), p. 87.
[4] Amy Clampitt, 'Stevie Smith: The Desolation of the Ordinary', *Predecessors, Et Cetera: Essays* (Ann Arbor: University of Michigan, 1991), p. 123.

suburban 'meelyoo', and death is the only welcome visitor. Yet Smith understood that a modern poet needed a persona, even if it was one that advertised its own marginality at every opportunity. While critics were both delighted and exasperated at her apparent idiosyncrasies, she countered them with shoulder-shrugging ordinariness: 'the poet is not an important fellow', she reminds us in the essay 'My Muse' (1960): 'there will always be another poet'.[5]

Another version of her life could equally cast her as a prolific book reviewer, a trenchant social critic, or a shrewd literary professional. At the height of her success in the 1960s, she was feted on both sides of the Atlantic, yet in interviews played the unconnected and isolated figure, ferried in from an unliterary suburb, trespassing on the modern day.[6] The editor who told her to 'go away and write a novel'[7] when faced with her unpublished poetry in 1935 offered better advice than he knew: *Novel on Yellow Paper* (1936), *Over the Frontier* (1938), and *The Holiday* (1949) gave her the opportunity to create the nearest the period could ever come to Wordsworth's *Prelude*. Her gift for self-fashioning turned Florence to Stevie in the 1920s, and then Stevie into Pompey Casmilus, the arch, brittle and conspiratorial protagonist of her first two novels. Hiding amongst the glittering conversational set-pieces of the first book (women's magazines, anti-Semitism, the ironies of staging Euripides at a girls' school) there is a poet eager for us to 'get the first look in'[8] at her work; Sylvia Plath's *The Bell Jar* (1963) would follow this example. In *Over the Frontier*, the spectre of war is accompanied by the anxieties of authorship and literary production. By the time we come to the plaintive Celia in *The Holiday*, the protagonist brings her

5 'My Muse', *Me Again: The Uncollected Writings of Stevie Smith*, eds. Jack Barbera and William McBrien (London: Virago, 1981), p. 126.
6 See Yvonne Thomas, 'A Polite Murder, Cookery, and Melancholy', *Evening Standard*, 3 December 1969, p. 22.
7 Stevie Smith to Hans Hausermann, 17 October 1957, University of Neuchâtel.
8 *Novel on Yellow Paper* (London: Virago, 1980), p. 25.

poems to life by recitation and performance. The question is no longer one of publication, but of posterity: a cancelled line in the manuscript confesses 'how these tunes bother me, how can I get them written down, and if I do not do that, when I am dead who will know how they should be sung?'[9] While Smith distanced herself from her novels later in her career, they alert us to the careful moves her poetry makes in situating her story. 'Reader, before you condemn, pause', she cautions in 'Infant', with a line that pauses, knowingly, after it has as good as condemned us. While lyrics like 'Not Waving but Drowning' can be flattened by biography, the cryptic allegory of 'The Crown of Gold' cannot be deciphered without it.

Smith is often remembered for her hymns to the suburbs, but once warned against 'letting [children] think it matters much *where* a writer lives',[10] and made her first novel's tutelary deity Hermes, the messenger god who speeds back and forth from the Underworld. 'To and fro'[11] is the most common co-ordinate in her work. Yet she is an inveterate chronicler of English places and their traditions. Her England is full of water, from the pashy ground of Lincolnshire and the Fenland drains to the rivers Yarrow, Deben, and Humber. While Britain is sometimes invoked in patriotic terms, her feelings are nationalist: she thought twice about publishing the anti-Welsh poem 'Soupir d'Angleterre', but not 'The Celts'. Her landscapes are sometimes fantastical, but those permitted to venture there are often her most pragmatic characters, like Joan in 'Deeply Morbid'. When the imagination becomes an unhealthy delusion, Smith is the first to disapprove: both 'Night Thoughts' and 'How do you see?' cast judgement on their troubled fantasists with the resigned understatement 'it is not good'.

[9] *The Holiday*, manuscript copy, The Stevie Smith Collection, Special Collections, McFarlin Library, University of Tulsa. Hereafter UT.

[10] 'Dear Spots', *New Statesman and Nation*, 17 May 1963, p. 766.

[11] See 'Up and Down', 'Little Boy Lost', 'The Deathly Child', 'Lot's Wife', 'A Shooting Incident', 'Le Singe Qui Swing', 'The Engine Drain', 'Cat Asks Mouse Out', and 'The Ballet of the Twelve Dancing Princesses'.

Contradictions abound, too, in the timbre of her poems. Early critics heard the visionary power of William Blake and Emily Dickinson alongside the epigrammatic comedy of Dorothy Parker and Ogden Nash.[12] Her work is distinctive, but it jangles with a range of voices and registers. She is pitch-perfect in her ventriloquism, whether voicing the distracted evasions of the English upper class, the self-satisfied entitlement of the literary critic, or even the harmless vanity of a preening bull. Not since Keats has English poetry had a voice that can make archaism so energetic (her closing rhyme of 'death/saith' at the end of 'The Bereaved Swan' is her affectionate gesture to 'The Eve of St Agnes'). Within a single poem, the same speaker might declaim 'Sepulchral ailment!' or complain about all the 'push and fuss' (p. 394). Yet these shifts are not just there for comic bathos: like Wallace Stevens, with whom Smith has more than a 'ho ho, thump thump' (p. 537) in common, her switches allow the possibility of seriousness. Her nomadic diction permits the solemn more often than the whimsical.

The range of Smith's poetic voice is matched by its polyphony. There are stoic dialogues, choruses, and chanting twins. Smith captivated 1960s poetry audiences by singing her poems to missionary hymns, self-penned drones, and folk ballads, but her musical range goes further: 'Death in the Rose Garden' is scored to Bizet, while 'The Dedicated Dancing Bull and the Water Maid' was inspired by Beethoven's horn and piano sonata. Like Smith's singing voice, the exchanges between Smith's speakers are uneven and off-kilter. Her poems are full of committed conversations, but often ones that turn on difference or mishearing:

> Struck by the shout
> That he may not know what it's about
> The deaf friend again
> Up-ends his hearing instrument to relieve the strain.

[12] See Patric Dickinson's introduction to *Scorpion* (London: Longmans, 1972).

What? Oh shock, ' "Pray for the Mute"?
I thought you said the newt.'
('In the Park')

Smith is most famous for the drowned man who goes unheard, but even the religious fanatics in 'Our Bog is Dood' find they 'never could agree'.

Her first collection includes a poem called 'Progression', and some of her greatest admirers have questioned whether her work really had any.[13] Although 1960s works such as 'The Last Turn of the Screw' and 'Watchful' marked a renewed interest in the long poem, a corpus that begins with an eerie trip to the pet shop and ends with a number of commissions to write children's animal poems does not tell the usual story. Her poems are haunted by the dangers of development deferred:

To carry the child into adult life
Is to be handicapped
('To Carry the Child')

We might read this psychological warning as authorial self-diagnosis. Yet the origins of individual poems challenge our understanding of chronology in more complicated ways. Some are Escher-like puzzles that seem to have been written before the idea for them came about: 'What is she writing? Perhaps it will be good' is Smith's only poem about a writer not worried about their reception, and yet it is one of her most self-conscious. 'Was it not curious?' constructs its central rhyme around Saint Aúgustin, only to conveniently remember in the final verse it has mistaken him for someone else:

Was it not curious of *Gregory*
Rather more than of Aúgustin?

[13] Seamus Heaney, 'A Memorable Voice', *Preoccupations: Selected Prose, 1968–1978* (London: Faber, 1984), p. 200.

It was not curious so much
As it was wicked of them.

Other poems disorientate us not with their synchronicity, but their gestation. 'Come on, Come back' begins its life in the 1920s as a draft called 'Incident in the Great War, 1991–7', but this futuristic vision of apocalypse is not completed for another thirty-five years, by which time a war as long as the one she imagined has come and gone. This is one of the many wormholes that war drills though Smith's work: the Trojan women quarrel to a soundtrack of 'we're here because, we're here because we're here' in 'I had a dream . . .'; a young Smith learns about trench warfare by reading Browning's 'Child Roland to the Dark Tower Came' in 'A Soldier Dear to Us'; while 'At School', a poem which introduces itself as a 'Paolo and Francesca' situation, is prompted by the Cold War. Smith's most topical poem, 'Angel Boley', explored the Moors Murders, but was also her most sustained attempt at a legend.

As these examples suggest, allusion is a tricky customer in Smith's poetry. The three roots most visible above ground are classical tragedy and epic (especially Dante, Euripides, and Racine), French symbolist poetry (Baudelaire, Mallarmé, Rimbaud), and the 'rag-bag' of quotations and biblical verse that came from school and home. Smith was brought up in the Palgrave's *Golden Treasury* tradition: Browning, Blake, Clare, Cowper, Shelley, Tennyson, and Wordsworth in particular. Yet her use of allusion flits between misremembered quotation and deliberate reversal; it's telling that 'Old Ghosts', a poem apparently about the burden of literary antecedents, makes very free and easy with its epigraph from De Quincey. In *Confessions of An English Opium-Eater* (1821), De Quincey praises a child for his ability to call up ghosts; Smith's misremembered quotation worries about whether they can be sent back. She removes the epigraph altogether for *Mother, What is Man?*, but reinstates a revised version in *Selected Poems*, now even more approximate. The poem is about being besieged by the past, but the allusion only asserts Smith's control. We find

similarly sharp-witted children throughout her work: 'The Orphan Reformed' suggests a poet more astute about placing themselves in a lineage than we have been:

> She looks at this pair and that
> Cries, Father, Mother,
> Likes these, does not like those,
> Stays for a time; goes.

The resemblance to Wordsworth's orphan-in-distress 'Alice Fell' (1807) beguiles us, and is meant to: her poetry claims then disavows kinships far and wide.

Sometimes Smith's poetic reversals are more deliberate, and more knowing. Tennyson rhapsodises 'The Dying Swan' (1830) in full-throated apostrophe, and Smith replies with the stubby monosyllables of 'The Bereaved Swan':

> The desolate creeks and pools among,
> Were flooded over with eddying song.
> (Tennyson, 'The Dying Swan')

> Wan
> Swan
> On a lake
> (Smith, 'The Bereaved Swan')

Romantic swansongs have their place, but more interesting to Smith are those left behind who have to 'go on'.[14] While the swansong risks self-indulgence and sentimentality, Smith's bereaved swan gives up the right to compassion. The voice of the abandoned is less grief-stricken than caustic.

Smith had little truck with poetic schools or movements, but chose her source material to place her in a wider tradition of wily

[14] See 'The Hostage', 'At School', 'Was He Married?', 'The Forlorn Sea', and 'The Galloping Cat'.

writers and writing: Coleridge's interruption by the Person from Porlock is revealed as an expedient excuse; an invented quotation about atheism by French novelist Jules Barbey d'Aurevilly prompts a poem about something-and-nothing in 'Ceci est digne de gens sans Dieu'; while 'Great Unaffected Vampires and the Moon' is written in response to a competition in *The Spectator* to introduce the title line, the line itself coming from a made-up poem in a spoof review by Hilaire Belloc.[15] Writers, like reformed orphans, are not averse to pulling the wool over our eyes when they have to. Sometimes, Smith is less allusive than she appears. One of her most celebrated poems, 'I Remember', seems to invoke Keats, Hardy, Larkin, and Edward Thomas, and was tellingly noted by an interviewer as being 'typical' of her style.[16] Yet she breezily dismissed it as a near transcription from Llewellyn Powys, and therefore could not claim to have written it (p. 761). Smith's poems are translations, reworkings, afterthoughts, disquisitions, interrogations, feelings recollected in anxiety. When we listen to them carefully, we hear not only the cadences of canonical Victorian verse, but also the fudged rhymes of Scottish child-poet Marjorie Fleming (p. 777), the quips of Billy Bunter (p. 766), or the ghost of a seventeenth-century French witch hunter (p. 751).

The furniture of Smith's poetry specialises in uncanny objects – plaster busts of dead mothers sitting on pianos, hats of surreal proportions, gas fires worthy of friendship, and toxic mushrooms. Her drawings are similarly disorientating. Sketches of enigmatic women look out from the page, like readers who have got there first but are unwilling to give up their secrets to us. Like her poetry, her drawings have eclectic starting points. Some are inspired by the epigrammatic underlines of Goya or the sketches of Georg Grosz, while others skirt closer to Edward Lear. While a few appear to be illustrations to the poems they accompany, many were added to her poems at proof stage or

[15] See 'Spectator Competition', *The Spectator*, 21 March 1952, p. 16, and Hilaire Belloc's *Caliban's Guide to Letters* (1903).
[16] Derek Parker to William McBrien, 19 September 1979, UT.

substituted for an apparently unrelated doodle, deliberately unsettling how we might understand a poem's speaker, tone, or addressee. As with her poems, they are as likely to put us on our guard as provide relief.

Her rhymes are also never quite at home: an early uncollected poem satirises a girl who

> only censures or approves
> In pompous hesitating sixth form syllables
> ('Portrait of a Fool')

The poem teases us for our tacit disapproval of the half-rhyme, and draws further attention to its excess of syllables. Sometimes Smith's most distinctive rhymes are hired out from her poetic ancestors. 'Suburb' warns us we will 'die remembering' when the time comes for our 'dismembering', which seems to be half-remembering Robert Browning's 'disemburdening' from 'Fra Lippo Lippi' (1855). Yet Smith's rhymes also wander far from home for other reasons: she delights in the rhyming antonym, and many of her drafts find her vacillating between two words close in sound but opposite in sense. 'Do Take Muriel Out' finds its protagonist led out by a 'deceiver' or a 'believer', depending on when Smith reads the poem, and to whom. The speaker in 'Look, Look' is either waiting 'happily' or 'impatiently'.[17]

Smith cares a great deal how her poems will be read, remembered, and sung, yet can be disarmingly off-hand about whether they've been published before, where the epigraphs might come from, or whether they should be collected in a book.[18] 'How do you see?', a poem specially commissioned by the *Guardian* in 1964, worried over the 'pious forgeries' interpolated into the Bible, yet saw fit to incorporate in full 'Oh Christianity,

[17] See poem drafts held at UT, and William May, *Stevie Smith and Authorship* (Oxford: Oxford University Press, 2010), pp. 106–7.
[18] See accounts in Spalding, *Stevie Smith*, p.252, and Jack Barbera and William McBrien, *Stevie: A Biography* (London: Heinemann, 1985), p. 241.

Christianity', a poem Smith had already published elsewhere. A faithless lover looks on with 'imperial carelessness' in 'Oh, If Only . . .': the phrase suggests the degree of authority Smith's apparent indifference might lend to her art. Both on the page and stage, Smith delighted in revising works for various audiences. A gathering of schoolchildren would prompt a careful reselection and rewriting of particular lines, although someone as clear-eyed about the savagery of infanthood as Smith often created her most uncompromising poems for her youngest audiences.[19] When selling individual poems to British and American newspapers, she changed words, titles or illustration to dodge copyright issues.[20] Putting together a new collection would then present her with the challenge of deciding between numerous versions of a poem. At times, her choices were pragmatic: which newspaper could supply the original illustration or copy first would determine which version made the proof. Yet she could be categorical, threatening to leave publishers when they refused to include drawings alongside her poems, as Diana Athill nearly found to her cost.[21] She adopted a series of postures towards her editors, from the author-in-distress, under siege from proliferating versions of poems and drawings, to the obstinate star-pupil. In truth, no writer was better served by choosing not to have an agent, a truth of which Smith was wryly aware.

Smith well understood the dangers a 'collected poems' might present for writers who dared to gamble with tone, rhyme and

[19] She describes the two versions of her poem 'The Donkey' when it is requested for a children's verse anthology by Anthony Thwaite: see correspondence dated 16 June 1969 in UT.

[20] 'Pretty Baby' was included in the US collection *The Best Beast* (Knopf, 1969) as a previously unpublished poem, though it had been published as 'Sweet Baby' in *The Sunday Times* (22 Dec 1968) and 'Pretty Baby' in *The Queen* (Christmas 1968).

[21] Smith threatened to renege on her contract with André Deutsch for *Not Waving but Drowning* (1957) unless Athill included drawings: see letter dated 22 November 1955, UT.

metre. While Smith would blanch at a reviewer comparing her to Thomas Hood, her 1940s radio programme on his collected poetry sounds a telling posthumous caution; 'certainly not a heavy volume in the intellectual sense, but be careful how you skip, you may miss something good, suddenly, unexpectedly'.[22] His 'all too faithfully collected' and 'unpruned' poems worry her lest readers take them in bad faith. Smith agonised over which poems and drawings to include in individual books or, more accurately, which to omit from them. While her most frequent rationale for exclusion was 'too light' or 'too sentimental',[23] she knew her particular poetic performance was a balancing act, and an off-rhyme in one poem might upset a clean quatrain on the following page. Yet other poems were denied book publication for more prosaic reasons: the *Observer* poetry editor had the only copy of her 1961 poem 'The Holiday', and a tight print deadline meant it never found its way into *Selected Poems* (1962). Mindful of these omissions, this edition includes unpublished and uncollected poetry in the appendix, including the sixty-four poems included in *Me Again* (1981).

There are more poems and drawings by Stevie Smith than can be contained in one book, and little sense from her own criticism that any poet is served well by having only one title in print. Her 1958 book of drawings and captions for Gabberbochus Press was entitled *Some Are More Human Than Others* (1958) and, of her own poems, she might be happy to say some are more collected than others.

WILL MAY

[22] Script for the programme 'Thomas Hood' for *Book of Verse, 87*, produced by John Arlott and broadcast on the BBC Eastern Service on 8 June 1946, held at the BBC Written Archives Centre, Reading.
[23] Stevie Smith to James Laughlin, 26 November 1963, UT.

A Note on the Text

Smith was clearest on editorial matters after seeing her poems in print, once decisions became errors. Several of Smith's personal copies of her books have emendations, as do the excised newspaper versions. While she never sent these post-publication versions to her editors, they were her reading editions for performances and broadcasts. As far as possible, these amended final versions have provided the source texts here. The punctuation in her first volume is very light, but when she began to perform her work she grew more concerned with how her poems might be misread, and punctuated accordingly. She revised a number of earlier poems for *Selected Poems, The Frog Prince and Other Poems*, and *Penguin Modern Poets 8*: I have followed the later version in each case, and note substantive variants.

The number of drawings included in each volume was often determined by Smith's publisher. When given the opportunity, she would include as many as she could, as in *The Frog Prince and Other Poems*. While this edition returns us to the layout and chronology of the original volumes, drawings that Smith added when republishing the poems have been included here. In a few instances, Smith removed earlier drawings, but the alternatives were substitutes rather than replacements, usually dictated by book make-up; all original drawings have been retained. Smith sometimes reused drawings for subsequent collections. In these cases, a note has been made.

Chronology

<table>
<tr><td>1902</td><td>Born on 20 September in Hull as Florence Margaret Smith to Charles Ward Smith (b.1872) and Ethel Spear (b.1876); her sister Ethel Mary Frances (Molly) was born in 1900</td></tr>
<tr><td>1905</td><td>Her father abandons them to work as a pantry boy on the White Star Line after his family business goes bankrupt</td></tr>
<tr><td>1906</td><td>Moves to 1 Avondale Road, Palmers Green, with her mother, sister and aunt, Madge Spear</td></tr>
<tr><td>1907</td><td>Contracts TB, and spends three years at a children's convalescent home in Broadstairs, Kent</td></tr>
<tr><td>1911</td><td>Attends Palmers Green High School; pupils are encouraged to recite Palgrave's Golden Treasury; wins literature prize in her final year and is given Thomas Carlyle's Sartor Resartus and On Heroes and Hero-Worship</td></tr>
<tr><td>1917</td><td>Follows her sister to North London Collegiate, although she does not receive a scholarship; the Smith family receive visits by soldiers convalescing in nearby Grovelands</td></tr>
<tr><td>1918</td><td>Florence is confirmed</td></tr>
<tr><td>1919</td><td>Her mother dies on 6 February, having suffered a heart attack</td></tr>
<tr><td>1920</td><td>Trains at Mrs Hoster's Secretarial Academy; by 1922, she has taken up her post as secretary to Arthur Pearson, the magazine publisher, and adopted the nickname 'Stevie'</td></tr>
<tr><td>1920s</td><td>Begins a period of sustained reading, and writes her first mature poems; these include 'Morbid Maltravers' (1924), 'The Everlasting Percy' (1925), and 'Huderina Elegans' (1925), a tribute to the American fantasy writer James Branch Cabell</td></tr>
<tr><td>1928</td><td>Her sister converts to Roman Catholicism; Stevie meets Karl Eckinger, a Munich student researching the Sonderbund War</td></tr>
<tr><td>1929</td><td>Travels to Germany, visiting Halle and Berlin in the period of economic crisis which saw the Nazi Party make its first major gains in power</td></tr>
<tr><td>1933</td><td>Begins seeing Eric Armitage ('Freddy' in Novel on Yellow Paper); she calls off their engagement, and he marries in 1935</td></tr>
</table>

1934 Sends poems to literary agency Curtis Brown; an anonymous reader finds them 'bitty' and 'so very ultra-1934'

1935 Ian Parsons from Chatto and Windus advises her to 'go away and write a novel' before they can consider her poems; she submits a manuscript by Christmas

1936 *Novel on Yellow Paper, or Work it Out for Yourself* published with Jonathan Cape ('Under the Haystack' and 'Pompey Casmilus' were both considered as titles); her poet-protagonist Pompey Casmilus links her name to Hermes, the messenger-god who can come and go freely from the Underworld; the book is an immediate critical and commercial success, and she begins a sequel

1937 Publishes *A Good Time Was Had By All*, which sells over 800 copies

1938 *Over the Frontier* published; begins her book reviewing career with work for *London Mercury*, *Life and Letters*, and *John O'London's Weekly*; starts work on a novel manuscript entitled 'Married to Death', which she abandons in 1939; publishes second volume of poetry, *Tender Only to One*, which sells around 400 copies

1940–1 Begins friendship with George Orwell and poet Mulk Raj Anand

1942 Publishes wartime poetry collection, *Mother, What is Man?* and begins work on *The Holiday*

1946 Embarks on an affair with Scottish-Canadian psychotherapist (known as 'Mary' in Frances Spalding's biography); *The Holiday* is rejected by Cape, and her friend Leo Khan unsuccessfully attempts to publish it (see 'The Crown of Gold')

1949 *The Holiday* is published by Chapman and Hall

1950 Publishes *Harold's Leap*; though reviewed well, it sells fewer copies than any previous volume

1951 Makes first BBC broadcast, 'Poems and Drawings'

1953 Makes unsuccessful suicide attempt at work, and is signed off with a full pension by Newnes

1954 Begins reviewing for the *Observer* and *The Spectator*; writes 'Not Waving but Drowning'

1957 Publishes *Not Waving but Drowning* with André Deutsch; renegotiates contract when Diana Athill objects to her drawings; gives her first poetry reading at the Oxford Union; delivers public lecture, 'The Necessity of Not Believing', at invitation of the Cambridge Humanists

1958 Publishes a book of drawings and captions with Gabberbochus Press entitled *Some Are More Human Than Others*

1959 Produces the radio play 'A Turn Outside', which imagines an interview with a mysterious interlocutor, eventually revealed as death

1962 Publishes *Selected Poems* with Longman, prompting a fan letter from Sylvia Plath

1964 James Laughlin publishes an American edition of *Selected Poems*, which draws praise from Marianne Moore and Ogden Nash

1965 Records an LP of poetry readings for Marvell Press

1966 Publishes *The Frog Prince and Other Poems* with Longman; included in *Penguin Modern Poets 8* alongside Geoffrey Hill and Edwin Brock; given the Cholmondeley Award for poetry

1968 Her aunt dies at 96 after a stroke

1969 Awarded the Queen's Medal for Poetry; Robert Gottlieb publishes *The Best Beast* in the US, choosing the title and selection; performs at the Poetry Society Gala Recital on 4 February with Basil Bunting, Ted Hughes, Brian Patten, and William Plomer; moves in with sister after Molly suffers a stroke

1970 Edits *The Batsford Book of Children's Verse* and begins work on *Scorpion* (published posthumously in 1972)

1971 Suffers from fainting fits and aphasia, later diagnosed as a brain tumour; dies on 7 March

ALL THE POEMS
OF STEVIE SMITH

A GOOD TIME WAS HAD BY ALL (1937)

The Hound of Ulster

Little boy
Will you stop
And take a look
In the puppy shop –
Dogs blue and liver
Noses aquiver
Little dogs big dogs
Dogs for sport and pleasure
Fat dogs meagre dogs
Dogs for lap and leisure.
Do you see that wire-haired terrier?
Could anything be merrier?
Do you see that Labrador retriever?
His name is Belvoir.
 Thank you courteous stranger, said the child.
 By your words I am beguiled,
 But tell me pray
 What lurks in the gray
 Cold shadows at the back of the shop?
Little boy do not stop
Come away
From the puppy shop.
For the Hound of Ulster lies tethered there
Cuchulain tethered by his golden hair
His eyes are closed and his lips are pale
Hurry little boy he is not for sale.

On the Death of a
German Philosopher

He wrote *The I and the It*
He wrote *The It and the Me*
He died at Marienbad
And now we are all at sea.

Papa Love Baby

My mother was a romantic girl
So she had to marry a man
 with his hair in curl
Who subsequently became my
 unrespected papa,
But that was a long time ago now.

What folly it is that daughters are always supposed to be
In love with papa. It wasn't the case with me
I couldn't take to him at all
But he took to me
What a sad fate to befall
A child of three.

I sat upright in my baby carriage
And wished mama hadn't made such a foolish marriage.
I tried to hide it, but it showed in my eyes unfortunately
And a fortnight later papa ran away to sea.

He used to come home on leave
It was always the same
I could not grieve
But I think I was somewhat to blame.

Bandol (Var)

Bandol (Var)
In the south of France, my dear,
Is full of the most awfully queer
Majors of the British Army, retired.

They live in boats tied up to the quay
(No income tax, no port dues here you see).

And they're always trying to buy or to sell each other things
And they hope what they lose on the roundabouts they'll make
 on the swings.

And they say
Quite in the best stage-army traditional way:
'England was quite a good place to live in before the War
Hawkahaw.'
They all seem to have got catarrh.

Bandol (Var)
How picturesque you are.

Egocentric

What care I if good God be
If he be not good to me,
If he will not hear my cry
Nor heed my melancholy midnight sigh?
What care I if he created Lamb,
And golden Lion, and mud-delighting Clam,
And Tiger stepping out on padded toe,
And the fecund earth the Blindworms know?
He made the Sun, the Moon and every Star.
He made the infant Owl and the Baboon,
He made the ruby-orbed Pelican,
He made all silent inhumanity,
Nescient and quiescent to his will,
Unquickened by the questing conscious flame
That is my glory and my bitter bane.
What care I if Skies are blue,
If God created Gnat and Gnu,
What care I if good God be
If he be not good to me?

Alfred the Great

Honour and magnify this man of men
Who keeps a wife and seven children on £2 10
Paid weekly in an envelope
And yet he never has abandoned hope.

Heber

I love little Heber
His coat is so warm
And if I don't speak to him
He'll do me no harm
But sit by my window
And stare in the street
And pull up a hassock for the comfort of his feet.

I love little Heber
His eyes are so wide
And if I don't speak to him
He'll stay by my side.
But oh in this silence
I find but suspense:
I must speak have spoken have driven him hence.

Mrs Simpkins

Mrs Simpkins never had very much to do
So it occurred to her one day that the Trinity wasn't true
Or at least but a garbled version of the truth
And that things had moved very far since the days of her youth.

So she became a spiritualist and at her very first party
Just to give her a feeling of confidence the spirit spoke up hearty:
'Since I crossed over dear friends' it said 'I'm no different to what
 I was before
Death's not a separation or alternation or parting it's just a
 one-handled door

We spirits can come back to you if your seance is orthodox
But you can't come over to us till your body's shut in a box
And this is the great thought I want to leave with you today
You've heard it before but in case you forgot death isn't a passing
 away
It's just a carrying on with friends relations and brightness
Only you don't have to bother with sickness and there's no
 financial tightness.'
Mrs Simpkins went home and told her husband he was a weak
 pated fellow
And when he heard the news he turned a daffodil shade of yellow
'What do you mean, Maria?' he cried, 'it can't be true there's
 no rest
From one's uncles and brothers and sisters nor even the wife of
 one's breast?'
'It's the truth,' Mrs Simpkins affirmed, 'there is no separation
There's a great reunion coming for which this life's but a
 preparation.'
This worked him to such a pitch that he shot himself through the
 head
And now she has to polish the floors of Westminster County Hall
 for her daily bread.

How far can you
Press a Poet?

How far can you press a poet?
To the last limit and he'll not show it
And one step further and he's dead
And his death is upon your head.

Forgive me, forgive me

Forgive me forgive me my heart is my own
And not to be given for any man's frown
Yet would I not keep it for ever alone.

Forgive me forgive me I thought that I loved
My fancy betrayed me my heart was unmoved
My fancy too often has carelessly roved.

Forgive me forgive me for here where I stand
There is no friend beside me no lover at hand
No footstep but mine in my desert of sand.

Progression

I fell in love with Major Spruce
And never gave a sign
The sweetest major in the force
And only 39.

It *is* Major Spruce
And he's grown such a bore, such a bore,
I used to think I was in love with him
Well, I don't think so any more.

It *was* the Major Spruce.
He died. Didn't I tell you?
He was the last of the Spruces,
And about time too.

To the Tune of the Coventry Carol

The nearly right
And yet not quite
In love is wholly evil
And every heart
That loves in part
Is mortgaged to the devil.

I loved or thought
I loved in sort
Was this to love akin
To take the best
And leave the rest
And let the devil in?

O lovers true
And others too
Whose best is only better
Take my advice
Shun compromise
Forget him and forget her.

The Suburban Classes

There is far too much of the suburban classes
Spiritually not geographically speaking. They're asses.
Menacing the greatness of our beloved England, they lie
Propagating their kind in an eightroomed stye.
Now I have a plan which I will enfold
(There's this to be said for them, they do as they're told)
Then tell them their country's in mortal peril
They believed it before and again will not cavil
Put it in caption form firm and slick
If they see it in print it is bound to stick:
'Your King and your Country need you Dead'
You see the idea? Well, let it spread.
Have a suitable drug under string and label
Free for every Registered Reader's table.
For the rest of the gang who are not patriotic
I've another appeal they'll discover hypnotic:
Tell them it's smart to be dead and won't hurt
And they'll gobble up drug as they gobble up dirt.

Spanish School

The painters of Spain
Dipped their brushes in pain
By grief on a gallipot
Was Spanish tint begot.

Just see how Theotocopoulos
Throws on his canvas
Colours of hell
Christ lifts his head to cry
Once more I bleed and die
Mary emaciated cries:
Are men not satiated?
Must the blood of my son
For ever run?
The sky turns to burning oil
Blood red and yellow boil
Down from on high
Will no hills fall on us
To hide that sky?
Y Luciente's pen
Traces the life of men
Christs crucified upon a slope
They have no hope
Like Calderon who wrote in grief and scorn:
The greatest crime of man's to have been born.
Dr Péral
In a coat of gray
Has a way
With his mouth which seems to say

A lot
But nothing very good to hear
And as for Doña Ysabel Corbos de Porcel
Well
What a bitch
This seems to me a portrait which
Might have been left unhung
Or at anyrate slung
A little higher up.

But never mind there's always Ribera
With his little lamb
(Number two-four-four)
To give a more
Genial atmosphere
And a little jam
For the pill –
But still.

Night-Time in the Cemetery

The funeral paths are hung with snow,
About the graves the mourners go
To think of those who lie below.
The churchyard pales are black against the night
And snow hung here seems doubly white.
I have a horror of this place,
A horror of each moonlit mourner's face,
These people are not familiar
But strange and stranger than strange, peculiar,
They have that look of a cheese, do you know, sour-sweet,
You can smell their feet.
Yet must I tread
About my dead,
And guess the form within the grave,
And hear the clank of jowl on jowl
Where low lies kin no love could save;
Yet stand I by my grave as they by theirs. Oh bitter Death.
That brought their love and mine unto a coffin's breadth.

The Songster

Miss Pauncefort sang at the top of her voice
(Sing tirry-lirry-lirry down the lane)
And nobody knew what she sang about
(Sing tirry-lirry-lirry all the same).

Up and Down

Up and down the streets they go
Tapping tapping to and fro
What they see I do not know

Up and down the streets they hurry
Push and rush and jerk and worry
Full of ineffectual flurry

Up and down the streets they run
From morning to the set of sun
I shall be glad when they have done

I shall be glad when there's an end
Of all the noise that doth offend
My soul. Night, don cloak, descend.

From the Greek

To many men strange fates are given
Beyond remission or recall
But the worst fate of all (tra la)
's to have no fate at all (tra la).

Alone in the Woods

Alone in the woods I felt
The bitter hostility of the sky and the trees
Nature has taught her creatures to hate
Man that fusses and fumes
Unquiet man
As the sap rises in the trees
As the sap paints the trees a violent green
So rises the wrath of Nature's creatures
At man
So paints the face of Nature a violent green.
Nature is sick at man
Sick at his fuss and fume
Sick at his agonies
Sick at his gaudy mind
That drives his body
Ever more quickly
More and more
In the wrong direction.

Intimation of Immortality

Never for ever, for ever never, oh
Say not aeonial I must for ever go
Sib to eternity, to confraternity
Of Time's commensurate multiples a foe.

Infant

It was a cynical babe
Lay in its mother's arms
Born two months too soon
After many alarms
Why is its mother sad
Weeping without a friend
Where is its father – say?
He tarries in Ostend.
It was a cynical babe. Reader before you condemn, pause,
It was a cynical babe. Not without cause.

God and the Devil

God and the Devil
Were talking one day
Ages and ages of years ago.
God said: Suppose
Things were fashioned in this way.
Well then, so and so.
The Devil said: No,
Prove it if you can.
So God created Man
And that is how it all began.
It has continued now for many a year
And sometimes it seems more than we can bear
But why should bowels yearn and cheeks grow pale?
We're here to point a moral and adorn a tale.

Es war einmal

I raised my gun
I took the sight
Against the sun
I shot a kite.

I raised my gun
I took the sight
A second one
I shot in flight.

I raised my gun
I shot a plover
I loaded up
And shot another.

Now round about me
Lay the dead
One more, one more,
Then home to bed.

Pray Heaven, said I
Send the best
That ever took
Lead to its breast.

Upon the word
Upon the right
Rose up a phoenix
Beaming bright.

I raised my gun
I took the sight
My lead unbarred
That breast of white.

Alas for awful
Magic art
The bullet bounced
Into my heart.

The phoenix bled
My heart can not
But heavy sits
Neath leaden shot.

Leave shooting, friend,
Or if you must
Shoot only what
Is mortal dust.

Pray not to Heaven
He stock your bag
Or you may feel
Your vitals sag.

Pray not to Heaven
For heavenly bird
Or Heaven may take you
At your word.

Dream

I came upon it in a dream
It was a sad and mournful scene
A mournfuller could not have been.

I rode my steed upon a plain
Against a bitter driving rain
So may I never ride again.

No man was there I rode alone
The icy wind cut to the bone
I came upon a funeral stone.

Deep in a yew tree grove it stood
And on its side were marks of blood
And at its foot the yellow mud.

I left the saddle, left my steed,
I went down on my hands to read
The tombstone's closely written screed, –

But oh from left and oh from right
Rang out a voice of ghostly might:
'Leave, lady, leave thy Leda light!'

The rain fell down with a heavy stroke,
I mounted up, my heart was broke.
I turned about and I awoke.

Numbers

A thousand and fifty-one waves
Two hundred and thirty-one seagulls
A cliff of four hundred feet
Three miles of ploughed fields
One house
Four windows look on the waves
Four windows look on the ploughed fields
One skylight looks on the sky
In that skylight's sky is one seagull.

From the
County Lunatic Asylum

The people say that spiritism is a joke and a swizz,
The Church that it is dangerous – not half it is.

Barlow

I'm growing much fonder of Barlow
And I think of him a lot
And sometimes I think I'm in love with him
And wish I was not.

For Barlow's my sister's fancy
The son of the Bishop of Bye
And if he should plump for the younger
That's me, the elder would die.

Oh I see by each curve and each wrinkle
Of each delicate lid of each eye
If Barlow should plump for the younger
The elder would certainly die.

Lament of a Slug-a-bed's Wife

Get up thou lazy lump thou log get up
For it is very nearly time to sup
And did the Saviour die that thou should'st be
In bed for breakfast, dinner lunch and tea?

The Bereaved Swan

Wan
Swan
On the lake
Like a cake
Of soap
Why is the swan
Wan
On the lake?
He has abandoned hope.

Wan
Swan
On the lake afloat
Bows his head:
O would that I were dead
For her sake that lies
Wrapped from my eyes
In a mantle of death,
The swan saith.

Correspondence between Mr Harrison in Newcastle and Mr Sholto Peach Harrison in Hull

Sholto Peach Harrison you are no son of mine
And do you think I bred you up to cross the River Tyne
And do you think I bred you up (and mother says the same)
And do you think I bred you up to live a life of shame
To live a life of shame my boy as you are thinking to
Down south in Kingston-upon-Hull a traveller in glue?
Come back my bonny boy nor break your father's heart
Come back and marry Lady Susan Smart
She has a mint in Anglo-Persian oil
And Sholto never more need think of toil.

You are an old and evil man my father
I tell you frankly Sholto had much rather
Travel in glue unrecompensed unwed
Than go to church with oily Sue and afterwards to bed.

Nature and Free Animals

I will forgive you everything.
But what you have done to my Dogs
I will not forgive.
You have taught them the sicknesses of your mind
And the sicknesses of your body
You have taught them to be servile
To hang servilely upon your countenance
To be dependent touching and entertaining
To have rights to be wronged
And wrongs to be righted.
You have taught them to be protected by a Society.
This I will not forgive,
Saith the Lord.
Well, God, it's all very well to talk like this
And I dare say it's all very fine
And Nature and Free Animals
Are all very fine,
Well all I can say is
If you wanted it like that
You shouldn't have created me
Not that I like it very much
And now that I'm on the subject I'll say,
What with Nature and Free Animals on the one side,
And you on the other,
I hardly know I'm alive.

The Parklands

Through the Parklands, through the Parklands
Of the wild and misty north,
Walked a babe of seven summers
In a maze of infant wrath.

And I wondered and I murmured
And I stayed his restless pace
With a courteous eye I held him
In that unfrequented place.

Questioning I drew him to me
Touched him not but with an eye
Full of awful adult power
Challenged every infant sigh.

'Of what race and of what lineage,'
Questioning I held him there,
'Art thou, boy?' He answered nothing
Only stood in icy stare.

Blue his eyes, his hair a flaxen
White fell gently on the breeze,
White his hair as straw and blue
His eyes as distant summer seas.

Steadfastly I gazed upon him
Gazed upon that infant face
Till the parted lips gave utterance
And he spake in measured pace:

'All abandoned are my father's
Parklands, and my mother's room
Houses but the subtle spider
Busy at her spinning loom.

'Dead my father, dead my mother,
Dead their son, their only child.'
'How is this when thou art living
Foolish boy, in wrath beguiled?'

'Ask me not,' he said, and moving
Passed into the distance dim.
High the sun stood in the heavens,
But no shadow followed him.

Eng.

What has happened to the young men of Eng.?
Why are they so lovey-dovey so sad and so domesticated
So sad and so philoprogenitive
So sad and without sensuality?
They love with a ci-devant feminine affection
They see in their dreams a little home
And *kiddies*
Ah the *kiddies*
They would not mind *having* babies:
It is unkind
Of Nature to lag behind.

Death Bereaves our Common Mother
Nature Grieves for my Dead Brother

Lamb dead, dead lamb,
He was, I am,
Separation by a tense
Baulks my eyes' indifference.
Can I see the lately dead
And not bend a sympathetic head?
Can I see lamb dead as mutton
And not care a solitary button?

Aubade

My dove, my doe,
I love you so,
I cannot will not
Let you go,
'Tis not the day lights yonder sky
It is too soon
I hear the cock's discordant cry,
He doodles to the moon.
It is not day
I say
It is the moon.

Alas, my love, it is the day,
Born twin to sun, but opening first
The womb of night.
There lies the day,
Her cheeks are gray,
Alas so soon it is the day.
And now in agony her dam will try
To bring forth sun, and in fulfilment die.
No easy birth is here,
Before our eyes
Night bleeds
And, born caesareanwise,
Her son in flaming gear
Comes forth and her succeeds.
Once more for man the heavenly twins are born,
Farewell, my love, adieu, it is the dawn.

Bag-Snatching in Dublin

Sisley
Walked so nicely
With footsteps so discreet
To see her pass
You'd never guess
She walked upon the street

Down where the Liffy waters' turgid flood
Churns up to greet the ocean-driven mud,
A bruiser in a fix
Murdered her for 6/6.

The River Deben

All the waters of the river Deben
Go over my head to the last wave even
Such a death were sweet to seven times seven.

Death sits in the boat with me
His face is shrouded but he smiles I see
The time is not yet, he will not come so readily.

But he smiles and I smile it is pleasant in the boat at night
There is no moon rising but from the east a light
Shines in the sky, is it dawn or dawn's twilight?

Over here the waters are dark as a deep chasm
Shadowed by cliffs of volcanic spasm
So dark so dark is the waves' fashion.

But the oars dip I am rowing they dip and scatter
The phosphorescence in a sudden spatter
Of light that is more actual than a piece of matter.

Up the Deben we row I row towards Waldringfield
It is a long way yet, my arms ache but will not yield
In this physical tiredness there is a happy shield.

Oh happy Deben, oh happy night, and night's companion Death,
What exultation what ecstasy is in thy breath
It is as salt as the salt silt that lies beneath.

Flow tidal river flow, draw wind from the east,
Smile pleasant Death, smile Death in darkness blessed,
But tarry day upon the crack of dawn. Thou comest unwished.

Death Came to Me

Death came to me and said
'Which will you choose?
Use one
Or all of these to summon me.
I'll come.'
And with a smile he'd gone.
There lay a knife
A labelled flask a gun.

I took the knife
Its cruel edge would bite
Into my flesh
Had I the resolution or the art
To bear the smart
And drive it to my heart?
Not I. I say
I love my flesh too much
For such
A way.

I took the flask and turned the label up –
Eastern Syrop – what a stirrup cup
For my short ride into eternity
And what a shame
To give a lordly drug so base a name
That better than this bottleful
Had decked a novelette by Mrs Hull.
For underneath the superscription lurked I knew
With pulses quickening and the blood thickening

For fear in every vein the deadly strychnine
It paralysed the heart at once they said, but I
Had not the heart to try.

I took the revolver in my hand and broke it open.
A Webley, service pattern, is a useful weapon
I liked it for the magazine chock-full
Of ammunition, liked the full
Shimmer of its barrel in the firelight's glimmer.
It had an air of quiet distinction lying there.
The handmaid of extinction
I snapped it to,
It weighed about a ton,
And two
Were on the trigger
Phew
I put it to my head
And now I'm dead.

No Respect

I have no respect for you
For you would not tell the truth about your grief
But laughed at it
When the first pang was past
And made a thing of nothing.
You said
That what had been
Had never been
That what was
Was not:
You have a light mind
And a coward's soul.

The Reason

My life is vile
I hate it so
I'll wait a while
And then I'll go.

Why wait at all?
Hope springs alive,
Good may befall
I yet may thrive.

It is because I can't make up my mind
If God is good, impotent or unkind.

I Like to Play with Him

I like to play with him
He would be so lovely to play with
He is so solemn sensitive conceited
He would be so lovely to play with
I could pretend
Say so-and-so and so-and-so
Watch his responses
How'd he take that today
And this tomorrow,
Mood, tense, you see
I'd conjugate His Inexcellency.

Oh on that evening you were
So charming enchanting touching
Lost wounded and betrayed
Oh that should have been only the beginning.

Analysand

He chases his tail
Like a puppy-fool
And wonders it tastes stale
The puppy-fool.

All thoughts that are turned inwards to their source
Bring one to self-hatred and remorse
Their punishment is suicide of course.

But first he'll tread
A calvary
From bed to bed
Of misery

And lying thinking on his bed of stone
No sleep will come to him he is alone
For evermore with every aching bone.

His spirit flags
His body slumps
His spirit nags
His mental dumps.

Self dedicated to self scrutiny
His every moment's an eternity
Of irritation and monotony.

For fuss and fret
His tears fall down

His brow is set
In savage frown.

Is it surprising Reader do you think?
Would you expect to find him in the pink?
Who's solely occupied with his own mental stink?

All Things Pass

All things pass
Love and mankind is grass.

Sunt Leones

The lions who ate the Christians on the sand of the arena
By indulging native appetites played what has now been seen a
Not entirely negligible part
In consolidating at the very start
The position of the Early Christian Church.
Initiatory rites are always bloody
And the lions, it appears
From contemporary art, made a study
Of dyeing Coliseum sands a ruddy
Liturgically sacrificial hue
And if the Christians felt a little blue –
Well people being eaten often do.
Theirs was the death, and theirs the crown undying,
A state of things which must be satisfying.
My point which up to this has been obscured
Is that it was the lions who procured
By chewing up blood gristle flesh and bone
The martyrdoms on which the Church has grown.
I only write this poem because I thought it rather looked
As if the part the lions played was being overlooked.
By lions' jaws great benefits and blessings were begotten
And so our debt to Lionhood must never be forgotten.

I do not Speak

I do not ask for mercy for understanding for peace
And in these heavy days I do not ask for release
I do not ask that suffering shall cease.

I do not pray to God to let me die
To give an ear attentive to my cry
To pause in his marching and not hurry by.

I do not ask for anything I do not speak
I do not question and I do not seek
I used to in the day when I was weak.

Now I am strong and lapped in sorrow
As in a coat of magic mail and borrow
From Time today and care not for tomorrow.

Lord Mope

What shall we say of this curious young man?
Scion of aristocracy sycophant of eld
Sitting at the feet of the old men because they are old
Warming his shivering behind at their gutted flame. . .
Brace up oh bunny heart, that man's no sage
Though the years heap on his head, be not deceived.
Each year is but a weight
To sky his empty pate
Nearer to heaven's gate
Nearer his god to him
(His god of prejudice and whim).
Oh fearful young man shivering ridiculously
What shall I say to give you heart oh poor young man?
No shield is in the old
Better to be young and cold
(Shivering ridiculously in your four-and-twenty years)
Better to be young, a Cry-baby, a Pet,
Than to be an old man, mouthing in a fret.
Better to be young and let the cold tears fall and ravage
Than to be an Old Boy, senile, simian and savage.

Feminine Charm

O never girl beneath the skies of Italy
Or maiden singing in the vales of Sicily
Or matron carding wool in Thessaly
Or skivvy washing up in Beverley
Gave man such joy as Bessie, Bessie Leigh,
Daughter of Mr and of Mrs Leigh.

To the Dog Belvoir

*whom I saw in a Dream Push Baby N. from
under a Brewer's Dray and Die in His Place*

The stricken Belvoir raised a paw and said:
I die a perfect gentle quadruped.

Never Again

Never again will I weep
And wring my hands
And beat my hands against the wall
Because
Me nolentem fata trahunt
But
When I have had enough
I will arise
And go unto my Father
And I will say to Him:
Father, I have had enough.

Little Boy Lost

The wood was rather old and dark
The witch was very ugly
And if it hadn't been for father
Walking there so smugly
I never should have followed
The beckoning of her finger.
Ah me how long ago it was
And still I linger
Under the ever interlacing beeches
Over a carpet of moss
I lift my hand but it never reaches
To where the breezes toss
The sun-kissed leaves above.
The sun?
Beware.
The sun never comes here.
Round about and round I go
Up and down and to and fro
The woodlouse hops upon the tree
Or should do but I really cannot see.
Happy fellow. Why can't I be
Happy as he?
The wood grows darker every day
It's not a bad place in a way
But I lost the way
Last Tuesday
Did I love father, mother, home?
Not very much; but now they're gone

I think of them with kindly toleration
Bred inevitably of separation.
Really if I could find some food
I should be happy enough in this wood
But darker days and hungrier I must spend
Till hunger and darkness make an end.

Does No Love Last?

I stand I fall
The depths appal
Upon my knees upon the bridge I fall.
Far down below
I see in fancy
My body spread
That in a frenzy
Down I cast.
'Tis broken now and bloody.
Does no love last?

Death of the Dog Belvoir

Belvoir thy coat was not more golden than thy heart
That beats no more
Now thy fled spirit
Delicate and suave
Thy virtue's core
Above the grave must soar.

Alas for baronet bereft
Of noble dog and left
To bear the mourner's part.

Let funeral smart
And dirge
Be all my song
And my song's urge
Ding dong.

For nobler heart beat never in more noble breast
And of beasts best
Thou with the least
In Death art dresst.

Farewell
Ding dong
Dear dog so ends my song.

Angel of Grace

I was talking one day
To a lady gay
When my Guardian Angel
Plucked me away:
Where can she be
Oh where does she wander
That lady of whom
I grow fonder and fonder?

Freddy

Nobody knows what I feel about Freddy
I cannot make anyone understand
I love him sub specie aeternitatis
I love him out of hand.
I don't love him so much in the restaurants that's a fact
To get him hobnob with my old pub chums needs too much tact
He don't love them and they don't love him
In the pub lub lights they say Freddy very dim.
But get him alone on the open saltings
Where the sea licks up to the fen
He is his and my own heart's best
World without end ahem.
People who say we ought to get married ought to get smacked:
Why should we do it when we can't afford it and have ourselves
 whacked?
Thank you kind friends and relations thank *you*,
We do very well as we do.
Oh what do I care for the pub lub lights
And the friends I love so well –
There's more in the way I feel about Freddy
Than a friend can tell.
But all the same I don't care much for his meelyoo I mean
I don't anheimate mich in the ha-ha well-off suburban scene
Where men are few and hearts go tumptytum
In the tennis club lub lights poet very dumb.
But there never was a boy like Freddy
For a haystack ivory's tower of bliss
Where speaking sub specie humanitatis
Freddy and me can kiss.

Exiled from his meelyoo
Exiled from mine
There's all Tom Tiddler's time pocket
For his love and mine.

Appetite

Let me know
Let me know
Let me go
Let me go
Let me have him
Let me have him
How I love him
How I love him.

From My Notes for a Series of
Lectures on Murder

It is not difficult to kill
Your enemy if you've sufficient will
But murderers are often in a hurry
And simply will not take the time to bury
The murderee. I'll indicate tomorrow
Just why this course is not for you to follow.

Is it Wise?

Is it wise
To hug misery
To make a song of Melancholy
To weave a garland of sighs
To abandon hope wholly?
No, it is not wise.

Is it wise
To love Mortality
To make a song of Corruptibility
A chain of linked lies
To bind Mutability?
No, it is not wise.

Is it wise
To endure
To call up Old Fury
And Pain for a martyr's dowry
When Death's a prize
Easy to carry?
No, it is not wise.

This Englishwoman

This Englishwoman is so refined
She has no bosom and no behind.

Lord Barrenstock

Lord Barrenstock and Epicene,
What's it to me that you have been
In your pursuit of interdicted joys
Seducer of a hundred little boys?

Your sins are red about your head
And many people wish you dead.

You trod the widow in the mire.
Wronged the son, deceived the sire.

You put a fence about the land
And made the people's cattle graze on sand.

Ratted from many a pool and forced amalgamation
And dealt in shares which never had a stock exchange quotation.

Non flocci facio, I do not care
For wrongs you made the other fellow bear:
'Tis not for these unsocial acts not these
I wet my pen. I would not have you tease,
With a repentance smug and overdue
For all the things you still desire to do,
The ears of an outraged divinity:
But oh your tie is crooked and I see
Too plain you had an éclair for your tea.

It is this nonchalance about your person –
That is the root of my profound aversion.

You are too fat. In spite of stays
Your shape is painful to the polished gaze;
Your uncombed hair grows thin and daily thinner,
In fact you're far too ugly to be such a sinner.

Lord Barrenstock and Epicene, consider all that you have done
Lord Epicene and Barrenstock, yet not two Lords but one,
I think you are an object not of fear but pity
Be good, my Lord, since you can not be pretty.

Maximilian Esterhazy

O Maximilian stern and wild
Wilt thou not look on me thy little child
Thy once so darling dear, so closely presst,
So cared for, so extravagantly dresst,
Raised up from nothing in thought to be
A furnished dwelling of felicity?
Now thou dost frown and all my walls descend
Like Jericho's and there is a swift end
Of comely donjon and of crested tops
Of flying buttresses and decorated props.
O never castle in the hills of Spain
Was half so much of nothing as thy Jane,
When thou dost turn away and no more look,
She is a song unsung, an unwrit book.

What is the Time?
or
St Hugh of Lincoln

What is the time, my limber lad,
What is the time, I pray?
I am old and blind
And weak in my mind,
But what is the time of day?

He took the youth by his golden hair
He dragged him up a crooked stair
Never more was *Hughie* seen,
Be warned, my child, while the grass is green.

Major Macroo

Major Hawkaby Cole Macroo
Chose
Very wisely
A patient Griselda of a wife with a heart of gold
That never beat for a soul but him
Himself and his slightest whim.

He left her alone for months at a time
When he had to have a change
Just had to
And his pension wouldn't stretch to a fare for two
And he didn't want it to.

And if she wept she was game and nobody knew it
And she stood at the edge of the tunnel and waved as his train
 went through it.

And because it was cheaper they lived abroad
And did he care if she might be unhappy or bored?
He did not.
He'd other things to think of – a lot.

He'd fads and he fed them fat,
And she could lump it and that was that.

He'd several boy friends
And she thought it was nice for him to have them,
And she loved him and felt that he needed her and waited
And waited and never became exasperated.

Even his room
Was dusted and kept the same,
And when friends came
They went into every room in the house but that one
Which Hawkaby wouldn't have shown.

Such men as these, such selfish cruel men
Hurting what most they love what most loves them,
Never make a mistake when it comes to choosing a woman
To cherish them and be neglected and not think it inhuman.

Private Means is Dead

Private Means is dead
God rest his soul,
Officers and fellow-rankers said.

Captive Good, attending Captain Ill
Can tell us quite a lot about the Captain,
If he will.

Major Portion
Is a disingenuous person
And as for Major Operation well I guess
We all know what *his* reputation is.

The crux and Colonel of the whole matter,
(As you can read in the Journal, if it's not tattered)

Lies in the Generals, Collapse, Debility, Panic and Uproar,
Who are too old in any case
To go to the War.

Bereavement

Maria Holt
Was not the dolt
That people thought her.
Her face was full
Her mind was not dull
She was my daughter.
She had so much to do so very much
And used to shuffle round upon a crutch,
The younger children always called her mother,
And so she was to sister and to brother
Poor wretch she's dead and now I am bereft
Of £60 each year to fill the place she left
I never paid a cent before; it is too bad,
It's worse to lose a lass than lose a lad.

Death of Mr Mounsel

I am dying Egypt dying
Keep my watch and send word home
Never mind about the funeral
Just a simple coping stone
Manly virtue needs no bushel
Baby hands that cling and tear
Better twenty years of Kathy
Than the fiend's own heart of fear
Solitude corrupting manners
Often has the tale been told
Memory paints a brighter pansy
Springing from the funeral mould
Let my grave with wrath no stranger
Visit not complaining come
Unmolested quit of danger
Quietly I slip hence and home
But when lights are glowing lower
Pressing downward through the gloom
And the porter shows the lady
To the first-class waiting-room
Then let every City Pretty –
You not least dear you not least –
Shed a tear for Mister Mounsel
Most unhappily deceased.

Who Killed Lawless Lean?

The parrot
Is eating a carrot
In his cage in the garret

Why is the parrot's
Cage in the garret?
He is not a sage
Parrot: his words enrage.

Downstairs
In his bed
Lies the head
Of the family
He is dead.

And the brothers gather
Mutter utter would rather
Forget
The words the parrot
Said.

When high in his cage swinging
From the lofty ceiling
Sat the pet screaming:
'Who killed Lawless Lean?'
It was not at all fitting.

So they put the parrot
In his cage in the garret
And gave him a carrot
To keep him quiet.
He should be glad they did not wring his neck.

Road Up

It seemed a curious place to rest one's body and take one's ease
Here in the very middle of Euston Road.
Now if it had been on the Thames' green bank, under poplar trees,
But here the traffic instead of the water flowed.
It was a British working man who lay full length on his back
And every now and then he turned and hit the road a thwack.
Was he dowser tapping for water I wonder,
Or was it a sudden spasm of rage that split his dreams asunder?

Mrs Osmosis

Mrs Osmosis
Is all right in small doses
Like what I was saying about Mrs Pale
There's a tell-tale
And for why?
Cos I blacked her eye
Last Fri –
day.
It don't sound natural to me
But they do say Mr P.
Well it all comes of her going with a fellow which ain't hardly
 so to say
Not that *he'd* cause to worry, seeing it was that way.

The Fugitive's Ride

Across the bridge across the dyke
Foresworn by friend and foe alike,
I ride
The field upon the further side
Stretches before me and its wide
Horizon dark against dark sky
Beckons me on. Dim homesteads lie
To left and right as I ride by.

It is a wet and steamy night,
More steamy night I have not seen,
More steamy night there has not been,
I have rode on for many a mile
And now it does not rain
And has not done for quite a while
And all the plain
Lies limpid underneath the stars
That give an eerie light
And make the plain seem to be bright.
With standing water, deep or shallow?
Deep lake, or river? Corn or fallow?
Lord, Lord, I cannot say
But warily I pick my way
This false starlight is worse than no light
To bewitch
The eyes and hide the gaping ditch.

What owl was that that howls upon
The trees athwart the stream
And have I been this way before
Or do I dream?
He seems to be a mournful one
That hoots to make a coward run
I hate to hear I hate to see
An owl that hoots so dismally
It makes my very blood run cold
No bird should dare to be so bold
I feel as fearful as he should
Who's done a dreadful deed of blood.

(Now hold up horse a moment pray,
Don't sidestep in that foolish way,
If you fall down upon the ground
There is a chance you will be drowned.)

A wetter plain I have not seen
A wetter plain there has not been
I say there has not been
A wetter plain
Since first I came
And may I die
If once again it does not rain.
In early dawn is this dark plain
Made darker still of darkness shorn
More dismaller but still the same
Lit by the ray that heralds day.

On my poor horse so lost so wan
That cannot understand
Why we must ride and ride and ride
And never yet come back home
On you must go until you drop
For since time won't, I dare not stop.

Suburb

How nice it is to slink the streets at night
And taste the slight
Flavour of acrity that comes
From pavements throwing off the dross
Of human tread.
Each paving stone sardonic
Grins to its fellow citizen masonic:
'Thank God they're gone,' each to the other cries
'Now there is nothing between us and the skies'.

Joy at this state transports the hanging heavens
And down to earth they rain celestial dew
The pavement darkly gleams beneath the lamp
Forgetful now of daylight's weary tramp.

Round about the streets I slink
Suburbs are not so bad I think
When their inhabitants can not be seen,
Even Palmers Green.
Nobody loves the hissing rain as I
And round about I slink
And presently
Turn from the sleek wet pavements to the utter slime
Where jerrybuilders building against time
Pursue their storied way,
Foundations and a pram,
Four walls and a pot of jam,
They have their sentries now
Upon a hundred hillocks.
Night watchman bad and old
Take rheumatism in exchange for gold.
Do you see that pub between the trees
Which advertises gin and cyclists' teas?
Down there I know a lane
Under the padding rain
Where leaves are born again
Every night
And reach maturity
In a remote futurity
Before dawn's light.
I have never seen
Anything quite so green
So close so dark so bright
As the green leaves at night.
I will not show you yet
Lest you should forget,
But when the time is come for your dismembering
I'll show you that you may die remembering.

Beware the Man

Beware the man whose mouth is small
For he'll give nothing and take all.

Breughel

The ages blaspheme
The people are weak
As in a dream
They evilly speak.

Their words in a clatter
Of meaningless sound
Without form or matter
Echo around.

The people oh Lord
Are sinful and sad
Prenatally biassed
Grow worser born bad

They sicken oh Lord
They have no strength in them
Oh rouse up my God
And against their will win them.

Must they lambs to the slaughter
Delivered be
With each son and daughter
Irrevocably?

From tower and steeple
Ring out funeral bells
Oh Lord save thy people
They have no help else.

The Blood Flows Back

The blood flows back behind my eyes
For fears I cannot recognise.

I stood upon the brink
And heard the clink
And clatter of my own thoughts.
Fear drove them on, the craven crew,
My soul was sick,
I knew it knew
For the first time
And saw
The thoughts that thronged its house
All fears and lies
All fears and craven subterfuge.
My soul was sick and wished to die.
Weeping its immortality
My soul stood there.

Ah me, ah me,
What use contempt and hate?
Myself is welded to a whole
And hidden thoughts must have their place
With Will and Soul.

Now Pine-Needles

Now pine-needles
You lie under the pine-trees
In the darkness of the pine-trees
The sun has not touched you
You are not brown because the sun has touched you
You are brown because you are dead.
The parent tree sighs in the wind
But it does not sigh for sadness
Only because the wind blows
The pine-tree sighs
Only because you are dead
You are brown.
Well, you do not know
That you were so and so
And are now so and so.
So why should I say
You were alive and are now dead
That your parent tree sighs in the wind?
I will sleep on you pine-needles,
Then I shall be
No more than the pine-tree
No more than the pine-tree's needles.

Portrait (1)

She was not always so unkind I swear
And keep this thought that's all I have of her
Who was upon a time my only thought and care.

Sweet memory hid from the light of truth
I'll keep thee, for I would not have thy worth
Questioned in Court of Law nor answer for it on my oath,

But hid in my fond heart I'll carry thee
And to a fair false thought I'll marry thee
And when thy time is done I'll bury thee.

Louise

Why is the child so pale,
Sitting alone in that sawny way
On an upturned valise
In a suburban sitting-room?
Louise,
Can't you give moma a smile?
Come and say How-do-you-do
To Mr Tease.

Why is the child so pale?
They have come overnight by rail
From Budapest;
Oh the poor child.

And the money has given out,
And they've telegraphed home for more,
And meanwhile they're having to stay
In a small-beerish way
With Mr and Mrs Tease, as I have said,
Of Harringay Park, instead
Of having a comfortable bed
At the Ritz.

The child is pale and precocious,
She knows all the capitals of Europe,
She knows all there is to know about Wagons-Lits
And First Class accommodation,
But she has never been long enough in any nation
Completely to unpack:

Always her thoughts are centred
On the nearest railway station.

Moma and nurse and Louise
A hatbox, a trunk, a valise,
And one was lost at Marseille.

　　'Oh if only I could stay
　　Just for two weeks in one place'
　　Thinks the child of the doleful face.

Moma has had a cup of tea,
She is feeling better
'Cheer up, girlie' she says
'I've a letter here from your poppa,
It will take him some time to raise the bucks . . .
Shucks, child,
Go and help nurse unpack,
We're here for two weeks at least
Then we leave for Athens and the Near East.'

In the suburban sitting-room
The poor child sits in a mazy fit:
Such a quick answer to a prayer
Shakes one a bit.

TENDER ONLY TO ONE (1938)

Tender Only to One

Tender only to one
Tender and true
The petals swing
To my fingering
Is it you, or you, or you?

Tender only to one
I do not know his name
And the friends who fall
To the petals' call
May think my love to blame.

Tender only to one
This petal holds a clue
The face it shows
But too well it knows
Who I am tender to.

Tender only to one,
Last petal's latest breath
Cries out aloud
From the icy shroud
His name, his name is Death.

O Happy Dogs of England

O happy dogs of England
Bark well as well you may
If you lived anywhere else
You would not be so gay.

O happy dogs of England
Bark well at errand boys
If you lived anywhere else
You would not be allowed to make such an infernal noise.

Darling Daughters

Darling daughters, listen to your mother,
I must go away and leave you to each other,
And one shall marry a rich man
And one shall go on an excursion to the Isle of Man
And one shall find her way home if she can.

The Bishops of the Church of England

I admire the Bishops of the Church of England
No man can be a Bishop of the Church of England
And a fool.
A man can be a Bishop of the Church of England
And a knave.
But
Fortunately
Few if any of the Bishops of the Church of England
Are men of ill will.
They do their best
To resolve wisely
To govern effectively.
They are the butt of the ignoramus,
Of the sentimentalist,
Of the man who makes
Of his own bad temper and incompetency
A Movement for the Amelioration of the Sufferings
Of the Oppressed Members of the Lower Middle Classes.

The Toll of the Roads

The angels wept to see poor Tolly dead
He was a harmless simple creature without a thought in his head.
Oh what is come upon him to make the road his death-bed?

Eulenspiegelei

To be so cold and yet not old
Oh what can ail the changeling child?
She has an eye that is too bold
Upon the night. She is beguiled.

The night is dark and the windowpane
Holds the rattle of the falling rain.
Oh look not forth but look within
Where the room lies safe from the stormwinds' din.

The tears upon the infant eyes
Are held in icy thrall
And when she speaks contrariwise
The rivven echoes fall:

Oh mother come not near me now
Nor lay thy hand on my cold cold brow
Few years if any heap on my head
But I am old as the newly dead.

Now louder far than the stormwinds' jar
And the voice of the mother and child
Is heard the scritch of the gravid bitch
That will be so wild.

Oh what can ail the gravid bitch
That howls upon the midnight stroke?
Dear mother dear I cannot say
Perhaps the devil gave her a poke.

The changeling child from her bed is gone
The mother weeps alone
And the stormwinds beat on the window pane
And mock the maternal moan.

Oh whither is fled thy changeling child
And by what witching craft?
It was the Eulenspiegel spake
And as he spake he laughed.

For well he knew that wrought it so,
The bitch and the changeling too
Are vanished away from the stormwinds' play
And the stricken mother's mew.

The Abominable Lake

Deep in the still mysterious waters of the lake a world lies
　　drowned.
How sombre and sad the silent world in the womb of the lake,
Not the reflection of Tellus, not the arch of heaven
But an earth and a heaven beyond the dominion of Time,
Beyond the soft sensual touch of the seasonal flow
And the inviolable sequence of midnight and noon.
Poor world, my heart breaks for your sealed inarticulate woe,
And the tears that are frozen in yours melt to flood in my eyes,
Overflow and descend and impinge on the waters of the lake,
And shatter at once the form of the silent world.
But the teardrops mingle, the waters shudder and close,
And again and again the sad world is revealed to my sight.
Then I know, and the knowledge transfixes my sensitive heart,
Not my tears, nor my prayers, nor my gold shall encompass
　　at last
A freedom unthought, manumission unhoped, undesired.

One of Many

You are only one of many
And of small account if any,
You think about yourself too much.
This touched the child with a quick touch
And worked his mind to such a pitch
He threw his fellows in a ditch.
This little child
That was so mild
Is grown too wild.

Murder in the first degree, cried Old Fury,
Recording the verdict of the jury.

Now they are come to the execution tree.
The gallows stand wide. Ah me, ah me.

Christ died for sinners, exclaimed the Prison Chaplain from
 his miscellany.
Weeping bitterly the little child cries: I die one of many.

Death's Ostracism

He stood in dream upon the brim
Of a deep sea, his mirth too young for him,
For all the people that he smiled upon
Cry: Fool. And they are gone.
With what hostility
And pride
They saw and fled.
He sighed.

The sea ran heavy on a core
Of hidden deep disturbance, ah before
The dream came had an earthquake first
The seabed burst.

Now from the depths
He sees
The sullied water rise.
All is disease.

And the long reaching waves swing wide,
Sick with death's taste upon the flooding tide,
And dead sea monsters with a deep appal
Of open wounds upon the water sprawl.

His foothold slips
The clay
Rank with long rains
Gives way.

But falling he will call the waves to friend,
Come cover over all and make an end.
No use, they will not do it, they swing aside.
Death's ostracism in a dream he must abide.

The Boat

The boat that took my love away
He sent again to me
To tell me that he should not sleep
Alone beneath the sea.

The flower and fruit of love and mine
The ant, the fieldmouse and the mole,
But now a tiger prowls without
And claws upon my soul.

Love is not love that wounded bleeds
And bleeding sullies slow.
Come death within my hands and I
Unto my love will go.

Parrot

The old sick green parrot
High in a dingy cage
Sick with malevolent rage
Beadily glutted his furious eye
On the old dark
Chimneys of Noel Park

Far from his jungle green
Over the seas he came
To the yellow skies, to the dripping rain,
To the night of his despair.
And the pavements of his street
Are shining beneath the lamp
With a beauty that's not for one
Born under a tropic sun.

He has croup. His feathered chest
Knows no minute of rest.
High on his perch he sits
And coughs and spits,
Waiting for death to come.
Pray heaven it won't be long.

The Doctor

You are not looking at all well, my dear,
In fact you are looking most awfully queer.
Do you find that the pain is more than you can bear?

Yes, I find that it is more than I can bear, so give me some bromide
And then I will go away for a long time and hide
Somewhere on the seashore where the tide

Coming upon me when I am asleep shall cover
Me, go over entirely,
Carry beyond recovery.

I
HATE
THIS
GIRL

I hate this girl.
She is so cold.
And yet her eyes say
She is not so good as gold.
I should like to kill her,
But what do I do?
Kiss her, kiss her,
And wish that she would kiss me too.

Infelice

Walking swiftly with the dreadful duchess,
He smiled too briefly, his face was as pale as sand,
He jumped into a taxi when he saw me coming,
Leaving me alone with a private meaning,
He loves me so much, my heart is singing.
Later at the Club when I rang him in the evening
They said: Sir Rat is dining, is dining, is dining,
No Madam, he left no message, ah how his silence speaks,
He loves me too much for words, my heart is singing.
The Pullman seats are here, the tickets for Paris, I am waiting.
Presently the telephone rings, it is his valet speaking,
Sir Rat is called away, to Scotland, his constituents,
(Ah the dreadful duchess, but he loves me best)
Best pleasure to the last, my heart is singing.
One night he came, it was four in the morning,
Walking slowly upstairs, he stands beside my bed,
Dear darling, lie beside me, it is too cold to stand speaking,
He lies down beside me, his face is like the sand,
He is in a sleep of love, my heart is singing.
Sleeping softly softly, in the morning I must wake him,
And waking he murmurs, I only came to sleep.
The words are so sweetly cruel, how deeply he loves me,
I say them to myself alone, my heart is singing.
Now the sunshine strengthens, it is ten in the morning,
He is so timid in love, he only needs to know,
He is my little child, how can he come if I do not call him,
I will write and tell him everything, I take the pen and write:
I love you so much, my heart is singing.

Come, Death (1)

Why dost thou dally, Death, and tarry on the way?
When I have summoned thee with prayers and tears, why dost
 thou stay?
Come, Death, and carry now my soul away.

Wilt thou not come for calling, must I show
Force to constrain thy quick attention to my woe?
I have a hand upon thy Coat, and will
Not let thee go.

How foolish are the words of the old monks,
In Life remember Death.
Who would forget
Thou closer hangst on every finished breath?
How vain the work of Christianity
To teach humanity
Courage in its mortality.
Who would not rather die
And quiet lie
Beneath the sod
With or without a god?

Foolish illusion, what has Life to give?
Why should man more fear Death than fear to live?

The Cock and the Hen

The Cock of the North
Has forgotten his worth
And come down south
In a month of drouth,
Woe for the Cock of the North.

The Cock of the Fen
Has forgotten his Hen
Has flown from his pen
And passed out of his ken,
Woe for the Cock of the Fen.

The Cock of the North
And the Cock of the Fen
Are one and the same,
And one is the bane
Of the Hen
Of the Cock of the North and the Fen
Who sits in a pen
Of forgotten worth
In a Fen in the North,
Woe for them both.

Silence and Tears

*A priestly garment, eminently suitable for
conducting funeral services in inclement weather.*
From a church outfitter's catalogue

The tears of the widow of the military man
Fell down to the earth as the funeral sentence ran.
Dust to dust, Oh how frightful sighed the mourners as the rain
 began.

But the grave yawned wide and took the tears and the rain,
And the poor dead man was at last free from all his pain,
Pee-wee sang the little bird upon the tree again and again.

Is it not a solemn moment when the last word is said,
And wrapped in cloak of priestly custom we dispose our dead,
And the earth falls heavy, heavy, upon the expensive coffin lined
 with lead?

And may the coffin hold his bones in peace that lies below,
And may the widow woman's tears make a good show,
And may the suitable priestly garment not let the breath of
 scandal through.

For the weather of their happening has been a little inclement,
And would people be so sympathetic if they knew how the story
 went?
Best not put it to the test. Silence and tears are convenient.

A Father for a Fool

to the tune 'Boys and Girls Come out to Play'

Little Master Home-from-School,
This is the Parkland you must rule.
What does it feel like to have a father for a fool?
Your father mortgaged the estate,
Lost his money, blamed fate
And shot himself through the head too late.
There's a father for a fool,
My little Master Home-from-School.

Why does Auntie wear such funny hats
And invert her sentences? Now that's
Positive proof she must be bats.
Why has Parker got all the horses out for me?
Why doesn't Ma meet the train as usually?
Here's hoping they give us shrimps for tea.

Little Master Home-from-School,
Your Ma lies dead, she lies too cool,
She's stone cold dead of a broken heart, the fool.
Jingle-jog the horses go,
And Parker's thinking what I know:
Here comes Master Home-from-School
That had a father for a fool.

Siesta

She went to bed
To doze,
And rose
To find that she was dead
How, no one knows.

Brickenden, Hertfordshire

Sitting alone of a summer's evening,
I thought
Of the tragedy of unwatered country.
O little village of Brickenden,
Where is thy stream,
Translucent drain of thy manorial sward?
Thy sward is green,
Its source of verdancy guessed but unseen.
Where is thy stream?
I have beat every bound of this wild wood.
I have trod down its spiteful and detaining undergrowth,
Seeking a broad stream and contented fish,
Seeking but finding not.
Now that the sun
Sou'westering in the sky
Tells me that evening is come,
I rest
Oppressed
By the wood's profligate viridity,
By thy wood's sap,
Child of a moisture that I cannot tap.

O woods of Brickenden, you have confounded me
By your appearance of humidity.
I see the pashy ground,
And round and round
My tired feet the rushes twine,
And frogs croak and the sweating slime

Is moved about by an ambiguous brood
Of low and legless life.
Hadst thou thy stream,
O wood of Brickenden,
This had been
Paradise.
But thy sap's virtue comes from dank earth's sweat,
And to be wet
Is not enough, O wood.
Hadst thou thy stream,
O little village of Brickenden,
Thy stream
Had salined thee
By virtue of destinatory sea,
And thou hadst been
A Paradise.
But lacking stream
Art but a suppuration of earth's humours.
Sitting alone on a summer's evening,
I wept
For the tragedy of unwatered country.
Take thou my tears, O Brickenden,
They are thy rank sweat's sea.

The Cousin

Standing alone on a fence in a spasm,
I behold all life in a microcosm.
Behind me unknown with a beckoning finger
Is the house and well timbered park. I linger
Uncertain yet whether I should enter, take possession,
 still the nuisance
Of a huge ambition; and below me is the protesting face
 of my cousin.

The Murderer

My true love breathed her latest breath
And I have closed her eyes in death.
It was a cold and windy day
In March, when my love went away.
She was not like other girls – rather diffident,
And that is how we had an accident.

Mother, among the Dustbins

Mother, among the dustbins and the manure
I feel the measure of my humanity, an allure
As of the presence of God. I am sure

In the dustbins, in the manure, in the cat at play
Is the presence of God, in a sure way
He moves there. Mother, what do you say?

I too have felt the presence of God in the broom
I hold, in the cobwebs in the room,
But most of all in the silence of the tomb.

Ah! but that thought that informs the hope of our kind
Is but an empty thing, what lies behind? —
Naught but the vanity of a protesting mind

That would not die. This is the thought that bounces
Within a conceited head and trounces
Inquiry. Man is most frivolous when he pronounces.

Well Mother, I shall continue to feel as I do,
And I think you would be wise to do so too,
Can you question the folly of man in the creation of God? Who
 are you?

Le Désert de l'Amour

I want to be your pinkie
I am tender to you
My heart opens like a cactus flower
Do you thinky I will do?

My heart is like a cactus
Not like a cactus flower
And I can kill love
Without entering her bower.

So they both thought. But he was silent and she said:
I cannot see which way you are pointing, the sky is so dark red,
And when the sandstorm is over I shall lie down on my bed.

Portrait (2)

My mother was Dutch
My father a Jew
And that is why I
Am so different from you.

I like to sit and pry and peer
And poke and watch the light of fear
Shine in your eyes
As I grow wise
And my sagacious fingers press
The very root and core of your distress.
Shall I make my fingers pause
Stay a while and turn and cause
The intellectual ray I so despise
Fade in your eyes,
Drowned by the tears that rise
Because my touch is wise?

To a Dead Vole

Now Vole art dead
And done is all thy bleeding.
Thy soul is sped
And all thy body's heeding
For daily bread
And comfortable bed
Has brought thee where there's no more thought of feeding,
And where the soil is thy last unappreciated quilt.

Arabella

White and yellow were the flowers
Shed on Arabella's bier.
Bright and mellow were the hours
Sped in which I called her Dear.
Oh my Arabella, why
Did you leave me here and die,
Leave me here beside your bier
To lick a salt and solitary tear?

The Deathly Child

The deathly child is very gay,
He walks in the sunshine but no shadow falls his way,
He has come to warn us that one must go who would rather stay.

Oh deathly child
With a heart of woe
And a smile on your face,
Who is it that must go?

He walks down the avenue, the trees
Have leaves that are silver when they are turned upon the breeze.
He is more pale than the silver leaves more pale than these.

He walks delicately,
He has a delicate tread.
Why look, he leaves no mark at all
Where the dust is spread.

Over the café tables the walk is going to and fro,
And the people smile and they frown, but they do not know
That the deathly child walks. Ah who is it that must go?

Reversionary

The Lion dishonoured bids death come,
The worm in like hap lingers on.
The Lion dead, his pride no less,
The world inherits wormliness.

Dear Karl

Dear Karl, I send you Walt Whitman in a sixpenny book.
'How dilettante', I hear you observe, 'I hate these selections
Arbitrarily made to meet a need that is not mine and a taste
Utterly antagonistic, wholly alien, egregiously coercionary
Of individualism's, egotism's, insolence's light-fingered
 traffickings.'
Put a leash on your indignation; hold it on a tight short leash,
Muzzle it in a tough criss-cross mesh of temporization and
 impartiality.
'God, I have no such dishonourable merchandise, such tinsel
 and tawdry in my shop window.'
So you say. Then borrow or steal a muzzle to muzzle your
 indignation,
A criss-cross wire mesh of temporization and suavity, and with
 a muzzled and leashed wrath
Hanging on your tapping heels: Listen.
If I had what hypocritical poetasters crocodilely whining call
 lucre and filthy,
But man, and it takes a man to articulate the unpalatable truth,
Means of support, if I had this and a little more,
I would give you Leaves of Grass, I would send
All of Walt Whitman to you with a smile that guesses it is
More blest to give than receive.
For I, I myself, I have no Leaves of Grass
But only Walt Whitman in a sixpenny book,
Taste's, blend's, essence's, multum-in-parvo's Walt Whitman.
And now sending it to you I say:
Fare out, Karl, on an afternoon's excursion, on a sixpenny
 unexplored uncharted road,

Over sixpennyworth of tarmac, blistered by an American sun,
 over irrupted boulders,
And a hundred freakish geology's superimpositions. Fare out on
 a strange road
Between lunchtime and dinner. Bon voyage, Karl, bon voyage.

In Canaan's Happy Land

Fair waved the golden corn
When I was stepping out,
And all the churchyard bells they rang
The day I turned about.

It's nice to get abroad,
It quickens and refines,
But now I find myself at home
My heart to peace inclines.

The bells ring for my friends
Who were untimely slain,
But I was luckier than they
And go my rounds again.

I take the cart I took,
I take another horse,
I sell my goods from door to door
And smother every curse.

Proud Death with Swelling Port

Proud Death with swelling port comes ruffling by,
He takes the worthy man and leaves the fond.
So many worthy men and they must die,
And all the foolish men stay still beyond
The shadow of Death's beckoning. O let *them* go
And save man's nobler sons and daughters from Death's blow.

Thou wilt not do it, Lord, still wilt thou take
First fruits of our integrity and strength,
Tithes of our wisdom thou wilt have, and make
Our loftiest sons sink to a coffin's length.
O spare them Lord, take toll of lesser men,
For it is certain *they* will come again.

Men of great moral stature are not born
So easily as men of lesser worth.
But in the steep captivity forlorn
Of Time's entrail they slowly draw to birth.
After such long gestation, hast no ruth
To eat them up on the first flower of youth?

O spare our nobler sons and daughters, give
Them space to grow and feel their sinews' might
And hearts' full beat. O Father, let them live
Throughout life's day, and in the cool of Night
That is the cloak of natural death take them away.
But while the song is up still let them stay.

My Soul

In the flame of the flickering fire
The sins of my soul are few
And the thoughts in my head are the thoughts of a bed
With a solitary view.
But the eye of eternal consciousness
Must blink as a bat blinks bright
Or ever the thoughts in my head be stilled
On the brink of eternal night.

Oh feed to the golden fish his egg
Where he floats in his captive bowl,
To the cat his kind from the womb born blind,
And to the Lord my soul.

In My Dreams

In my dreams I am always saying goodbye and riding away,
Whither and why I know not nor do I care.
And the parting is sweet and the parting over is sweeter,
And sweetest of all is the night and the rushing air.

In my dreams they are always waving their hands and saying
 goodbye,
And they give me the stirrup cup and I smile as I drink,
I am glad the journey is set, I am glad I am going,
I am glad, I am glad, that my friends don't know what I think.

Noble and Ethereal

Noble and ethereal he sped upon his way,
And never Bishop blithe as he about the meadows gay.
He thought upon the Saviour's blood so freely spent for him,
And with a thankful heart he trod about the river's brim,
There for a moment, stood at stare, with meditative eye
He saw within the limpid stream the fishes hurry by.
And all Creation seemed to him a tranquil joyous song
Where never plain had place at all or spite of Ancient Wrong.
He savoured that sweet moment's pause, all Heaven in a day,
And knowing yet his hour not come, he bravely turned away.

Dear Female Heart

Dear Female Heart, I am sorry for you,
You must suffer, that is all that you can do.
But if you like, in common with the rest of the human race,
You may also look most absurd with a miserable face.

How Slowly Time Lengthens

How slowly time lengthens from a hated event.
In my youth I was humiliated in a guilty association –
Insinuator, flatterer, Board of Trade Surveyor, hypocrite,
Aha, Hildreth Parker, how have the years dealt with you?

The Man Saul

The man Saul
Is very tall.
He stands at the cross-bar where the shadows fall.

He stands in the shadows, he is a shadowed man,
God haunted since he first began,
God daunted, now he is looking very wan.

Deep are the furrows on his brow.
He stands like the figurehead at a ship's prow.
This ship has been wrecked a long time now.

Shadowed Saul, I am sorry for him.
He is the victim of a God's whim.
He was exalted and now he is cast down, now he is very dim.

And only for the memory of a glory
That was not his, they tell the story.
Ah, he must clench his hands so tight his nails are grown gory.

Blood flows beneath his finger nails,
Blood is beating in his head, he rails.
But for all his vaunt he knows that all within him fails,

Fails and grows faint and turns to death.
He is betrayed from within, there is no thought beneath
That crowned crest that does not pant upon last breath.

I am sorry for Saul,
There is no help for him at all.
He stands where the shadows fall.

The River Humber

No wonder
The river Humber
Lies in a silken slumber.

For it is dawn
And over the newly warm
Earth the mists turn,

Wrapping their gentle fringes
Upon the river where it hinges
Upon the perfect sleep of perfected images.

Quiet in the thought of its felicity,
A graven monument of sufficiency
Beautiful in every line the river sleeps complacently.

And hardly the dawn distinguishes
Where a miasma languishes
Upon the waters' farther reaches.

Lapped in the sleeping consciousness
Of its waves' happiness
Upon the mudbanks of its approaches,

The river Humber
Turns again to deeper slumber,
Deeper than deeps in joy without number.

La Gretchen de Nos Jours (1)

Would he might come
Again and I
Upon his breast
Again might lie.

Would I had not
In foolish wrath
Driven him ever
From my path.

Would that the sun
His day's course over,
Might that same day's
Lost dawn recover.

As vain as this
Vain prayer are all
Vain prayers that would
Past days recall.

Never shall sun
Now sunk away
Rise up again
On yesterday.

Never shall love
Untimely slain
Rise from the grave
And live again.

Nourish Me on an Egg

Nourish me on an Egg, Nanny,
And ply with bottled stout,
And I'll grow to be a man
Before the secret's out.

Nourish me on an egg, Nanny,
With bottled stout to drink,
And I'll grow to be a man
Before you can think.

Nourish me on an egg, Nanny,
Don't wring your hands and weep,
Bring me a glass of stout,
And close my eyes in sleep.

Dear Muse

Dear Muse, the happy hours we have spent together.
I love you so much in wet or fine weather.
I only wish sometimes you would speak louder,
But perhaps you will do so when you are prouder.
I often think that this will be the next instant,
Meanwhile I am your most obliging confidante.

Souvenir de Monsieur Poop

I am the self-appointed guardian of English literature,
I believe tremendously in the significance of age;
I believe that a writer is wise at 50,
Ten years wiser at 60, at 70 a sage.
I believe that juniors are lively, to be encouraged with discretion
 and snubbed,
I believe also that they are bouncing, communistic, ill mannered
 and, of course, young.
But I never define what I mean by youth
Because the word undefined is more useful for general purposes
 of abuse.
I believe that literature is a school where only those who apply
 themselves diligently to their tasks acquire merit.
And only they after the passage of a good many years (see above).
But then I am an old fogey.
I always write more in sorrow than in anger.
I am, after all, devoted to Shakespeare, Milton,
And, coming to our own times,
Of course
Housman.
I have never been known to say a word against the established
 classics,
I am in fact devoted to the established classics.
In the service of literature I believe absolutely in the principle of
 division;
I divide into age groups and also into schools.
This is in keeping with my scholastic mind, and enables me to
 trounce

Not only youth
(Which might be thought intellectually frivolous by pedants) but
 also periodical tendencies,
To ventilate, in a word, my own political and moral philosophy.
(When I say that I am an old fogey, I am, of course, joking.)
English literature, as I see it, requires to be defended
By a person of integrity and essential good humour
Against the forces of fanaticism, idiosyncrasy and anarchy.
I perfectly apprehend the perilous nature of my convictions
And I am prepared to go to the stake
For Shakespeare, Milton,
And, coming to our own times,
Of course
Housman.
I cannot say more than that, can I?
And I do not deem it advisable, in the interests of the editor to
 whom I am spatially contracted,
To say less.

Vater Unser

to the tune of the 'Londonderry Air'

Vater Unser,
Du Der im Himmel wohnst,
Behold thy child,
His prayers and his complaint.
He was conceived
In sin and born to set it on,
This sin is his,
His strength to act upon.
Oh, Father, heed
Thy child, let not the grave
Seal him in sin
Beyond they power to save.
Strike at his strength,
Leave weakness only for her vaunt,
Vater Unser,
Du Der im Himmel wohnst.

Gnädiges Fräulein

In the cold light of morning she was looking rather queer,
In the cold light of morning, with a ribbon round her hair,
And her youth lay behind her a long time for many a year.

For when she was young, they took her love away
And sent him to work, beyond the Mexique Bay,
And she thought of him and lost her wits and now her hair is gray

With an, Oh, if I think of him he'll come again to me,
And an, Oh, it was but a whim that took him o'er the sea;
And an, Oh, for all my eyes are dim they can look lovingly.

The Friend

We needs must love the highest when we see it,
And having seen it knowing lower flee it.
But whither flee
Exiled from bliss
In these sad days
Of nothingness,
Shall we,
Trailing the tired wing of happier flights,
Hemmed in by lower presents mourn past heights,
And in a phrase
Of bitterness
Throw
All our woe?
No, gentle soul,
If fate and all the world have wronged thee,
And every spectre of despite has thronged thee,
Keep fast
Thy visionary past,
A part of present's whole
And but a part.
Thus happiness

And grief in thy stout heart
Shall range thee higher than th'angelic bands
Who know bliss but no smart
And serve
With happy but not midnight clenched hands
A lower place deserve.
But thou of present depth and former height
Has highest height attained and needst no flight.

The Lads of the Village

The lads of the village, we read in the lay,
By medalled commanders are muddled away,
And the picture that the poet makes is not very gay.

Poet, let the red blood flow, it makes the pattern better,
And let the tears flow, too, and grief stand that is their begetter,
And let man have his self-forged chain and hug every fetter.

For without the juxtaposition of muddles, medals and clay,
Would the picture be so very much more gay,
Would it not be a frivolous dance upon a summer's day?

Oh sigh no more: Away with folly of commanders.
This will not make a better song upon the field of Flanders,
Or upon any field of experience where pain makes patterns the
 poet slanders.

Upon a Grave

to the tune 'Upon a bank in the greenwood as I lay'

Upon a grave
In the churchyard as I lay,
An angel out of heaven
Came to me and he did say:
Your child is dead,
He singeth far away,
In Death is sorrow shed,
In Death is sorrow shed.

I raised my head
And mournfully I cried:
My son is dead
I was with him when he died.
He lies alone,
And worms his flesh divide.
In life is sorrow known,
In life is sorrow known.

Bye Baby Bother

Bye Baby Bother
Where is your brother?

They so-and-so and so-and-so
And twisted his guts
In a nasty way
Because he said they were nuts.

Bye Baby Bother
How shall I keep them from your pother?

I will be quiet now, Mother, but when there is a general
 mobilization
Dozens of chaps like me will know what to do with our
 ammunition.

Dozens by hundreds will be taken and torn,
Oh would the day had died first when you were born.

The Photograph

They photographed me young upon a tiger skin
And now I do not care at all for kith and kin,
For oh the tiger nature works within.

Parents of England, not in smug
Fashion fancy set on a rug
Of animal fur the darling you would hug,

For lately born is not too young
To scent the savage he sits upon,
And tiger-possessed abandon all things human.

'. . . and the clouds return after the rain'

to the tune 'Worthy the Lamb'

In a shower of tears I sped my fears
And lost my heavy pain,
But now my grief that knew relief
Is sultried o'er again.

Of leaf and flower of that first shower
No memories remain.
The clouds hang down in heavy frown
But still it does not rain.

Happy the man of simple span
Whose cry waits on his pain,
But there are some whose mouths are dumb
When the clouds return again.

Out of Time

It is a formal and deserted garden
With many a flower bed and winding path.
A cupid stands and draws a bow at venture
Upon a marble bath.

All round his feet the eager ivy grows,
Stretches upon the stone, above the ground,
And in the ivy flowers the busy bee
Makes a melodious sound.

The air is ponderous with summer scents
And still it lies upon the garden all
As still and secret as it stayed upon
A funeral.

The sun shines brightly in the upper air
And casts his beams upon the garden grass.
There spilled they lie a carpet of dull gold
Where shadows pass.

The garden gives to these primaeval beams
That strew its floor a plastered yellow tone
As of too mellow sunshine that brings on
A thunder stone.

It is an ominous enchanted garden
That can transmogrify the healthful rays,
Can hold and make them an essential part
Of unquiet days.

Ah me, the unquiet days they tread me down,
The hours and minutes beat upon my head.
I have spent here the time of three men's lives
And am not dead.

And even as I count the days that pass
I lose the total and begin again.
It is an evil garden out of Time
A place of pain.

'I'll have your heart'

I'll have your heart. If not by gift, my knife
Shall carve it out; I'll have your heart, your life.

Flow, Flow, Flow

Flow, flow, flow,
Deep river running
To the sea.
Go, go, go,
Let all thy waters go
Over my head,
And when my bones are dead
Long may they lie
Upon the ocean bed,
Thy destiny.

The Children of the Cross

Oh cold and ferocious are the children of the cross,
They have captured us and bound us and their gain is our loss.
But straining to death
In the stench of the fire's breath
We leave lonely for ever the children of the cross.

Fallen, Fallen

The angel that rebellion raised
In moment of ecstatic rage
Is fallen, is fallen; his power is gauged.

Noted, by rote is had, the word is spoken.
Nothing remains but a falling star for a token,
A tale told by the fireside, a sword that is broken.

Rothebât

Rothebât, Rothebât, the days that are gone
Have taken my heart with them, I am twisted and torn.
But no longer I linger, and no longer I long,
If Rothebât will put a finger on the pang of my wrong.
Rothebât, Rothebât, the winds blew back the name that she cried,
Rothebât, Rothebât, and cast it to the ocean wide.

Look, Look

He flies so high
Upon the sky
Like winged piggywig
Above his sty.

The sky is
Too high for you. Is
Not the world
A good sty for you?

Tableau de l'Inconstance des
Mauvais Anges

Brightest and best are the sons of the morning,
They wait on our footsteps and show us no ill.
But waking or sleeping
We are in their keeping
And sooner and later they will do as they will.

Will Ever?

Will ever the stormy seas and the surges deep,
Swinging from left to right over the world,
Stay in their idiot pacing, silently sleep
In a memorial silence of precreation?

Alas for the crafty hand and the cunning brain
That took from silence and sleep the form of the world,
That bound eternity in a measuring chain
Of hours reduplicate and sequential days.

Would that the hours of time as a word unsaid
Turning had turned again to the hourless night,
Would that the seas lay heavy upon the dead,
The lightless dead in a grave of a world new drowned.

Ceux qui luttent . . .

Ceux qui luttent ce sont ceux qui vivent.
And down here they luttent a very great deal indeed.
But if life be the desideratum, why grieve, ils vivent.

Suicide's Epitaph

Oh Lord have mercy on my soul
As I had none upon my body.
And you who stand and read this rhyme
How do you do, Tomnoddy?

Sois punie par où tu as tant péché,
dit-il, en me regardent d'une
manière froide et enigmatique.

Come

Venez vite
Avec moi
To the street
Of the cow.

Little Boy Sick

I am not God's little lamb
I am God's sick tiger.
And I prowl about at night
And what most I love I bite,
And upon the jungle grass I slink,
Snuff the aroma of my mental stink,
Taste the salt tang of tears upon the brink
Of my uncomfortable muzzle.
My tail my beautiful, my lovely tail,
Is warped.
My stripes are matted and my coat once sleek
Hangs rough and undistinguished on my bones.
O God I was so beautiful when I was well.
My heart, my lungs, my sinews and my reins
Consumed a solitary ecstasy,
And light and pride informed each artery.
Then I a temple, now a charnel house.
Then I a high hozannah, now a dirge.
Then I a recompense of God's endeavour,
Now a reproach and earnest of lost toil.
Consider, Lord, a tiger's melancholy
And heed a minished tiger's muted moan,
For thou art sleek and shining bright
And I am weary.
Thy countenance is full of light
And mine is dreary.

The Violent Hand

Angel most cynical
Cold and inimical
With a smile of brass
On your cruel face

I think you will irritate me.
So much that you will make me
Risk at a touch
All that is at stake for me.
If I clutch
With violent hand the rosary
You dangle out of reach for me
I shall find out what it must be
Taken not given freely, injury.

Fuite d'Enfance

I have two loves,
There are two loves of mine,
One is my father
And one my Divine.
My father stands on my right hand,
He has an abstracted look.
Over my left shoulder
My Divine reads me like a book.
Which shall I follow . . .
And following die?
No longer count on me
But to say goodbye.

A leur insu
Je suis venue
Faire mes adieux
Adieu, adieu, adieu.

MOTHER, WHAT IS MAN? (1942)

Human Affection

Mother, I love you so.
Said the child, I love you more than I know.
She laid her head on her mother's arm,
And the love between them kept them warm.

A King in Funeral Procession

He blinks he sighs
He is alive, they cry.

Give us the body
Let us see him breathe
Show us the heartbeat
And the dedicated sleeve.
He looks ill
They are satisfied he is looking that way
It is no more than he should
He looks ill
O.K.

De profundis
The solemn music the tune
Clamavi
I have cried unto thee on the loud bassoon
Clamavi a toto corde meo Domine
From the desert the stones
From the rift of this affectionate people
From my bones.

Lift the baby
Let her see him
Lift up the baby
Give her a lift up then.

Oh Lord I am not high minded
I have no proud looks
Not one proud look they have left me
I am their picture book.

La Gretchen de Nos Jours (2)

O Queen of Heaven,
Have pity on me,
My heart is bared
For you to see.

Forgive, forgive
The heart that lies
In anguish bared
Before your eyes.

Mother of God
Behold my heart,
Its sin and stain,
Its bitter smart;

In pity turn
Your pitying gaze
Upon my heart,
And its hopes raze.

Quite to the ground,
For there are yet
Some hopes that are
Too highly set.

O lop each hope
And lay it low,
And quench the fire
Of my heart's glow.

For still I hope
He may return,
And while I hope,
Still must I burn

All with desire
That waits on hope
As doth the hangman
On the rope.

Hope and desire,
All unfulfilled,
Have more than rope
And hangman killed.

Murder

Farewell for ever, well for ever fare,
The soul whose body lies beneath this stone!
'Tis easy said by one who had a care
Soul should doff flesh. That has another tone?
My hand brought *Reggie Smith* to this strait bed –
Well, fare his soul well, fear not I the dead.

Girls!

Girls! although I am a woman
I always try to appear human

Unlike Miss So-and-So whose greatest pride
Is to remain always in the VI Form and not let down the side

Do not sell the pass dear, don't let down the side
This is what this woman said and a lot of balsy stuff beside
(Oh the awful balsy nonsense that this woman cried.)

Girls! I will let down the side if I get the chance
And I will sell the pass for a couple of pence.

Where are you going?

Oh where are ye going ye human faces,
Where are ye going, to what far places,
Where are ye going, to what distances?

The boat takes the boatman,
The deep-sea fisher
Has taken away
The old world preacher,

This tedious old person who asked such questions
As drove everybody to exasperation.
No wonder they all of them cried, Good riddance!

Autumn

He told his life story to Mrs Courtly
Who was a widow. 'Let us get married shortly,'
He said. 'I am no longer passionate,
But we can have some conversation before it is too late.'

Poet!

Poet, thou art dead and damned,
That speaks upon no moral text.
I bury one that babbled but; –
Thou art the next. Thou art the next.

Bog-Face

Dear little Bog-Face,
Why are you so cold?
And why do you lie with your eyes shut? –
You are not very old.

I am a Child of this World,
And a Child of Grace,
And Mother, I shall be glad when it is over,
I am Bog-Face.

The Zoo

The lion sits within his cage,
Weeping tears of ruby rage,
He licks his snout, the tears fall down
And water dusty London town.

He does not like you, little boy,
It's no use making up to him,
He does not like you any more
Than he likes Nurse, or Baby Jim.

Nor would you do if you were he,
And he were you, for don't you see
God gave him lovely teeth and claws
So that he might eat little boys.

So that he might
In anger slay
The little lambs
That skip and play
Pounce down upon their placid dams
And make dams flesh to pad his hams.

So that he might
Appal the night
With crunching bones
And awful groans
Of antelope and buffalo,
And the unwary hunter whose 'Hallo'
Tells us his life is over here below.

There's none to help him, fear inspired,
Who shouts because his gun misfired.
All this the lion sees, and pants
Because he knows the hot sun slants
Between the rancid jungle-grass,
Which never more shall part to let him pass
Down to the jungle drinking-hole,
Wither the zebra comes with her sleek foal.

The sun is hot by day and has his swink,
And sops up sleepy lions' and tigers' stink,
But not this lion's stink, poor carnivore,
He's on the shady shelf for ever more.

His claws are blunt, his teeth fall out,
No victim's flesh consoles his snout,
And that is why his eyes are red
Considering his talents are misusèd.

Advice to Young Children

'Children who paddle where the ocean bed shelves steeply
Must take great care they do not,
Paddle too deeply.'

Thus spake the awful aging couple
Whose heart the years had turned to rubble.

But the little children, to save any bother,
Let it in at one ear and out at the other.

The Face

There is a face I know too well,
A face I dread to see,
So vain it is, so eloquent
Of all futility.

It is a human face that hides
A monkey soul within,
That bangs about, that beats a gong,
That makes a horrid din.

Sometimes the monkey soul will sprawl
Athwart the human eyes,
And peering forth, will flesh its pads,
And utter social lies.

So wretched is this face, so vain,
So empty and forlorn,
You may well say that better far
This face had not been born.

If I lie down

If I lie down upon my bed I must be here,
But if I lie down in my grave I may be elsewhere.

The Sad Mother

Darling little baby child,
You lie upon my breast so mild,
Later you must learn to creep,
But now you are entirely free to wake or sleep.

Ah, will the Saviour . . . ?

The cross begot me on the stone,
My heart emits no further moan,
But fortified by funeral thought
Awaits the doom of the distraught.

Ah! will the Saviour never come
To unlock me from the tomb,
To requite the tears that falter
For a birth I could not alter?

Conviction (I)

Christ died for God and me
Upon the crucifixion tree
For God a spoken Word
For me a Sword
For God a hymn of praise
For me eternal days
For God an explanation
For me salvation.

Conviction (II)

I walked abroad in Easter Park,
I heard the wild dog's distant bark,
I knew my Lord was risen again, –
Wild dog, wild dog, you bark in vain.

Conviction (III)

The shadow was so black
I thought it was a cat,
But once in to it
I knew it
No more black
Than a shadow's back.

Illusion is a freak
Of mind;
The cat's to seek.

Conviction (IV)

I like to get off with people,
I like to lie in their arms,
I like to be held and tightly kissed,
Safe from all alarms.

I like to laugh and be happy
With a beautiful beautiful kiss,
I tell you, in all the world
There is no bliss like this.

The Virtuoso

The portrait of my mother
In plaster lightly scored,
Has always protected me
From anything untoward;
In Manchester or Italy,
Wherever I have toured,
Upon its plinth
It beholds the zenith
Of my success on the pianoforte;
I ask no further reward,
I ask no further reward.

Villains

Profit and Batten
Had coats lined with satin,
And no wonder either,
For they never owed a stiver;
If folks owed them rent,
They owed at ten per cent.
Sing Batten and Profit
If you've got a hat, doff it.

Le Majeur Ydow

'Eh bien! Marche!', fit le Majeur Ydow,
'Any more gentlemen like that? *I'll see them off!*'

But there were no gentleman really, only the
 phantoms
He warred with in his perpetual tantrums.

The Little Daughters of America

Pearl Harbor, 1941

Admirals Curse-You and No-More
Set their compasses and sailed for war.

I am sorry that all the little daughters of America
Should be involved in a thing like this; upon my word.

She said . . .

She said as she tumbled the baby in:
There, little baby, go sink or swim,
I brought you into the world, what more should I do?
Do you expect me always to be responsible for you?

Quand on n'a pas ce que l'on aime,
il faut aimer ce que l'on a –

Cold as no love, and wild with all negation –
Oh Death in Life, the lack of animation.

The Sad Heart

I never learnt to attract, you see,
And so I might as well not be,
A dreary future I see before me,
'Tis pity that ever my mother bore me.

The Conventionalist

Fourteen-year-old, why must you giggle and dote,
Fourteen-year-old, why are you such a goat?
I'm fourteen years old, that is the reason,
I giggle and dote in season.

Study to Deserve Death

Study to deserve Death, they only may
Who fought well upon their earthly day,
Who never sheathed their swords or ran away.

See, such a man as this now proudly stands,
Pale in the clasp of Death, and to his hands
Yields up the sword, but keeps the laurel bands.

Honour and emulate his warrior soul,
For whom the sonorous death-bells toll;
He after journeying has reached his goal.

Prate not to me of suicide,
Faint heart in battle, not for pride
I say Endure, but that such end denied
Makes welcomer yet the death that's to be died.

Dirge

From a friend's friend I taste friendship,
From a friend's friend love,
My spirit in confusion,
Long years I strove,
But now I know that never
Nearer I shall move,
Than a friend's friend to friendship,
To love than a friend's love.

Into the dark night
Resignedly I go,
I am not so afraid of the dark night
As the friends I do not know,
I do not fear the night above,
As I fear the friends below.

La Speakerine de Putney

This heap of ashes was a learned girl;
Oh how the ashes shift to the words' smoke-curl!
Blow wind, blow, blow away the frightful form, scatter
The false girl-form and the words' mutter.

Distractions and the Human Crowd

Ormerod was deeply troubled
When he read in philosophy and religion
Of man's lust after God,
And the knowledge of God,
And the experience of God
In the achievement of solitary communion and the loss of self.
For he said that he had known this knowledge,
And experienced this experience,
Before life and death;
But that here in temporal life, and in temporal life only, was
 permitted,
(As in a flaw of divine government, a voluntary recession),
A place where man might impinge upon man,
And be subject to a thousand and one idiotic distractions.
And thus it was that he found himself
Ever at issue with the Schools,
For ever more and more he pursued the distractions,
Knowing them to be ephemeral, under time, peculiar,
And in eternity, without place or puff.
Then, ah then, he said, following the tea-parties,
(And the innumerable conferences for social rearrangement),
I knew, and shall know again, the name of God, closer than close;
But now I know a stranger thing,
That never can I study too closely, for never will it come again, –
Distractions and the human crowd.

Be off!

I'm sorry to say my dear wife is a dreamer,
And as she dreams she gets paler and leaner.
'Then be off to your Dream, with his fly-away hat,
I'll stay with the girls who are happy and fat.'

Love Me!

Love me, Love me, I cried to the rocks and the trees,
And Love me, they cried again, but it was only to tease.
Once I cried Love me to the people, but they fled like a dream,
And when I cried Love me to my friend, she began to scream.
Oh why do they leave me, the beautiful people, and only the
 rocks remain,
To cry Love me, as I cry Love me, and Love me again.

On the rock a baked sea-serpent lies,
And his eyelids close tightly over his violent eyes,
And I fear that his eyes will open and confound me with a
 mirthless word,
That the rocks will harp on for ever, and my Love me never
 be heard.

The Wild Dog

The City Dog goes to the drinking trough,
He waves his tail and laughs, and goes when he has had
 enough.
His intelligence is on the brink
Of human intelligence. He knows the Council will give him
 a drink.

The Wild Dog is not such an animal,
Untouched by human kind, he is inimical,
He keeps his tail stiff, his eyes blink,
And he goes to the river when he wants a drink.
He goes to the river, he stamps on the mud,
And at night he sleeps in the dark wood.

The Heavenly City

I sigh for the heavenly country,
Where the heavenly people pass,
And the sea is as quiet as a mirror
Of beautiful beautiful glass.

I walk in the heavenly field,
With lilies and poppies bright,
I am dressed in a heavenly coat
Of polished white.

When I walk in the heavenly parkland
My feet on the pasture are bare,
Tall waves the grass, but no harmful
Creature is there.

At night I fly over the housetops,
And stand on the bright moony beams;
Gold are all heaven's rivers,
And silver her streams.

Lady 'Rogue' Singleton

Come, wed me, Lady Singleton,
And we will have a baby soon
And we will live in Edmonton
Where all the friendly people run.

I could never make you happy, darling,
Or give you the baby you want,
I would always very much rather, dear,
Live in a tent.

I am not a cold woman, Henry,
But I do not feel for you,
What I feel for the elephants and the miasmas
And the general view.

Mother

I have a happy nature,
But Mother is always sad,
I enjoy every moment of my life, –
Mother has been had.

My Heart was Full

My heart was full of softening showers,
I used to swing like this for hours,
I did not care for war or death,
I was glad to draw my breath.

Croft

Aloft,
In the loft,
Sits Croft;
He is soft.

Rencontres Funestes

I fear the ladies and gentlemen under the trees,
Could any of them make an affectionate partner and not tease? –
Oh, the affectionate sensitive mind is not easy to please.

The Film Star

Donnez à manger aux affamées
It is a film star who passes this way
He is looking so nice the women would like
To have him on a tray
Donnez à manger aux affamées.

The Bottle of Aspirins

'I look at the bottle, when mournful I feel.'
'C'est une ressource contre tout,' ajouta-t-il,
(Avec le sombre gaité du pays des suicides
D'où il était), – 'two hundred and I am freed,'
He said, 'from anxiety.'

The Governess

The milky love of this bland child
Her governess has quite beguiled,
And now they spend the hours talking,
Sometimes winding wool and sometimes walking.

The Actress

I can't say I enjoyed it, but the pay was good.
Oh how I weep and toil in this world of wood!
Longing in the city for the pursuit of beautiful scenery,
I earn my bread upon the Stage, amid painted greenery.
I have a poet's mind, but a poor exterior,
What goes on inside me is superior.

The Devil-my-Wife

to the tune of 'Golden Slumbers'

The nervous face of my dear wife
Is covered with a fearful grin,
And nods and becks
Come without checks
As the devils pop out and in.

Gush, then, gush and gabble,
Vanity is your dabble,
And in mediocrity
Is your cruelty.

The Repentance of Lady T

I look in the glass
Whose face do I see?
It is the face
Of Lady T.

I wish to change,
How can that be?
Oh Lamb of God
Change me, change me.

The Smile

When ancient girl is garbed in spite
And turns to rend, and lives to bite,
Oh what can end the marriage night?

Wait, wait (and with a smile); the dawn
Shall come again, and day return
As fair as any that has gone.

But if the nature of that smile
Be mockery, contempt and guile
Should such a one my face defile?
No! Rather let me *call* her – Crocodile!

Forgot!

There is a fearful solitude
Within the careless multitude,
And in the open country too,

He mused, and then it seemed to him
The solitude lay all within;
He longed for some interior din:

Some echo from the worldly rout,
To indicate a common lot,
Some charge that he might be about,
But oh he felt that he was quite forgot.

A Man I Am

I was consumed by so much hate
I did not feel that I could wait,
I could not wait for long at anyrate.
I ran into the forest wild,
I seized a little new born child,
I tore his throat, I licked my fang,
Just like a wolf. A wolf I am.

I ran wild for centuries
Beneath the immemorial trees,
Sometimes I thought my heart would freeze,
And never know a moment's ease,
But presently the spring broke in
Upon the pastures of my sin,
My poor heart bled like anything.
The drops fell down, I knew remorse,
I tasted that primordial curse,
And falling ill, I soon grew worse.
Until at last I cried on Him,
Before whom angel faces dim,
To take the burden of my sin
And break my head beneath his wing.

 Upon the silt of death I swam
And as I wept my joy began
Just like a man. A man I am.

The Broken Heart

'Oh, Sing to me Gypsy'

He told me he loved me,
He gave me red roses,
Twelve crimson roses
As red as my blood.

The roses he gave me,
The roses are withered,
Twelve crimson roses
As red as my blood.

The roses are withered,
But here on my breast, far
Redder than they is
The red of my heart's blood.

He told me he loved me,
He gave me red roses,
Twelve crimson roses
As red as my blood.

The White Thought

I shall be glad to be silent, Mother, and hear you speak,
You encouraged me to tell too much, and my thoughts are weak,
I shall keep them to myself for a time, and when I am older
They will shine as a white worm shines under a green boulder.

In the Night

I longed for companionship rather,
But my companions I always wished farther.
And now in the desolate night
I think only of the people I should like to bite.

The Magic Morning

The boating party
Started at dawn from Clarté.
Lightly lightly they stepped into the green boat
(The Lady Marion has left behind her golden coat)
Marion d'Arcy and Charley Dake
Were the only ones. He rowed her upon the lake.
He rowed her across the lake until the green shallows
Paled in a waxed lily litter striped with swallows.
And now the morning sun flecks the dark trees
And lightly the mauve sedge moves in a little breeze.

Charley Dake loves the ducal girl
But her eyelids flick flick upon his thoughts' whirl.

Oh my ducal girl, cries Charley in a fit
Of love-spasm. He is Cupid-hit.
But the Lady Marion smiles and smiles
And so they go again upon the watery miles.

'Oh Charley, Charley, do not go upon the water'
Cries a friendly swan, 'with the Duke's daughter.
You wish to marry er, my boy-carrier? you can not support er
Oh do not go with the Duke's daughter.'

There is an island in the lake, old brick walled,
Where the laurestina climbs and is not spoiled.
What man will spoil the brick walls of their yellow brim?
Such a one as is nervy bold and grim.
(Such a one, says the swan, as has something in store for him.)

Flick, flick, the eyelids of the lady mark
Where a dark angel flies across her father's park.
All the green grass shivers in a warning,
Flee, Charley, flee the magic morning.

But Charley is folly-blind to the visitation
Of the dark angel of consternation.
Boldly he plucks a golden cup
Throws it in Marion's lap and does not look up.

Ah then the thunder peals and waters bound
For who took the flower, the angel says, must be drowned.
So up rears the lake water and drags him underneath
Where in suffering he draws his last breath.
'Never more,' cries the swan, 'shall Charley be seen,
He is underneath the waters of the mise-en-scène'

(And 'Charley, Charley, Charley' cry the swan-instructed curlews
Ever after as they fly to their nests in the purlieus).

But the ducal girl comes safe to land and takes her coat
And goes off in the likeness of a slim stoat.

Après la Politique, la Haine
des Bourbons

Count Flanders
Was eaten up with pride;
His dog Sanders
Thought only of his inside.

They were a precious couple
And let the people feed on straw and
 rubble.

Bitter was the weather,
Bitter the people,
When they flung Count Flanders
From the church steeple.
Bitter was the weather,
Iron the ground,
When Dog Sanders died – of a stomach
 wound.

The Poets are Silent

There's no new spirit abroad,
As I looked, I saw;
And I saw that it is to the poets' merit
To be silent about the war.

The Pleasures of Friendship

The pleasures of friendship are exquisite
How pleasant to go to a friend on a visit!
I go to my friend, we walk on the grass,
And the hours and moments like minutes pass.

Happiness

Happiness is silent, or speaks equivocally for friends,
Grief is explicit and her song never ends,
Happiness is like England, and will not state a case,
Grief like Guilt rushes in and talks apace.

Lot's Wife

'In that rich, oil-bearing region, it is probable that Lot's wife was turned into a pillar of asphalt – not salt.'

SIR WILLIAM WHITEBAIT, MEMBER OF THE
INSTITUTE OF MINING ENGINEERS

I long for the desolate valleys,
Where the rivers of asphalt flow,
For here in the streets of the living,
Where my footsteps run to and fro,
Though my smile be never so friendly,
I offend wherever I go.

Yes, here in the land of the living,
Though a marriage be fairly sprung,
And the heart be loving and giving,
In the end it is sure to go wrong.

Then take me to the valley of asphalt,
And turn me to a river of stone,
That no tree may shift to my sighing,
Or breezes convey my moan.

The Fool

A couple of women is one too many,
Oh, how I wish I could do without any!

Old Ghosts

'By one half as much power as the Roman Centurion.'
DE QUINCEY

I can call up old ghosts, and they will come,
But my art limps,— I cannot send them home.

Death in the Rose Garden

God in Heaven, forgive my death, it lies
Not on any hand, but mine, but mine!

No More People

Passing at my pleasure's pace
Among each moping angel face,
Above the sun on the lily-bright air
I fly my aeroplane here and there.
The heaven-born plod the heavens over,
But I, the son of mischief's lover,
Let the engine carry me. The angels, wing sore,
Look glum, I guess wish they were earth-born more and
 more.
But sometimes I have a feeling that my busy clatter
Has a mocking echo.
Than earth-born engine-borne, heaven-born wing-borne is
 better?
Do they look sideways because they know
That they will live to see the day when there are no more
 people?
All right. All right.
(I drop my bomb upon a church steeple.)

Hast Du dich verirrt?

My child, my child, watch how he goes,
The man in Party coloured clothes.

Satin-Clad

Satin-clad, with many a pearl,
Is this rich and wretched girl.
Does she weep? Her tears are crystal,
And she counts them as they fall.

Unpopular, lonely and loving

Unpopular, lonely and loving,
Elinor need not trouble,
For if she were not so loving,
She would not be so miserable.

'Ceci est digne de gens sans Dieu'

(Allen)

These hands so well articulated
By brother's life-blood are contaminated
And still he walks, and still the shadows fall,
He clasps them. There is nothing there at all.

When the Sparrow Flies

When the sparrow flies to the delicate branch
He seems to be a heavy one alighting there,
It is March, and the fine twigs dance
As the boisterous sparrow plunges masterfully.

Fly again to my heart oh my beloved,
My heart flies too high when you are absent.

Voices against England in the Night

'England, you had better go,
There is nothing else that you ought to do,
You lump of survival value, you are too slow.

England, you have been here too long,
And the songs you sing now are the songs you sung
On an earlier day. Now they are wrong.

And as you sing the sliver slips from your lips,
And the governing garment sits ridiculously on your hips.
It is a pity that you are still too cunning to make slips.'

Dr Goebbels, that is the point,
You are a few years too soon with your jaunt,
Time and the moment is not yet England's daunt.

Yes, dreaming Germany with your Urge and Night,
You must go down before English and American might.
It is well, it is well, cries the peace kite.

Perhaps England our darling will recover her lost thought
We must think sensibly about our victory and not be distraught,
Perhaps America will have an idea, and perhaps not.

But they cried: Could not England, once the world's best,
Put off her governing garment and be better dressed
In a shroud, a shroud? O history turn thy pages fast!

'N'est-ce pas assez de ne me point haïr?'

Stand off, Mother, let me go!
The clock upon the shelf is slow
There wants but half a moment
E'er I am celled and barred in thy heart's convent.

Mother, if mother-love enclosure be,
It were enough, my dear, not quite to hate me.

The Failed Spirit

To those who are isolate
War comes promising respite
Making what seems to be up to the moment the most
 successful endeavour
Against the fort of the failed spirit that is alone for ever.
Spurious failed spirit, adamantine wasture,
Crop, spirit, crop thy stony pasture.

The Sliding Mountain

The terrors of the scenery,
The black rocks of the sliding mountain,
Are hid from the man of family
Who lives beneath the fountain.
His name is Domesticity,
He's married to an ivy tree,
And the little children laugh and scream,
For they do not know what these things mean.

The Recluse

My soul within the shades of night,
Like a languid plant with a fungoid blight,
Shone out in unearthly damp a bright white light;
Pashy the ground underfoot where I trod,
Musing as I passed of the nature of God,
But on my reverent reveries and fruitful plod
Of tear-strewn steps, like a wrathful rod
Fell the touch of a girl, young in years and officious,
Who broke at once at a touch my chain of delicious
Melancholy. Away flew every ecstasy.
With ridiculous intention she drew me to the sun,
My soul's rich langours decried,
And, e'er I could chide, away did run,
Leaving my soul undone.
Oh too much sun, Oh wretched presumption,
Oh too little wisdom and too much compunction.

'I could let Tom go – but what about the children?'

Since what you want, not what you ought,
Is the difficult thing to decide,
I advise you, Amelia, to persevere
With Duty for your guide.

Christmas

A child is born, they cry, a child
And he is Noble and not Mild
(It is the child that makes them wild).

The King sits brooding on his throne
He looks around and calls a man:
My men bring me a heavy stone.

My men bring me a purple robe
And bring me whips and iron goad.
They brought them to him where he strode.

My men bring gold and bring incense
And fetch all noble children at once
That I shall never take offence.

The men fetched the noble children away
They lifted them up and cried: Hurray.
The King sat back and clapped their play.

All noble mild children are brought home
To the wicked King who has cast them down
And ground their bones on the heavy stone.

But the child that is Noble and not Mild
He lies in his cot. He is unbeguiled.
He is Noble, he is not Mild,
And he is born to make men wild.

Uncle Torquemada,
does Beppo know about Jesus?

HAROLD'S LEAP (1950)

The Roman Road

a Christian speaks to a Lion in the Arena

Oh Lion in a peculiar guise,
Sharp Roman road to Paradise,
Come eat me up, I'll pay thy toll
With all my flesh, and keep my soul.

The Castle

I married the Earl of Egremont,
I never saw him by day,
I had him in bed by night,
And cuddled him tight.

We had two boys, twins,
Tommy and Roly,
Roly was so fat
We called him Roly-poly.

Oh that was a romantic time,
The castle had such a lonely look,

The estate,
Heavy with cockle and spurge,
Lay desolate.

The ocean waves
Lapped in castle caves.

Oh I love the ramshackle castle,
And the room
Where our sons were born.

Oh I love the wild
Parkland,
The mild
Sunshine.

Underneath the wall
Sleeps our pet toad,
There the hollyhocks grow tall.

My children never saw their father,
Do not know,
He sleeps in my arms each night
Till cockcrow.

Oh I love the ramshackle castle,
And the turret room
Where our sons were born.

To Dean Inge Lecturing on Origen

Listen, all of you, listen, all of you,
This way wisdom lies,
To reconcile with the simplicity of God
His contingent pluralities.

Oh, the wise man sat in his chair,
And oh, the people they would not hear,
They said, It is much too deep for us,
As they turned to the Differential Calculus.

Oh, if the people had only heard
Him,
Oh, if that wise man's word was not blurred,
Not dimmed.

Behind the Knight

Behind the Knight sits hooded Care,
And as he rides she speaks him fair,
She lays her hand in his sable muff,
Ride he never so fast he'll not cast her off.

The Warden

to the tune of 'They played in the beautiful garden . . .'

They played in the beautiful garden
Those children of high degree,
But she sighed as she swam with the Warden
In the depths of the Zuyder Zee.

Oh why did you take me away
From the children I loved so well?
I had other plans in my heart, dear,
For the child of my latest spell.

The Warden has decked her with seaweed,
And shells of an ancient design,
But she sighs as she presses his fingers,
My heart can never be thine.

He sits in the golden chair
With the child he would call his own,
But the beautiful child has expired,
He nurses a sea-green stone.

Harold's Leap

Harold, are you asleep?
Harold, I remember your leap,
It may have killed you
But it was a brave thing to do.

Two promontories ran high into the sky,
He leapt from one rock to the other
And fell to the sea's smother.

Harold was always afraid to climb high,
But something urged him on,
He felt he should try.
I would not say that he was wrong,
Although he succeeded in doing nothing but die.
Would you?

Ever after that steep
Place was called Harold's Leap.

It was a brave thing to do.

A Mother's Hearse

The love of a mother for her child
Is not necessarily a beautiful thing
It can be compounded of pride and show
And exalt the self above every thing.

Oh why is that child so spoilt and horrible?
His mother has never neglected the trouble
Of giving him his will at every turn
And that is why his eyes do burn.

His eyes do burn with a hungry fire
His fingers clutch at the air and do not tire
He is a persecuting force
And as he grows older he grows worse.

And for his sake the friends are put down
And the happy people do not come round,
In pride and hostility against the world
This family upon itself is now curled.

Oh wretched they and wretched the friend
And this will continue without end
And all for a mother's love it was,
I say it were better a mother's hearse.

Touch and Go

Man is coming out of the mountains
But his tail is caught in the pass,
Why does he not free himself
Is he not an ass?

Do not be impatient with him
He is bowed with passion and fret
He is not out of the mountains
He is not half out yet.

Look at his sorrowful eyes
His torn cheeks, his brow
He lies with his head in the dust
Is there no one to help him now?

No, there is no one to help him
Let him get on with it
Cry the ancient enemies of man
As they cough and spit.

The enemies of man are like trees
They stand with the sun in their branches
Is there no one to help my creature
Where he languishes?

Ah, the delicate creature
He lies with his head in the rubble
Pray that the moment pass
And the trouble.

Look he moves, that is more than a prayer,
But he is so slow
Will he come out of the mountains?
It is touch and go.

Man is a Spirit

Man is a spirit. This the poor flesh knows,
Yet serves him well for host when the wind blows,
Why should this guest go wrinkling up his nose?

Thought is Superior

Thought is superior to dress and circumstance,
It is thought proud thought that sets the world in a dance.
And what is the greatest thought since the world begun?
The discovery that the earth goes round the sun.

The River God of the River Mimram
in Hertfordshire

I may be smelly and I may be old,
Rough in my pebbles, reedy in my pools,
But where my fish float by I bless their swimming
And I like the people to bathe in me, especially women.
But I can drown the fools
Who bathe too close to the weir, contrary to rules,
And they take a long time drowning
As I throw them up now and then in a spirit of clowning.
Hi yih, yippity-yap, merrily I flow,
Oh I may be an old foul river but I have plenty of go.
Once there was a lady who was too bold,
She bathed in me by the tall black cliff where the water runs cold,
So I brought her down here
To be my beautiful dear.

Oh will she stay with me will she stay
This beautiful lady, or will she go away?
She lies in my beautiful deep river bed with many a weed
To hold her, and many a waving reed.
Oh who would guess what a beautiful white face lies there
Waiting for me to smooth and wash away the fear
She looks at me with. Hi yih, do not let her
Go. There is no one on earth who does not forget her
Now. They say I am a foolish old smelly river
But they do not know of my wide original bed
Where the lady waits, with her golden sleepy head.
If she wishes to go I will not forgive her.

Cool as a Cucumber

Cool as a cucumber calm as a mill pond sound as a bell
Was Mary
When she went to the Wishing Well.

But a fairy came up out of the well
And cursed her up hill and down dale
And cursed her from midnight to morning hail.

And now she gets worse and worse
Ever since she listened to the fairy's curse
She is nervy grim and bold
Looks over her left shoulder and does not do as she is told.

She is quite unfit for marriage
Of course
Since she listened to the fairy's curse
She grows worse and worse.

Starts off by herself each day
In a most unusual way
But nobody seems to know which way.

She looks pale, really unhealthy,
And moves so queerly, rather stealthy.

Mary come back to me,
Cried one who loved her.
He is the miller's son.

And when she heard him she broke into a run.

She has not been seen since then.
If you ask me she'll not be seen again.

The Orphan Reformed

The orphan is looking for parents
She roams the world over
Looking for parents and cover.
She looks at this pair and that
Cries, Father, Mother,
Likes these, does not like those,
Stays for a time; goes.
Crying, Oh hearts of stone.
But really she is better alone.
Orphan, the people who will not
 be your parents are not evil,
Not the devil.
But still she cries, Father, Mother
Must I be alone for ever?
Yes you must. Oh wicked orphan, oh rebellion,
Must an orphan not be alone is that your opinion?
At last the orphan is reformed. Now quite
Alone she goes; now she is right.
Now when she cries, Father, Mother, it is only to please.
Now the people do not mind, now they say she is a mild tease.

A Shooting Incident

Man does not live by bread alone
Nor die alone for lack of it
For he may be well fed, and die,
Well housed, well married, still may die.
There is a hunger of the heart
Will slay him, though each day he feast
On bread and wine, and go well dresst,
And such a one was Colonel Yeast.
He was a noble simple man
But all within his heart was black
And as he walked the way along
He cried, alas alack,
And cried and sighed and sighed and cried,
I am a long-delayèd suicide.
It was as though a fiend had swung
Him by the toe when he was young
And swung him so
And to and fro
And swore and said he should be most oppressed
When most against a loving friend he pressed.
And now he walks with gun and roar –
He is a colonel in the Indian Army –
Sporting upon a tiger's spoor
And with him goes his faithful escort, Harmi.
Oh Harmi dear I love the sun
And all the crooked jungle path
But most the water holes I love
With creatures peering from above.
Why do I pick the wilder animal?

It is because he is not fanciful.
I had a dog in England once,
I loved him well, his name was Bunce,
And now I think I see him here,
And as I think, the scene grows clear,
An English scene. The colonel sighed.
The misty fells lay open wide
Upon his loving thought,
And dog Bunce ran again to start
The timid hare, and play his part
As he was taught.
Wild creatures' eyes, the colonel said,
Are innocent and fathomless,
And when I look at them I see
That they are not aware of me,
And oh I find and oh I bless
A comfort in this emptiness.

They only see me when they want
To pounce upon me in the hunt.
But in the tame variety
There couches an anxiety
As if they yearned, yet knew not what
They yearned for, nor they yearned for not.
And so my dog would look at me
And it was pitiful to see
Such love and such dependency.
The human heart is not at ease
With animals that look like these.
The colonel paused and wiped his brow,
He felt his words were too dramatic
But as he knew no English they
Were lost upon the Asiatic.
Ah me, the bitter bitter love,
Why must it be so bitter
Or animal, or man, or tree –
Would not no love be better?
And still in recollection bound
The Colonel gazed upon the ground
It seemed his senses in a swound
Had left him quite,
Then turning to his gun again
And stamping on his heavy pain,
He loaded up and in the sight
Beheld a tiger stepping bright.
He steps so brightly to his death,
The colonel shot him through the teeth.
I had a dream I beat dear Bunce,
He said, with many a weal
Until he lay down at my feet
All red from toe to heel

Then in my dream I rose and fled,
Crying, The dog, the dog is dead.
Now, Harmi, mark, when daylight came,
My night and dream to shatter through
My dog came and so looked at me
I said, Why, Bunce, what's the matter with you?
Oh day and night, oh Holy Dove,
We slay the thing we most do love,
And it is pitiful to see
Our friends live but in memory.
But they are safe in memory
And are they not? the colonel said,
He turned and looked at Harmi so
That Harmi dropped his gun and fled.
When he came back again he found
The colonel dying of a wound,
And crying close upon the ground:
Oh bright bright blood that flows so bright
Within the wound myself did make
Oh jungle grass that drinks it up
And with my life thy thirst doth slake
Why has my hand this hour postponed
That sees me now with dust conjoined?
The Indian's tears fell like a blot
Upon the colonel's face
And carefully before he left
He put his hands in place.
Later upon the tomb, now grave now gay,
He daily danced to keep the fiends away.

'Oh stubborn race of Cadmus' seed . . .'

It is the bird of burial
I invoke for my brother's funeral.
I throw the dust in Creon's eyes
Not my father is blind but my uncle is.
And when they have killed me I shall stand in the Dark Hall
And cry: Orcus, see that my sister does not suffer at all.

The Ambassador

'known also among the Phoenicians as Casmilus'
LEMPRIÈRE

Underneath the broad hat is the face of the Ambassador
He rides on a white horse through hell looking two ways.
Doors open before him and shut when he has passed.
He is master of the mysteries and in the market place
He is known. He stole the trident, the girdle,
The sword, the sceptre and many mechanical instruments.
Thieves honour him. In the underworld he rides carelessly.
Sometimes he rises into the air and flies silently.

Persephone

I am that Persephone
Who played with her darlings in Sicily
Against a background of social security.

Oh what a glorious time we had
Or had we not? They said it was sad
I was born good, grown bad.

Oh can you wonder can you wonder
I struck the doll-faced day asunder
Stretched out and plucked the flower of winter thunder?

Then crashed the sky and the earth smoked
Where are father and mother now? Ah, croaked
The door-set crone, Sun's cloaked.

Up came the black horses and the dark King
And the harsh sunshine was as if it had never been
In the halls of Hades they said I was queen.

My mother, my darling mother,
I loved you more than any other,
Ah mother, mother, your tears smother.

No not for my father who rules
The fair fields of Italy and sunny fools
Do I mourn where the earth cools.

But my mother, I loved and left her
And of a fair daughter bereft her,
Grief cleft her.

Oh do not fret me
Mother, let me
Stay, forget me.

But still she seeks sorrowfully,
Calling me bitterly
By name, Persephone.

I in my new land learning
Snow-drifts on the fingers burning.
Ice, hurricane, cry: No returning.

Does my husband the King know, does he guess
In this wintriness
Is my happiness?

Do Take Muriel Out

Do take Muriel out
She is looking so wan
Do take Muriel out
All her friends have gone.

And after too much pressure
Looking for them in the Palace
She goes home to too much leisure
And this is what her life is.

All her friends are gone
And she is alone
And she looks for them where they have never been
And her peace is flown.

Her friends went into the forest
And across the river
And the desert took their footsteps
And they went with a believer.

Ah they are gone they were so beautiful
And she can not come to them
And she kneels in her room at night
Crying, Amen.

Do take Muriel out
Although your name is Death
She will not complain
When you dance her over the blasted heath.

The Weak Monk

The monk sat in his den
He took his mighty pen
And wrote: 'Of God and Men'.

One day the thought struck him
It was not according to Catholic doctrine;
His blood ran dim.

He wrote till he was ninety years old
Then he shut the book with a clasp of gold
And buried it under the sheepfold.

He'd enjoyed it so much, he loved to plod,
And he thought he'd a right to expect that God
Would rescue his book alive from the sod.

Of course it rotted in the snow and rain,
No one will ever know now what he wrote of God and Men.

For this the monk is to blame.

Le Singe Qui Swing

to the tune of 'Green-sleeves'

Outside the house
The swinging ape
Swung to and fro,
Swung to and fro,
And when midnight shone so clear
He was still swinging there.

Oh ho the swinging ape,
The happy peaceful animal,
Oh ho the swinging ape,
I love to see him gambol.

Pad, pad

I always remember your beautiful flowers
And the beautiful kimono you wore
When you sat on the couch
With that tigerish crouch
And told me you loved me no more.

What I cannot remember is how I felt when you were unkind
All I know is, if you were unkind now I should not mind.
Ah me, the capacity to feel angry, exaggerated and sad
The years have taken from me. Softly I go now, pad pad.

The Broken Friendship

'My heart is fallen in despair'
Said Easter Ross to Jolie Bear.
Jolie answered never a word
But passed her plate as if she had not heard.

Mrs Ross is took to her bed
And kept her eye fixed on the bed-rail peg
'When I am dead roll me under the barrow,
And who but pretty Jolie shall carry the harrow.'

Jolie Bear is gone away
Easter Ross's heart is broke,
Everything went out of her
When Jolie never spoke.

'Duty was his Lodestar'

a song

Duty was my Lobster, my Lobster was she,
And when I walked out with my Lobster
I was happy.
But one day my Lobster and I fell out,
And we did nothing but
Rave and shout.

Rejoice, rejoice, Hallelujah, drink the flowing champagne,
For my darling Lobster and I
Are friends again.

Rejoice, rejoice, drink the flowing champagne-cup,
My Lobster and I have made it up.

The After-thought

Rapunzel Rapunzel let down your hair
It is I your beautiful lover who am here
And when I come up this time I will bring a
 rope ladder with me
And then we can both escape to the dark
 wood immediately.
This must be one of those things, as Edgar
 Allan Poe says somewhere in a book,
Just because it is perfectly obvious one is certain to overlook.

I wonder sometimes by the way if Poe isn't a bit introspective,
One can stand about getting rather reflective,
But thinking about the way the mind works, you know,
Makes one inactive, one simply doesn't know which way to go;
Like the centipede in the poem who was corrupted by the toad
And ever after never did anything but lie in the
 middle of the road,
Or the old gurus of India I've seen, believe it or
 not,
Standing seventy five years on their toes until
 they dropped.
Or Titurel, for that matter, in his odd doom
Crying: I rejoice because by the mercy of the
 Saviour I continue to live in the tomb.

What's that, darling? You can't hear me?
That's odd. I can hear you quite distinctly.

The Wanderer

Twas the voice of the Wanderer, I heard her exclaim,
You have weaned me too soon, you must nurse me again,
She taps as she passes at each window pane,
Pray does she not know that she taps in vain?

Her voice flies away on the midnight wind,
But would she be happier if she were within?
She is happier far where the night-winds fall
And there are no doors and no windows at all.

No man has seen her, this pitiful ghost,
And no woman either, but heard her at most,
Sighing and tapping and sighing again,
You have weaned me too soon, you must nurse me again.

No Categories!

I cry I cry
To God who created me
Not to you Angels who frustrated me
Let me fly, let me die,
Let me come to Him.

Not to you Angels on the wing,
With your severe faces,
And your scholarly grimaces,
And your do this and that,
And your exasperating pit-pat
Of appropriate admonishment.

This is not what the Creator meant,
In the day of his gusty creation
He made this and that
And laughed to see them grow fat.

Plod on, you Angels say, do better aspire higher
And one day you may be like us, or those
 next below us,
Or nearer the lowest,
Or lowest,
Doing their best.

Oh no no, you Angels, I say,
No hierarchies I pray.

Oh God, laugh not too much aside
Say not, it is a small matter.
See what your Angels do; scatter
Their pride; laugh them away.

Oh no categories I pray.

The Deserter

The world is come upon me, I used to keep it a long way off,
But now I have been run over and I am in the hands of the
 hospital staff.
They say I have not been run over as a matter of fact it's
 imagination,
But they all agree I should be kept in bed under observation.
I must say it's very comfortable here, nursie has such nice hands,
And every morning the doctor comes and lances my tuberculous
 glands.
He says he does nothing of the sort, but I have my own feelings
 about that,
And what they are if you don't mind I shall continue to keep
 under my hat.
My friend, if you call it a friend, has left me; he says I am a
 deserter to ill health,
And that the things I should think about have made off for ever,
 and so has my wealth.
Portentous ass, what to do about him's no strain
I shall quite simply never speak to the fellow again.

 I rode with my darling. . .

I rode with my darling in the dark wood at night
And suddenly there was an angel burning bright
Come with me or go far away he said
But do not stay alone in the dark wood at night.

My darling grew pale he was responsible
He said we should go back it was reasonable
But I wished to stay with the angel in the dark wood at night.

My darling said goodbye and rode off thoughtfully
And suddenly I rode after him and came to a cornfield
Where had my darling gone and where was the angel now?
The wind bent the corn and drew it along the ground
And the corn said, Do not go alone in the dark wood.

Then the wind drew more strongly and the black clouds covered
 the moon
And I rode into the dark wood at night.

There was a light burning in the trees but it was not the angel
And in the pale light stood a tall tower without windows
And a mean rain fell and the voice of the tower spoke,
Do not stay alone in the dark wood at night.

The walls of the pale tower were heavy, in a heavy mood
The great stones stood as if resisting without belief.

Oh how sad sighed the wind, how disconsolately,
Do not ride alone in the dark wood at night.

Loved I once my darling? I love him not now.
Had I a mother beloved? She lies far away.
A sister, a loving heart? My aunt a noble lady?
All all is silent in the dark wood at night.

God and Man

Man is my darling, my love and my pain,
My pleasure, my excitement, and my love again,
My wisdom, my courage, my power, my all,
Oh Man, do not come to me until I call.

In man is my life, and in man is my death,
He is my hazard, my pride and my breath,
I sought him, I wrought him, I pant on his worth,
In him I experience indeterminate growth.

Oh Man, Man, of all my animals dearest,
Do not come till I call, though thou weariest first.

Mr Over

Mr Over is dead
He died fighting and true
And on his tombstone they wrote
Over to You.

And who pray is this You
To whom Mr Over is gone?
Oh if we only knew that
We should not do wrong.

But who is this beautiful You
We all of us long for so much
Is he not our friend and our brother
Our father and such?

Yes he is this and much more
This is but a portion
A sea-drop in a bucket
Taken from the ocean

So the voices spake
Softly above my head
And a voice in my heart cried: Follow
Where he has led

And a devil's voice cried: Happy
Happy the dead.

My Cats

a Witch speaks

I like to toss him up and down
A heavy cat weighs half a Crown
With a hey do diddle my cat Brown.

I like to pinch him on the sly
When nobody is passing by
With a hey do diddle my cat Fry.

I like to ruffle up his pride
And watch him skip and turn aside
With a hey do diddle my cat Hyde.

Hey Brown and Fry and Hyde my cats
That sit on tombstone for your mats.

Drugs Made Pauline Vague

Drugs made Pauline vague,
She sat one day at the breakfast table
Fingering in a baffled way
The fronds of the maidenhair plant.

Was it the salt you were looking for dear?
Said Dulcie, exchanging a glance with the
 Brigadier.

Chuff chuff Pauline what's the matter?
Said the Brigadier to his wife
Who did not even notice
What a handsome couple they made.

Our Bog is Dood

Our Bog is dood, our Bog is dood,
They lisped in accents mild,
But when I asked them to explain
They grew a little wild.
How do you know your Bog is dood
My darling little child?

We know because we wish it so
That is enough, they cried,
And straight within each infant eye
Stood up the flame of pride,
And if you do not think it so
You shall be crucified.

Then tell me, darling little ones,
What's dood, suppose Bog is?
Just what we think, the answer came,
Just what we think it is.
They bowed their heads. Our Bog is ours
And we are wholly his.

But when they raised them up again
They had forgotten me
Each once upon each other glared
In pride and misery
For what was dood, and what their Bog
They never could agree.

Oh sweet it was to leave them then,
And sweeter not to see,
And sweetest of all to walk alone
Beside the encroaching sea,
The sea that soon should drown them all,
That never yet drowned me.

Wretched Woman

Wretched woman that thou art
How thou piercest to my heart
With thy misery and graft
And thy lack of household craft.

Lightly Bound

You beastly child, I wish you had miscarried,
You beastly husband, I wish I had never married.
You hear the north wind riding fast past the window? He calls me.
Do you suppose I shall stay when I can go so easily?

Le Revenant

My Uncle from the realms of Death
Returned to draw an earthly breath
And as he walked upon the heath
The wild wind whistled through his teeth.

He came unto a habitation
That was the centre of the nation
He knocked upon each house and said:
It is much better to be dead.

And when they stoned him from the door
He vowed he would come back no more.

Friskers
or
Gods and Men

Oh what can be happening pray what are they at?
Oh why am I slowly turning into a cat?
Is it Zeus responsible, tired of my love
Does he send me outside with the puss cats to rove?
Or indifferent rather, quite sick of it all,
Is he simply letting Hera have her way with a rival?
Oh look at my beautiful coat and my handsome whiskers,
I shall be most loved of all the young cats and I shall be called
 Friskers.

Cool and Plain

Cool and plain
Cool and plain
Was the message of love
 on the window pane.
Soft and quiet
Soft and quiet
It vanished away in the fogs of night.

To School!

Let all the little poets be gathered together in classes
And let prizes be given to them by the Prize Asses
And let them be sure to call all the little poets young
And worse follow what's bad begun
But do not expect the Muse to attend this school
Why look already how far off she has flown, she is
 no fool.

To an American Publisher

You say I must write *another* book? But I've just written this one.
You liked it so much that's the reason? Read it again then.

The Rehearsal

I always admire a beautiful woman
And I've bought you some flowers for your beautiful bosom.

Death-bed of a Financier

Deal not with me God as I have dealt with Man
In the prosperity which thou hast given me
Helpless in his need a careless course I ran
And now oh Lord that thou hast driven me
To my last gasp, I pray for all I am not worth
Deal not with me as I have dealt on earth.

The Hat

I love my beautiful hat more than anything
And through my beautiful hat I see a wedding ring
The King will marry me and make me his own before all
And when I am married I shall wear my hat and walk on the
 palace wall.

Thank You

We have no father and no mother
We are often taken for one another
What are we looking for over the wall?
We are not looking for anything at all.

The Ride

Riding slowly along the banks of a canal
Where the dredges had been at work and the slime lay piled,
I rode in Egypt slowly, slowly with Captain Fairchild,
Under a black sun, on an oppressive afternoon.
Pricking our dull horses to an even pace
We rode beside the black slide, mile upon mile,
Between the slime mounds, beside the black deep water.
Suddenly the captain turning smiled into my face,
Smiling with a black smile, pale beneath his burnt skin,
Smiling he said, if the Sultana of Istanbuol
Had in her Household a Grand Vizier so old
That he was alive in the Napoleonic Wars,
What is it, he said, she would most wish him to forget?
My hand for a moment lay slack upon the rein,
And my horse checking stood still with lowered head,
Oh, I said carelessly, the slime and the black slime,
The slime and the length and the slime
Of the ramshackle Ottoman Empire.
Well my dear chap, said the Captain smiling,
It always comes to that, but we know do we not,
That the slime and the black slime is something we can parry
With a Byronic connotation and a note in time.

I Am

Far from normal far from normal far from normal I am
He sighed as he stood on the river bank and watched where
 the fishes swam
But ever the wind in the willow trees whispered, I am: I am.
He saw the variety of nature
The ant the mole and the sky
And resignedly hurried upon his way
Crying: I, I; I, I;

Then a priest came and told him if he was good
And thought as he ought and did as he should
He should be saved by the Lamb's fresh blood.

Oh I know, I know the poor man cries,
I know the worth of the heavenly prize
And I know the strength of the race to be run
But my black heart cleaves to the strength of my gun.

Then he put his gun to his head and shot
Crying absurdly, I am not.

The Crown of Bays

They gave him a crown of bays and dressed him up,
But he was listless though famous, he had had enough.
He looked at the audience, they are clapping knaves,
And turning to the Winged Form, Who are you? he says.
'I am the Angel of the Considered Bays.'
When you go back I will follow you, he said.
'To do that, you must be dead.'
I ask it; this people is a basket.

He laid his head in the angel's lap,
Oh let me come with you, let me come.
'Can you say farewell to the people in deep slumbers
Who travel by the Underground railway with happy faces in
 numbers?'
These, and these
He said (thinking of the sleepers and the audience) tease,
Let me come with you.
'Only those who expect everything are prepared to take nothing,'
Said the angel slyly, as posing a conundrum,
'Death may be that.'
Still lead; I follow, pat pat.
'Can you say farewell to the Natural Beauties?'
Yes, I look at them through a glass cage, the glaze sullies.

The angel waves a hand and under a tree,
A mighty chestnut whose fine branches
The spring with white flowers enhances,
Lay the bay-crowned Misery.

Oh Angel of Bays, he cries, weeping bitterly,
You have forged a dagger with your visions for my penalty,

Crack my heart, pierce throat, I will come with you,
I only used to think it was worth while living for the view.
How beautiful the sky is that is bright blue
Through the green leaves, and the sun warms through and through
Before a man hangs they give him what he likes to eat,
So you have given me what I like to see, the trees and no street,
Now to the scaffold, Angel, do your part,
I will come with you. (The angel stabs him to the heart.)

As he lay bleeding his last into the untrod earth
He smiled a happy smile and said:
I had a philosophy of use and wont, it was bad;
I conceded that life was a balance with
Only three ha'pence to the liver's credit.
But to live with three ha'pence was a merit.
I held that nothing to have not wholly bad not wholly good
Was a young man's dream and juvenile aspiration,
Now I am come to the young man's situation,
And expecting everything gladly receive annihilation.

'You receive what I do not know,'
Said the angel, and with this word
Flies away and leaves him lying upon the sward.
But over his shoulder airborne came these last words, 'Briefly
In my opinion for what it is worth, you die trivially.'

Homage to John Cowper Powys

This old man is sly and wise,
He knows the truth, he tells no lies,
He is as deep as a British pool.
And Monsieur Poop may think him a fool.

Little Child of Brightest Face

Little Child of brightest face
Do you do you know your place?
Underneath the table pray
Where the little fishes play.

Our Office Cat

Our Office cat is a happy cat
She has had two hundred kittens
And every one has been adopted into happy homes
By our cat-loving Britons.

A Jew is Angry with his Friend who does not Believe in Circumcision

Oh ho uncircumciséd Sadducee I see
In all created time not one as thee
Befoul the cradle whence he came
Take a great name and make it a great shame
Take it and make it on the lips of the heathen a gibe
Not the name of a sect, not Sadducee, Pharisee or Scribe
But Jew Jew Jew
Should have taught you all that we knew
With a racial knowledge in the Pentateuchal days of old
Before the time had come for Sadducees to be so very bold
As to be so bold as to be too modern for circumcision
Oh mockery of Greek and Roman, oh derision
Of the derided
Now I have you, manikin, depend
I'll dock you of your foreskin and something else that will end
All hope of posterity, no little Sadducees will you beget
When I've finished with you, but sit in a eunochy fret
Waiting for death to relieve you of a hated life
You look a little pale? What ho, a knife, a knife.

From the Coptic

Three angels came to the red red clay
Where in a heap it formless lay,

Stand up, stand up, thou lazy red clay,
Stand up and be Man this happy day.

Oh in its bones the red clay groaned,
And why should I do such a thing? it said,
And take such a thing on my downy head?
Then the first angel stood forth and said,

Thou shalt have happiness, thou shalt have pain,
And each shall fall turn and about again,
And no man shall say when the day shall fall
That thou shalt be happy or not at all.

And the second angel said much the same
While the red clay lay flat in the falling rain,
Crying, I will stay clay and take no blame.

Then the third angel rose up and said,
Listen thou clay, raise thy downy head,
When thou hast heard what I have to say
Thou shalt rise Man and go man's way.

What have you to promise? the red clay moans,
What have you in store for my future bones?
I am Death, said the angel, and death is the end,
I am Man, cries clay rising, and you are my friend.

A Humane Materialist at the Burning
of a Heretic

When shall that fuel fed fire grown fatter
Burn to consumption and a pitter patter
Of soft ash falling in a formless scatter
Telling Mind's death in a dump of Matter.

In Protocreation

In protocreation
Is my imagination
And in my world's first emergence from gaseous fire
My desire.
Then heaved the earth
In a first vegetable birth
Later according to the record
Experimental animals walked abroad.
The awkward pterodactyl
The brontosaurus
The mammoth and the early lizard
Were before us.
Oh had it but stopped then
Oh had there not come men.
Earth fired
And the seas smoked
Heavy heavy swung the swamp
Crust broke and the mountains poked.
Oh had it but stopped then
Oh had there not come men.
In that high and early time
There was no good deed and no crime
No oppression by informed mind
No knowledge and no human kind.

Do Not!

Do not despair of man, and do not scold him,
Who are you that should so lightly hold him?
Are you not also a man, and in your heart
Are there not warlike thoughts and fear and smart?
Are you not also afraid and in fear cruel,
Do you not think of yourself as usual,
Faint for ambition, desire to be loved,
Prick at a virtuous thought by beauty moved?
You love your wife, you hold your children dear,
Then say not that Man is vile, but say they are.
But they are not. So is your judgement shown
Presumptuous, false, quite vain, merely your own
Sadness for failed ambition set outside,
Made a philosophy of, prinked, beautified
In noble dress and into the world sent out
To run with the ill it most pretends to rout.
Oh know your own heart, that heart's not wholly evil,
And from the particular judge the general,
If judge you must, but with compassion to see life,
Or else, of yourself despairing, in death flee strife.

The Death Sentence

Cold as No Plea,
Yet wild with all negation,
Weeping I come,
To my heart's destination,
To my last bed
Between th'unhallowed boards –
The Law allows it
And the Court awards.

The Commuted Sentence

Shut me not alive away
From the light of every day
Hang me rather by the neck to die
Against a morning sky.

Oh shut me not behind a prison wall
I have a horror of this sort of place
Where I may sit and count the hours pass
And never see a smiling human face.

Here is all straight and narrow as a tomb
Oh shut me not within a little room.

The Celtic Fringe

Kathleen ni Houlihan
Walking down the boule-igan
Ran into a hooligan
Ah ha, Kathleen ni Houlihan.

She went with the rat-ican
And very soon they had a brat-ican
Ah ha, Kathleen ni Houlihan
How goes it now?

They called him Rebel-can
Oh he was a devil-can
Kathleen ni Houlihan
Your son.

And the big black cat-ican
That sat on the mat-ican
With a pit and a pati-can
Spit. Spat.

Was the chief sport
Oh the Houlihan sort
And chiefly did Rebel-can
Twitch his tail, the devil-can.

All up the boule-igan
Runs Kathleen ni Houlihan
For flirting his tail the cat is gone,
They are alone.

And that is how the Houlihan
Fell out in the boule-igan
Whose tail shall they twitch now?
Eh, Kathleen, the cat is gone.

The Leader

Men fear the hollow man at the top of the tree
He is supported they say by a phoney majority
But the squirrel brings nuts and the mole brings meal
And the cock brings the spur from the tip of his heel
And they none of them dare say what they feel
For he kills as he wills does that horrible He
Who sits at the top of the old oak tree.

Oh foolish they are who keep his rules
And bring him food, they are surely fools
When it is plain as a pikestaff bold
They should run him out in the cold, cold, cold
Or burn him up in the hot fury
Of a flame that will lick to the top of a tree.

Oh if only they had some sense
The squirrel might store for her own expense
The cock at his heel find a use for the spur
And the mole with the meal sleek the young mole's fur.

But they will not do it, they are so frightened
Of what they have raised and the tree has heightened
Then come along with a sigh and a leap
For this people runs mad in the Fuehrer Prinzip.

Yes they will have a lord and it matters not who
Be he hollow as a drum he will do, do, do.

Oh, If Only . . .

The intellectual Englishman shrank away from the bedside.
There in the bed lay the Englishwoman Blah in the arms of Captain
 Thomas.
Oh, the ineffable smug look of Blah (thought the young intellectual)
The satisfaction, the noble-animal dignity, the imperial carelessness!
As Blah lay smiling in her sleep, a shadow crossed the face of
 Thomas.
He awoke, and putting his arms across Blah's breast
He stared in a sullen and offended manner at the young intellectual.
Go to hell, cried Thomas. Go to hell, cried the young intellectual.
A purely nervous situation for you I fancy, sneered Thomas.
The young intellectual crept weeping away,
Oh, if he could only experience emotional extravagance!

Who Shot Eugenie?

We had ridden three days Eugenie and I
And kept hidden
By an unnecessary habitual caution
The papers of our commission.

How blank is the heart when on service bent
Empty of all but official content
So inappropriate is all individual consideration
So impossible in the individual a communal realization
Of states', peoples', any group-mind's preoccupation,
That a girl in the service of her country at war
Must have a mind as blank as a wall
Apt only to carry
The terms of her commission and hurry.

Eugenie and I in an open deserted country
Had travelled till nightfall of the third day
When putting our horses at a hedge at the top of a hill,
Up and over,
We found ourselves under cover
Of a mighty forest whose pines' green needles
Fallen carpeted the ground and silenced our horses' footfall.

Now night was entrenched and over our head the stars
Shone out their fitful rather disturbing light
That hardly served to penetrate the gloomy thread
Of the long forest ride we rode upon.

Why is it starlight so disturbs our kind
Dissipates the purposes of the human mind

Emptying familiar things of all significance
Setting the thoughts in an inconsequent dance
And making the loftiest and ruling of them sit mumchance?

I said no word of this to her nor she to me,
We were old campaigners both of us you see,
Only we rode, she as I, distracted
And the heart had gone out of us both and the virtue,
We rode in silence.

Hour by hour of the night we rode and the sickle moon
Clearing the feathered treetops soared overhead
And the path we followed led always towards the north,
Skirting a lake. We saw where the arms of trees
Old wood and rotten and allowed to rot and to fall

When it should have been chopped and cherished in the service
 of nations
(According to the best interpretation of King's Regulations)
Broke surface.
Over our shoulders from the right the moonlight shimmered
Down and across the waters of the forest lake
Making in semblance more sombre the shadowy margin.
We were glad to leave it, the sombre sinister pool,
And rose till daylight came and the cold dawn wind,
And the stars grew pale, and the moon sank down on the west.

In the gray of the early day we dismounted and watered our
 beasts,
And breakfasted there by the side of the cold clear spring,
And tethered our horses, and lay and rested and slept,
The sleep of exhaustion. And still no sound,
No least hurry or flurry of wild birds moving,
Spoke of the alien presence of human beings,
The forest enclosed us around and my dreams were always
Of ways without ending and passively hostile Nature,
Of forests deploying and advancing with the power of death
In the huddle of trees and the treacherous undergrowth.

The sun was hot on my face when I woke, and Eugenie was
 dead,
Shot, with a bullet through her head.
Yet every chamber in her revolver was full to plenty.
And only in my own is there one that is empty.

Full Well I Know

Full well I know the flinty heart
That beats beneath those gentle airs
That asks the people to her hearth
But for a writer's cares
That asks them from below above
But only to observe, not love.

Then also as a writer she must fail
Since art without compassion don't avail?

Voices about the Princess Anemone

Underneath the tangled tree
Lies the pale Anemone.

She was the first who ever wrote
The word of fear, and tied it round her throat.

She ran into the forest wild
And there she lay and never smiled.

Sighing, Oh my word of fear
You shall be my only dear.

They said she was a princess lost
To an inheritance beyond all cost.

She feared too much they said, but she says, No,
My wealth is a golden reflection in the stream below.

She bends her head, her hands dip in the water
Fear is a band of gold on the King's daughter.

Deeply Morbid

Deeply morbid deeply morbid was the girl who typed the letters
Always out of office hours running with her social betters
But when daylight and the darkness of the office closed about her
Not for this ah not for this her office colleagues came to doubt her
It was that look within her eye
Why did it always seem to say goodbye?

Joan her name was and at lunchtime
Solitary solitary
She would go and watch the pictures
In the National Gallery
All alone all alone
This time with no friend beside her
She would go and watch the pictures
All alone.

Will she leave her office colleagues
Will she leave her evening pleasures
Toil within a friendly bureau
Running later in her leisure?
All alone all alone
Before the pictures she seems turned to stone.

Close upon the Turner pictures
Closer than a thought may go
Hangs her eye and all the colours
Leap into a special glow
All for her, all alone
All for her, all for Joan.

First the canvas where the ocean
Like a mighty animal
With a really wicked motion
Leaps for sailors' funeral

Holds her panting. Oh the creature
Oh the wicked virile thing
With its skin of fleck and shadow
Stretching tightening over him.
Wild yet captured wild yet captured
By the painter, Joan is quite enraptured.

Now she edges from the canvas
To another loved more dearly
Where the awful light of purest
Sunshine falls across the spray,
There the burning coasts of fancy
Open to her pleasure lay.
All alone, all alone
Come away, come away
All alone.

Lady Mary, Lady Kitty
The Honourable Featherstonehaugh
Polly Tommy from the office
Which of these shall hold her now?
Come away, come away
All alone.

The spray reached out and sucked her in
It was a hardly noticed thing

That Joan was there and is not now
(Oh go and tell young Featherstonehaugh)
Gone away, gone away
All alone.

She stood up straight
The sun fell down
There was no more of London Town
She went upon the painted shore
And there she walks for ever more
Happy quite
Beaming bright
In a happy happy light
All alone.

They say she was a morbid girl, no doubt of it
And what befell her clearly grew out of it
But I say she's a lucky one
To walk for ever in that sun
And as I bless sweet Turner's name
I wish that I could do the same.

The Ghost of Ware

I look in the mirror,
Whose face is there?
It is the face
Of the Ghost of Ware.
This is an old house,
The river flows below placidly,
I am enchanted completely
By this ancient city.
I will never leave you,
Dear town of Ware,
I will look into the mirror
Another afternoon and there
I shall see the smiling face
Of the Ghost of Ware.

NOT WAVING BUT DROWNING (1957)

Not Waving but Drowning

Nobody heard him, the dead man,
But still he lay moaning:
I was much further out than you thought
And not waving but drowning.

Poor chap, he always loved larking
And now he's dead
It must have been too cold for him his heart gave way,
They said.

Oh, no no no, it was too cold always
(Still the dead one lay moaning)
I was much too far out all my life
And not waving but drowning.

The English Visitor

In the graveyard, in the graveyard
By the tomb of Alan Blair
On the mighty Scottish mountain
Knelt the English visitor.

Oh my darling why did you leave me
To lie so cold where I cannot come,
I only wished to have you by me
In the busy town.

How beautiful are the Scottish mountains
Their backs are like ancient mammoths so quiet
And I should like to walk on the mountain
While it is light.

The people frowned to see her looking,
Alas for Alan that fell in with such a woman
Why is she here, what has brought her?
She has no thought for him.

The Englishwoman rose up quickly
And ran through the gates of the cemetery
And leapt on the mountain boulders
With quick step lightly,
Is that an eagle in the sky wheeling?
No, it is not wheeling but weaving
And it's too small for an eagle, it is not hard
To tell it is a buzzard.

Oh why are the people so hostile, why are they angry?
They say I come too late
And that Alan's blood is upon me
But chiefly it is my walking they hate.

Then the beautiful woman ran up the mountainside
As over the top she was spinning
And the people said she would never think of Alan again
And it was typical of Englishwomen.
But No, said an angel, you are wrong
She will think of him freely and frequently
She is not less sorry than you are
Only she was brought up differently.

'What is she writing?
Perhaps it will be good'

What is she writing? Perhaps it will be good,
The young girl laughs: 'I am in love.'
But the older girl is serious: 'Not now, perhaps later.'
Still the young girl teases: 'What's the matter?
To lose everything! A waste of time!'
But now the older one is quite silent,
Writing, writing and perhaps it will be good.
Really neither girl is a fool.

The Fairy Bell

A renegade poet, having taken to journalism
for more money, is rebuked by his Muse in the form
of an old gentleman; he cuts her throat.

A dismal bell hung in the belfry
And clanged a dismal tune
And back and forth the bats did fly
Wherever there was room.

He seemed a melancholy but a reasonable creature,
Yet I could see about his hat
As it were this belfry steeple.

The agony through which I go
(He said) is something that you ought to know
And something that you will know too
When I have finished telling you.

He took my hand, I could not choose but stand,
Perhaps for his own sake he should not have done this?
Yet I thought Death was the best prize, if he won this.

Oh, the sad music of the backward and forth
Flying of the bats, pleading for worth,
But in this perhaps again I was wrong?
That there was for him some enjoyment in their song?

It is done now and I cannot trouble to rue it,
I took his gullet in my hand and with my knife cut through it.

But still in my head I sometimes hear the soft tune
Of the belfry bats moaning to find more room,
And the ding-dong of that imaginary sound
Is as grateful as a fairy bell, tolling by waters drowned.

The New Age

Shall I tell you the signs of a New Age coming?
It is a sound of drubbing and sobbing
Of people crying, We are old, we are old
And the sun is going down and becoming cold
Oh sinful and sad and the last of our kind
If we turn to God now do you think He will mind?
Then they fall on their knees and begin to whine
That the state of Art itself presages decline
As if Art has anything or ever had
To do with civilisation whether good or bad.
Art is wild is as a cat and quite separate from civilisation
But that is another matter that is not now under consideration.
Oh these people are fools with their sighing and sinning
Why should Man be at an end? he is hardly begining.
This New Age will slip in under cover of their eyes.
Well, say geological time is a one-foot rule
 Then Man's only been here about half an inch to play the fool
 Or be wise if he likes, as he often has been
 Oh heavens how these crying people spoil the beautiful
 geological scene.

The Blue from Heaven

a legend of King Arthur of Britain

King Arthur rode in another world
And his twelve knights rode behind him
And Guinevere was there
Crying: Arthur, where are you, dear?

Why is the King so blue?
Why is he this blue colour?
It is because the sun is shining
And he rides under the blue cornflowers.

High wave the cornflowers
That shed the pale blue light
And under the tall cornflowers
Rides King Arthur and his twelve knights.

And Guinevere is there
Crying: Arthur, where are you, dear?

First there were twelve knights riding
And then there was only one
And King Arthur said to the one knight,
Be gone.

All I wish for now, said Arthur,
Is the beautiful colour blue
And to ride in the blue sunshine
And Guinevere I do not wish for you.

Oh lord, said Guinevere
I do not see the colour blue
And I wish to ride where our knights rode,
After you.

Go back, go back, Guinevere,
Go back to the palace, said the King.
So she went back to the palace
And her grief did not seem to her a small thing.

The Queen has returned to the palace
Crying: Arthur, where are you, dear?
And every day she speaks of Arthur's grandeur
To the knights who are there.

That the King has fallen from the power
Of his grandeur all agree
And the falling off of Arthur
Becomes their theme presently.

As if it were only temporarily
And it was not for ever
They speak, but the Queen knows
He will come back never.

Yes, Arthur has passed away,
Gladly he has laid down his reigning power,
He has gone to ride in the blue light
Of the peculiar towering cornflowers.

The Lady of the Well-Spring

Renoir's 'La Source'

He is quite captive to the Lady of the Well-Spring,
Who will rescue him?
Into the French drawing-room the afternoon sun shone
And as the French ladies laughed their white faces
Barred by the balcony shadows seemed to make grimaces.
In the far corner of the room
Sat the English child Joan
As far away as she could get but without exasperation
Only to be freed from the difficulty of conversation.
'Quite captive to the lady of the Well-Spring
Who will rescue him?'
Now I have an excuse to go
Said Joan, and walked out of the window
Down the iron staircase and along the path
And then she began to run through the tall wet grass.
Overhead the hot sun slanting
Fell on Joan as she ran through the fields panting,
Faster faster uphill she goes hoping
That as the ground goes uphill steeply sloping
She will find the well-spring. Into a little wood
She runs, the branches catching at her feet draw blood
And there is a sound of piping screaming croaking clacking
As the birds of the wood rise chattering.
And now as she runs there is the bicker
Of a stream growing narrower in a trickle
And a splash and a flinging, it is water springing.
Now with her feet in deep moss Joan stands looking
Where on a bank a great white lady is lying

A fair smooth lady whose stomach swelling
Full breasts fine waist and long legs tapering
Are shadowed with grass-green streaks. The lady smiles
Lying naked. The sun stealing
Through the branches, her canopies, glorifies
The beautiful rich fat lady where she lies.
Never before in history
In a place so green and watery
Has lady's flesh and so divine a lady's as this is
With just such an admiring look as Joan's met with.
'Quite captive to the Lady of the Well-Spring'?
What nonsense, it is a thing
French ladies would say
In sophisticated conversation on a warm day.
I do not wish to rescue him, blurts Joan,
The lady lolls, Do you wish to go home?
No, says Joan, I should like to live
Here. Right, says the lady, you are my captive.
The child Joan fully sees the beauty her eye embraces
Do not think of her as one who loses.

The Queen and the Young Princess

Mother, mother, let me go
There are so many things I wish to do.
My child, the time is not yet ripe
You are not yet ready for life.
But what is my life that is come to be?
Much the same, child, as it has been for me.
But Mother you often say you have a headache
Because of the crown you wear for duty's sake.
So it is, so it is, a headache I have
And that is what you must grow up to carry to the grave.
But in between Mother do you not enjoy the pleasant weather
And to see the bluebottle and the soft feather?
Ah my child, that joy you speak of must be a pleasure
Oh human statue, not the measure
Of animals', who have no glorious duty
To perform, no headache and so cannot see beauty.
Up, child, up, embrace the headache and the crown
Marred pleasure's best, shadow makes the sun strong.

A Dream of Comparison

after reading Book Ten of 'Paradise Lost'

Two ladies walked on the soft green grass
On the bank of a river by the sea
And one was Mary and the other Eve
And they talked philosophically.

'Oh to be Nothing,' said Eve, 'oh for a
Cessation of consciousness
With no more impressions beating in
Of various experiences.'

'How can Something envisage Nothing?' said Mary,
'Where's your philosophy gone?'
'Storm back through the gates of Birth,' cried Eve,
'Where were you before you were born?'

Mary laughed: 'I love Life,
I would fight to the death for it,

That's a feeling you say? I will find
A reason for it.'

They walked by the estuary,
Eve and the Virgin Mary,
And they talked until nightfall,
But the difference between them was radical.

My Hat

Mother said if I wore this hat
I should be certain to get off with the right sort of chap
Well look where I am now, on a desert island
With so far as I can see no one at all on hand
I know what has happened though I suppose Mother wouldn't see
This hat being so strong has completely run away with me
I had the feeling it was beginning to happen the moment I put it on
What a moment that was as I rose up, I rose up like a flying swan
As strong as a swan too, why see how far my hat has flown me
 away
It took us a night to come and then a night and a day
And all the time the swan wing in my hat waved beautifully
Ah, I thought, How this hat becomes me.
First the sea was dark but then it was pale blue
And still the wing beat and we flew and we flew
A night and a day and a night, and by the old right way
Between the sun and the moon we flew until morning day.
It is always early morning here on this peculiar island
The green grass grows into the sea on the dipping land
Am I glad I am here? Yes, well, I am,
It's nice to be rid of Father, Mother and the young man
There's just one thing causes me a twinge of pain,
If I take my hat off, shall I find myself home again?
So in this early morning land I always wear my hat
Go home, you see, well I wouldn't run a risk like that.

The Engine Drain

a Fenland memory

It was the mighty Engine Drain, the Engine Drain, the Engine
 Drain,
Down which the water went, the water went, the mighty waters
 of the inland sea.
But still in memory I see, the inland sea, the inland sea
That did reflect the summer sky, when it was summer time, of
 Cambridgeshire.
The sky was blue, the sea was blue, the inland sea, the inland sea,
All blue and flat and blue and flat it lay for all to see.
The trees stood up, the reeds stood too, and were reflected in the
 mere
As you might call the inland sea, you might have said it was a
 mere.
And in and out the branches all
The little birds did swoop and swing
Did swoop and swing and call
And oh it was a pretty thing to see them swoop and swing.
Oh ho the inland sea, the inland sea, the mighty mere that moved
 so prettily.

When winter came the water rose,
And rose and rose and rose and rose
And all about the cottage floors
It flowed and rose and flowed and rose
Till in their beds at night you'd see
Quite half afloat the midnight peasantry
That got their living hardily
And died of ripe old age rheumatically,
Oh it was quite surprising how

They'd live to ripe old age rheumatically.
It was because they early learnt
To put their boots on properly
While still in bed, while still in bed.
They learnt to put their boots on properly
Afloat in bed upon the inland sea.

And now I do remember how
Looking from shallow banks below
You'd see the little water-snakes
A-swimming to and fro,
So many little water-snakes
Careering round about
No man might stand to count them there
Careering in the pretty mere.

Oh it was merry in that day
To see the water-fowl play
Upon the inland sea,
Chip-chopping in the sea;
Or see them ride the water-race
In winter, till the winds in chase
Drove them ashore. Oh ho the wind upon the mere
It wound the waves in heaps and tossed the spray
That was half froze, upon the darkening day
Whipping the waters up till you might see
A mile away the whitecaps of the inland sea,
The whitecaps of the mere.

Ah me alas the day is past, is past and long ago
And no man living now may say he saw the waters flow,
And all are gone, the Engine Drain
Has took them to the cruel salt sea

And what is left behind?
A fertile flat and farming land,
A profitable farming land
Is what is left behind.
It took some time, as you might guess,
But not so long as you would guess,
A day or two, or two or three,
To take these waters to the sea
To take them to the Wash.

Why was it called the Engine Drain, the Engine Drain, the Engine
 Drain?
It was because the others were,
The other drains of Cambridgeshire,
Controlled by air, by windmills blowing there,
But oh this Engine was a force, a mighty engineering force,
It took the waters of the mere and brought them to the Wash,
It took them, did the Engine Drain, these waters of the inland sea,
And droppt 'em in the cruel salt sea.
The cruel salt sea.

Saint Anthony and the Rose of Life

a Desert Vision

A dark rose grew in the desert
A red and velvety flower
And opened her petals one by one
In the midnight hour.

Her leaves were a beautiful bright dark green
And this might only be seen
Because the full moon riding high
Threw a delicate beam.

The rose grew in a sand
Of a horrible gray yellow
For the moon that had made the red rose red
Made the sand sallow.

A strapping life heavy and bright
Bulged in the rose and her leaves
And up from the roots of the substantial plant
The bold drops ran like thieves.

Like burly thieves in a shadowy night
In a night of profound shades
They have carried aloft the colours of life
To flaunt in the deathly glades.

Oh rose oh leaves so much alive,
What are you doing here,
And why did you vanish at once away
In the light of a repentant tear?

Anger's Freeing Power

I had a dream three walls stood up wherein a raven bird
Against the walls did beat himself and was this not absurd?

For sun and rain beat in that cell that had its fourth wall free
And daily blew the summer shower and rain came presently

And all the pretty summer time and all the winter too
That foolish bird did beat himself till he was black and blue

Rouse up, rouse up, my raven bird, fly by the open wall
You make a prison of a place that is not one at all.

I took a raven by the hand, O home, I said, my Raven,
And I will take you by the hand and you shall fly to heaven.

But oh he sobbed and oh he sighed and in a fit he lay
Until two fellow ravens came and stood outside to say:

You wretched bird, conceited lump
You well deserve to pine and thump.

See now a wonder, mark it well
My bird rears up in angry spell,

Oh do I then? he says, and careless flies
O'er flattened wall at once to heaven's skies.

And in my dream I watched him go
And I was glad, I loved him so,

Yet when I woke my eyes were wet
To think Love had not freed my pet

Anger it was that won him hence
As only Anger taught him sense.

Often my tears fall in a shower
Because of Anger's freeing power.

Fafnir and the Knights

In the quiet waters
Of the forest pool
Fafnir and the dragon
His tongue will cool

His tongue will cool
And his muzzle dip
Until the soft waters lave
His muzzle tip

Happy single creature
In his coat of mail
With a mild bright eye
And a waving tail

Happy the dragon
In the days expended
Before the time had come for dragons
To be hounded

Delivered in their simplicity
To the Knights of the Advancing Band
Who seeing the simple dragon
Must kill him out of hand

The time has not come yet
But must come soon
Meanwhile happy Fafnir
Take thy rest in the afternoon

Take thy rest
Fafnir while thou mayest
In the green grass
Where thou liest

Happy knowing not
In thy simplicity
That the knights have come
To do away with thee.

When thy body shall be torn
And thy lofty spirit
Broken into pieces
For a knight's merit

When thy lifeblood shall be spilt
And thy Being mild
In torment and dismay
To death beguiled

Fafnir, I shall say then,
Thou art better dead
For the knights have burnt thy grass
And thou couldst not have fed.

Songe d'Athalie

from Racine

It was a dream and shouldn't I bother about a dream?
But it goes on, you know, tears me rather.
Of course I try to forget it but it will not let me.
Well it was on an extraordinary dark night at midnight
My mother Queen Jezebel appeared suddenly before me
Looking just as she did the day she died, dressed grandly.
It was her pride you noticed, nothing she had gone through
 touched that
And she had the look of being most carefully made up
She always made up a lot she didn't want people to know how
 old she was.
She spoke: Be warned my daughter, true girl to me, she said,
Do you not suppose the cruel God of the Jews has finished with
 you,
I am come to weep your falling into his hands, my child,
With these appalling words my mother,
This ghost, leant over me stretching out her hands
And I stretched out my hands too to touch her
But what was it, oh this is horrible, what did I touch?
Nothing but the mangled flesh
 and the breaking bones
Of a body that the dogs tearing
 quarrelled over.

The Hostage

You hang at dawn, they said,
You've done nothing wrong but at dawn you will be hung.
You'll pass tonight in this cell
With Father Whatshisname. He'll look after you well.

There were two truckle beds in the room, on one sat Father W.,
Reclining against a bolster. The lady sat on the other.

I should like you to hear my confession, Father, I'm not of your
 persuasion
I'm a member of the Church of England, but on this occasion
I should like to talk to you, if you'll allow, nothing more,
Just a talk, not really a confession, but my heart is sore.
No, it's not that I have to die, that's the trouble, I've always
 wanted to
But it seems so despondent you know, ungracious too,

She sighed. Daughter, proceed,
Said the father. I am here at your need.

Even as a child, said the lady, I recall in my pram
Wishing it was over and done with. Oh I am
Already at fault. Wonderful how 'bright' they keep,
I'd say of the other children, quite without rancour, then turn
 again to sleep.
Yet life is so beautiful. Oh the scenery.
Have you ever seen the sun getting up in the greenery
Of a summer day, in Norfolk say,
And the mild farm animals lumbering in the thistles.

Presently the Five-Thirty Milk in the station whistles,
You can hear the clank of the cans. In the wood
Trees drip to the stream, the fish rise up for food,
Shap, the old fly's caught. Et cetera. Oh it's busy,
Life bustles in the country, you know; it should be easy.
But I was outside of it, looking, finding no place,
No excuse at all for my distant wandering face.

When I came to London West-Eight, it was much the same
Oh the beautiful faces of others in the falling rain,
In the buses, no fuss there, no question they weren't at home,
Oh why should it only be I that was sent to roam?
I tell you, Father, I trod out the troughs of despair,
I'd rush out of doors in a fit, hurry, anywhere,
Kiss in my mind the darlings, beg them to stop . . .
Till the wind came up hard and blew my beauties off.
The wind blew hard. I snuffed it up and liked it,
Oh yes I liked it, that was the worst of it.

Of course I never dared form any close acquaintance.
Marriage? Out of the question. Well for instance
It might be infectious, this malaise of mine (an excuse?).
 Spread
That? I'd rather be dead.

But will the Lord forgive me? Is it wrong?
Will He forgive me do you think for not minding being hung,
Being glad it will soon be over,
Hoping he isn't the Ruler, the busy Lover,
Wishing to wake again, if I must at all,
A vegetable leaning against a quiet wall,
Or an old stone, so old it was here before Man,
Or a flash in the fire that split out world from the sun?

I find nothing to instruct me in this in Holy Writ,
Said Father W., only, Remember life not to cling to it.

Well I don't you know, said the lady, then aware of something
 comical
Shot him a look that made him feel uncomfortable
Until he remembered she came from the British Isles,
Oh, he said, I've heard that's a place where nobody smiles.
But they do, said the lady, who loved her country, they laugh
 like anything
There is no one on earth who laughs so much about everything.

Well I see, said the Father, the case is complicated,
I will pray for you, Daughter, as I pray for all created
Meanwhile, since you want to die and have to, you may go on
 feeling elated.

Away, Melancholy

Away, melancholy
Away with it, let it go.

Are not the trees green,
The earth as green?
Does not the wind blow,
Fire leap and the rivers flow?
Away melancholy.

The ant is busy
He carrieth his meat,
All things hurry
To be eaten or eat
Away, melancholy.

Man, too, hurried,
Eats, couples, buries,
He is an animal also
With a hey ho melancholy,
Away with it, let it go.

Man of all creatures
Is superlative
(Away melancholy)
He of all creatures alone
Raiseth a stone
(Away melancholy)
Into the stone, the god,
Pours what he knows of good

Calling, good, God.
Away melancholy, let it go.

Speak not to me of tears,
Tryanny, pox, wars,
Saying, Can God
Stone of man's thought, be good?

Say rather it is enough
That the stuffed
Stone of man's good, growing,
By man's called God,
Away, melancholy, let it go.

Man aspires
To good,
To love
Sighs;

Beaten, corrupted, dying
In his own blood lying
Yet heaves up an eye above
Cries, Love, love.
It is his virtue needs explaining,
Not his failing.

Away, melancholy,
Away with it, let it go.

Dido's Farewell to Aeneas

from Virgil

I have lived and followed my fate without flinching, followed it
 gladly
And now, not wholly unknown, I come to the end.
I built this famous city, I saw the walls rise,
As for my abominable brother, I don't think I've been too
 lenient.
Was I happy? Yes, at a price, I might have been happier
If our Dardanian Sailor had condescended to put in elsewhere.
Now she fell silent, turning her face to the pillow,
Then getting up quickly, the dagger in her hand,
I die unavenged, she cried, but I die as I choose,
Come Death, you know you must come when you're called
Although you're a god. And this way, and this way, I call you.

Childe Rolandine

Dark was the day for Childe Rolandine the artist
When she went to work as a secretary-typist
And as she worked she sang this song
Against oppression and the rule of wrong:

It is the privilege of the rich
To waste the time of the poor
To water with tears in secret
A tree that grows in secret
That bears fruit in secret
That ripened falls to the ground in secret
And manures the parent tree
Oh the wicked tree of hatred and the secret
The sap rising and the tears falling.

Likely also, sang the Childe, my soul will fry in hell
Because of this hatred, while in heaven my employer does well
And why should he not, exacerbating though he be but
 generous
Is it his fault I must work at a work that is tedious?
Oh heaven sweet heaven keep my thoughts in their night den
Do not let them by day be spoken.

But then she sang, Ah why not? tell all, speak, speak,
Silence is vanity, speak for the whole truth's sake.

And rising she took the bugle and put it to her lips, crying:
There is a Spirit feeds on our tears, I give him mine.
Mighty human feelings are his food
Passion and grief and joy his flesh and blood
That he may live and grow fat we daily die
This cropping One is our immortality.

Childe Rolandine bowed her head and in the evening
Drew the picture of this spirit from heaven.

The Jungle Husband

Dearest Evelyn, I often think of you
Out with the guns in the jungle stew
Yesterday I hittapotamus
I put the measurements down for you but they got lost in the fuss.
It's not a good thing to drink out here
You know, I've practically given it up, dear.
Tomorrow I am going alone a long way
Into the jungle. It is all grey
But green on top,
Only sometimes when a tree has fallen
The sun comes down plop, it is quite appalling.
You never want to go in a jungle pool
In the hot sun, it would be the act of a fool.
Because it's always full of anacondas, Evelyn, not looking ill-fed
I'll say. So no more now, from your loving husband, Wilfred.

'Come on, Come back'

incident in a future war

Left by the ebbing tide of battle
On the field of Austerlitz
The girl soldier Vaudevue sits
Her fingers tap the ground, she is alone
At midnight in the moonlight she is sitting alone on a round flat
 stone.

Graded by the Memel Conference first
Of all humane exterminators
M.L.5.
Has left her just alive
Only her memory is dead for evermore.
She fears and cries, Ah me why am I here?
Sitting alone on a round flat stone on a hummock there.

Rising, staggering, over the ground she goes
Over the seeming miles of rutted meadow
To the margin of a lake
The sand beneath her feet
Is cold and damp and firm to the waves' beat.

Quickly – as a child, an idiot, as one without memory –
She strips her uniform off, strips, stands and plunges
Into the icy waters of the adorable lake.
On the surface of the water lies
A ribbon of white moonlight
The waters on either side of the moony track
Are black as her mind.

Her mind is as secret from her
As the water on which she swims,
As secret as profound as ominous.

Weeping bitterly for her ominous mind, her plight
Up the river of white moonlight she swims
Until a treacherous undercurrent
Seizing her in an icy amorous embrace
Dives with her, swiftly severing
The waters which close above her head.

An enemy sentinel
Finding the abandoned clothes
Waits for the swimmer's return
('Come on, come back')
Waiting, whiling away the hour
Whittling a shepherd's pipe from the hollow reeds.

In the chill light of dawn
Ring out the pipe's wild notes
'Come on, come back.'

Vaudevue
In the swift and subtle current's close embrace
Sleeps on, stirs not, hears not the familiar tune
Favourite of all the troops of all the armies
Favourite of Vaudevue
For she had sung it too
Marching to Austerlitz
'Come on, come back.'

Why are the Clergy . . . ?

Why are the clergy of the Church of England
Always altering the words of the prayers in the Prayer Book?
Cranmer's touch was surer than theirs, do they not respect him?
For instance last night in church I heard
(I italicize the interpolation)
'The Lord bless you and keep you *and all who are dear unto
 you*'
As the blessing is a congregational blessing and meant to be
This is questionable on theological grounds
But is it not offensive to the ear and also ludicrous?
The 'unto' is a particularly ripe piece of idiocy
Oh how offensive it is. I suppose we shall have next
'Lighten our darkness we beseech thee oh Lord *and the darkness
 of all who are dear unto us.*'
It seems a pity. Does Charity object to the objection?
Then I cry, and not for the first time to that smooth face
Charity, have pity.

I Remember

It was my bridal night I remember,
An old man of seventy-three
I lay with my young bride in my arms,
A girl with t.b.
It was wartime, and overhead
The Germans were making a particularly heavy raid on
 Hampstead.
What rendered the confusion worse, perversely
Our bombers had chosen that moment to set out for Germany.
Harry, do they ever collide?
I do not think it has ever happened,
Oh my bride, my bride.

But Murderous

A mother slew her unborn babe
In a day of recent date
Because she did not wish him to be born in a world
Of murder and war and hate
'Oh why should I bear a babe from my womb
To be broke in pieces by the hydrogen bomb?'

I say this woman deserves little pity
That she was a fool and a murderess
Is a child's destiny to be contained by a mind
That signals only a lady in distress?

And why should human infancy be so superior
As to be too good to be born in this world?
Did she think it was an angel or a baa-lamb
That lay in her belly furled?

Oh the child is the young of its species
Alike with that noble, vile, curious and fierce
How foolish this poor mother to suppose
Her act told us aught that was not murderous

(As, item, That the arrogance of a half-baked mind
Breed murder; makes us all unkind.)

This is Disgraceful and Abominable

Of all the disgraceful and abominable things
Making animals perform for the amusement of human beings is
Utterly disgraceful and abominable.

Animals are animals and have their nature
And that's enough, it is enough, leave it alone.

A disgraceful and abominable thing I saw in a French circus
A performing dog
Raised his back leg when he did not need to
He did not wish to relieve himself, he was made to raise his leg.
The people sniggered. Oh how disgraceful and abominable.
Weep for the disgrace, forbid the abomination.

The animals are cruelly trained,
How could patience do it, it would take too long, they are
 cruelly trained.
Lions leap through fire, it is offensive,
Elephants dance, it is offensive
That the dignified elephant should dance for fear of hot plates,
The lion leap or be punished.
And how can the animals be quartered or carted except cheaply?
Profit lays on the whip of punishment, money heats the
 prodding iron,
Cramps cages. Oh away with it, away with
 it, it is so disgraceful and abominable.
Weep the disgraces. Forbid the
 abominations.

God the Eater

There is a god in whom I do not believe
Yet to this god my love stretches,
This god whom I do not believe in is
My whole life. My life and I am his.

Everything that I have of pleasure and pain
(Of pain, of bitter pain and men's contempt)
I give this god for him to feed upon
And he is my whole life and I am his.

When I am dead I hope that he will eat
Everything I have been and have not been
And crunch and feed upon it and grow fat
Eating my life all up as it is his.

God the Drinker

porque fue sensible

I like to see him drink the gash
I made with my own knife
And draw the blood out of my wrist
And drink my life.

Who is this One who drinks so deep?
His name is Death, He drinks asleep.

(She has taken the sweet knife far away,
The knife bleeds by night and day,
Night and day the blade drips,
I put the sweet knife to my lips.)

It was a god, he drank my health,
He came in shadows and by stealth.

Will Man Ever Face Fact and not Feel Flat?

The rocks and trees in silence stood
To see where Man ran by,
A creature weak as this one is
What can he do but die?
But as they stood and scornful smiled
They heard an angel call:
'The tender creature needeth love,
He needeth love above all.'

This made the rocks and trees laugh more
Until they saw the force of it,
Saw Man disembowelling the earth
And killing because of it.

Ah then they found Man admirable,
'But,' said the angel 'is he?'
And weeping cried, 'The need of love
Makes Man too busy.'

Then God said, 'You are wrong all,
The need of love is meant to call
Man to me, I am love, I,
If it does not, for lack of love he'll die.'

But then came a little wind sneaking along
That was older than all and infamously strong,
'Oh what an artistic animal is our little Man,'
Sneered the wind, 'It is wonderful how he can
Invent fairy stories about everything, pit pat,
Will he ever face fact and not feel flat?'

Every Lovely Limb's a Desolation

I feel a mortal isolation
Wrap each lovely limb in desolation,
Sight, hearing, all
Suffer a fall.

I see the pretty fields and streams, I hear
Beasts calling and birds singing, oh not clear
But as a prisoner
Who in a train doth pass
And through the glass
Peer;
Ah me, so far away is joy, so near.

Break, break the glass, you say?
These thoughts are but a mood
Blow them away, go free?
They are my whole soul's food.

Ghost's food! Sepulchral ailment!
Thou sleekst in me Death's tegument
And so art bent
To do, and this I know.

Yet there are days, oh brief,
When thought's caught half-asleep
(Most merrily) and drowsing
Set in a meadow browsing.

Ah then, like summer breeze in lovely trees
That comes in little pants unequally,
Or like the little waves of summer seas
That push and fuss
In heaven knows what sort of busyness,
Idly, idly, my thoughts bring me to sleep,
On sunny summer day, to sleep. In sun
I fall asleep.

But I must wake and wake again in pain
Crying – to see where sun was once all dust and stain
As on a window pane –

All, all is isolation
And every lovely limb's a desolation.

A Dream of Nourishment

I had a dream of nourishment
Against a breast
My infant face was presst
Ah me the *suffisance* I drew therefrom
What strength, what glory from that fattening fluid,
The fattening most
Was to my infant taste
For oh the sun of strength beat in my veins
And swelled me full, I lay in brightest sun
All ready to put forth, all bursting, all delight.

But in my dream the breast withdrew
In darkness I lay then
And thin,
Thin as a sheeted ghost
And I was famished,
Hankered for a dish
I thought, of blood, as in some classicist's
Old tale
To give me hue and substance, make me hale.

Oh breast, oh Best
That I held fast
Oh fattening draught
Timely repast
Quaffed, presst
And lost.

The breast was withdrawn violently
And oh the famishment for me.

The Airy Christ

Who is this that comes in grandeur, coming from the burning
 East?
This is he we had not thought of, this is he the airy Christ.

Airy in an airy manner, in an airy parkland walking,
Others take him by the hand, lead him, do the talking.

But the Form, the airy One, frowns an airy frown
What they say he knows must be, but he looks aloofly down,

Looks aloofly at his feet, looks aloofly at his hands,
Knows they must, as prophets say, nailèd be to wooden bands,

As he knows the words he sings, that he sings so happily,
Must be changed to working laws, yet sings he ceaselessly.

Those who truly hear his voice, the words, the happy song,
Never shall need working laws to keep from doing wrong.

Deaf men will pretend sometimes they hear the song, the words,
And make excuse to sin extremely; this will be absurd.

Heed it not. Whatever foolish men may do the song is cried
For those who hear, and the sweet singer does not care that he
 was crucified.

For he does not wish that men should love him more than
 anything
Because he died; he only wishes they would hear him sing.

It Filled my Heart with Love

When I hold in my hand a soft and crushable animal, and feel
the fur beat for fear and the soft feather, I cannot feel unhappy.

In his fur the animal rode, and in his fur he strove,
And oh it filled my heart my heart, it filled my heart with love.

i. An Agnostic

(of his religious friend)

He often gazes on the air
And sees quite plain what is not there
Peopling the wholesome void with horrid shapes
Which he manoeuvres in religious japes.
 And yet he is more gracious than I,
 He has such a gracious personality.

ii. A Religious Man

(of his agnostic friend)

He says that religious thought and all our nerviness
Is because of the great shock it was for all of us
Long, long ago when animal turned human being
Which is more than enough to account for everything . . .
 And yet he is more gracious than I,
 He has such a gracious personality.

Dear Little Sirmio

Catullus recollected

Dear little Sirmio
Of all capes and islands
Wherever Neptune rides the coastal waters and the open sea
You really are the nicest.

How glad I am to see you again, how fondly I look at you.

No sooner had I left Bithynia – and what was the name of the
 other place?
And was safely at sea
I thought only of seeing you.

Really is anything nicer
After working hard and being thoroughly worried
Than to leave it all behind and set out for home
Dear old home and one's comfortable bed?

Even if one wears oneself out paying for them.

'Great Unaffected Vampires and the Moon'

It was a graveyard scene. The crescent moon
Performed a devil's purpose for she shewed
The earth a-heap where smooth it should have lain;
And in and out the tombs great witches' cats
Played tig-a-tag and sang harmoniously.
Beneath the deathly slopes the palings stood
Catching the moonlight on their painted sides,
Beyond, the waters of a mighty lake
Stretching five furlongs at its fullest length
Lay as a looking-glass, framed in a growth
Of leafless willows; all its middle part
Was open to the sky, and there I saw
Embosomed in the lake together lie
Great unaffected vampires and the moon.
A Christian crescent never would have lent
Unchristian monsters such close company
And so I say she was no heavenly light
But devil's in that business manifest
And as the vampires seemed quite unaware
I thought she'd lost her soul for nothing lying there.

The Celts

I think of the Celts as rather a whining lady
Who was beautiful once but is not so much so now
She is not very loving, but there is one thing she loves
It is her grievance which she hugs and takes out walking.

The Celtic lady likes fighting very much for freedom
But when she had got it she is a proper tyrant
Nobody likes her much when she is governing.

The Celtic lady is not very widely popular
But the English love her oh they love her very much
Especially when the Celtic lady is Irish they love her
Which is odd as she hates them then more than anyone else.
When she's Welsh the English stupidly associate her chiefly
With national hats, eisteddfods and Old Age Pensions.
(They don't think of her at all when she is Scotch, it is rather
 a problem).

Oh the Celtic lady when she's Irish is the one for me
Oh she is so witty and wild, my word witty,
And flashing and spiteful this Celtic lady we love
All the same she is not so beautiful as she was.

The Passing Cloud

from the Royal Bethlehem Hospital

I thought as I lay on my bed one night, I am only a passing cloud
And I wiped the tear from my sorrowful eye and merrily cried aloud
Oh the love of the Lord is a fearful thing and the love of the Lord is
 mine
And what do I care for the sins of men and the tears of our guilty
 time
I will sail my cloud in the bright blue sky, in the bright blue sky I
 sail
And I look at the sea so merrily swung in the path of the Arctic
 whale
On the tropic belt of the uttermost wild the sea rings a merry peal
And the fish leaps up and the sharks pursue in Creation's happy reel
Oh I dance on my cloud and I cry aloud to the careless creative gust
That made us all and made the fish and the ocean that holds them
 fast
Hurrah hurrah for the grand old heavenly gusty creator Lord
Who said to Job, Don't bother me son, I'll do as a I please my
 word.
Oh never was happiness like to mine as I pelt along on my cloud
In the sky-blue path of the high winds' breath, no wonder I cry
 aloud
With joy I cried and my cheeks were wet and the air was a singing
 space
And I thought as we shot to the upper reach, My lord, it's a lick of
 a pace.
When we swept out of sight of the troublesome earth, was I afraid,
 oh no,
I was glad to see the parochial thing pack up its traps and go

And now I go round and round I go in the merry abyss of the sky
Piercing the grand primaeval dust of the stars in their infancy
I tunnel, I borrow, I offer my dust as a dust for creation's choice
And in the ding-dong of the universe I pipe my innocent voice
I pipe my innocent voice I pipe, I pipe and I also sing
Till I'd sung too loud and woke myself up and that is another
 thing.
Oh I woke with a bump and they brought me here to
 Bethlehem's Royal precincts
And do I care? Not I, not I, I have shed all careful instincts,
I will laugh and sing, or be dumb if they please, and await at the
 Lord's discretion
The day I'll be one, as one I'll be, in an infinite regression
One, ha ha, with a merry ha ha, skip the fish and amoeba where
 are we now?
We are very far out, in a rarefied place, with the thin thin dust
 in a giddy chase,
The dust of Continuous Creation, and how is that for
 identification?
You'll like it; you must, you know,
That merry dust does jig so.

Loin de l'Être

You don't look at all well, quite loin de l'être in fact
Poor pale-face what's the matter, don't they know?
Oh they don't know, but still I don't feel well
Nor ever shall, my name is *Loin de l'Être*.

They stood on the empty terrace above the precipice
When this conversation took place
Between the affectionate but exasperated friend
And the invalid. It is not possible to be
Ill and merry, poor *Loin de l'Être* sighed
And forced a smile, but oh she was so tired.
So tired, called Echo, so tired.

Now pull yourself together, cried the friend
Together cried Echo,
I must leave you now for a tick, she said
Mind you don't get edgy looking at the precipice.
The lovely invalid sighed, Loin de l'être,
And Echo taking the form of a handsome young man
Cried, *Loin de l'Être* and took her away with him.

Nipping Pussy's Feet in Fun

This is not Kind

Oh Mr Pussy-Cat
My, you are sweet!
How do you get about so much
On those tiny feet?
Nip, nip; miaou, miaou,
Tiny little feet,
Nip, nip pussy-cat
My, you are sweet!

Cat Asks Mouse Out

But then Neither is This

Mrs Mouse
Come out of your house
It is a fine sunny day
And I am waiting to play.

Bring the little mice too
And we can run to and fro.

My Cat Major

Major is a fine cat
What is he at?
He hunts birds in the hydrangea
And in the tree
Major was ever a ranger
He ranges where no one can see.

Sometimes he goes up to the attic
With a hooped back
His paws hit the iron rungs
Of the ladder in a quick kick
How can this be done?
It is a knack.

Oh Major is a fine cat
He walks cleverly
And what is he at, my fine cat?
No one can see.

Parents

Parents who can barely afford it
Should not send their children to public schools ill will reward it
That skimping and saving and giving up
That seems so unselfish will buy you a pup
Oh what an ugly biting bow-wow
Well Colonel, how does it go now?
Your son aged twenty-two wears a glittering blazer
His conversation about ponds and ducks, oh happy fool,
Is interrupted to speak of his school
As if at fault he'd allowed
Momentarily that pond to draw him from being proud.
Ah, so hardly won through to it, Colonel,
Is to attach too much importance to it.
But he's saved; ponds, duck, fish in dark water
Have a tight hold of him. It is your daughter
Colonel, who is wholly corrupted.
Women when they are snobbish do not loaf
Look at fish, are not oafish
But are persistently mercenary, cold, scheming and calculating,
This in a young girl is revolting.
Oh beautiful brave mother, the wife of the colonel,
How could you allow your young daughter to become aware of
 the scheming?
If you had not, it might have stayed a mere dreaming
Of palaces and princes, girlish at worst.
Oh to become sensible about social advance at seventeen is to
 be lost.

To a Lady in a Train

She is not Indian, she's ill
'Tis Death hath darkened that pale cheek of hers,
No sun of Indian summer in a trench
Of climate tropical hath made her brown
That was so pale and fair, a northern girl.

Now look more close. That colour's gray not brown
Death certainly hath hold of her, his fingers
Stop up the blood to blacken where it lingers
Death hath her now till gray to black shall turn.

Ah then her soul now ruffling up befeathered
In practice for the flight when Death hath done
Flying shall mock all those who stay at home
And cry: Begone,
Cast off from fleshy station,
Death untethered,
To heaven flown.

Seeing her now this day so soon to go
I would go too
And I say true,

If being Indian not ill had put it on
I should not so much envy her complexion.

Adelaide Abner

Adelaide Abner is cruel
She is grown into a cruel beast
She does not ask me to her parties now
She wants to be first at the feast.

But oh the parties were so beautiful
And I did not monopolize the faces
I was only happy to be delivered for a time
From silence.

Silence at depth is cold
It is misty and full of pain
And because of Adelaide Abner's cruelty
I am in silence again.

Then the girl knelt down and repented
Of what she had said about Adelaide,
Was I a true friend? she wondered,
Yes, I was a true friend, she said.

I was looking for a venial motive,
Vanity might change like the weather,
But oh her heart is cold
And so it is goodbye for ever.

The English

Many of the English,
The intelligent English,
Of the Arts, the Professions and the Upper Middle Classes,
Are under-cover men,
But what is under the cover
(That was original)
Died; now they are corpse-carriers.
It is not noticeable, but be careful,
They are infective.

King Hamlet's Ghost

'It would be spoke to.'

Poor noble Ghost that comes from place of pain
Of so much pain and foul and fiery,
To tread again in mournful armour clad
Thy soft gray fields upon a winter's night
Thou wouldst be spoke to, for unless one speaks
Thou canst not; *must* be spoke to then or go
Unheard, uncomforted to Misery.
I pity thy royal brow, thy temper too,
Thy crownèd brow and the sharp savagery
That, when thy son had spoke, found out in words
A long expression of revengefulness,
'Kill, kill the murderers'. All those who go
In midnight fields of melancholy thought
Where friends pass distantly and do not speak
May cry 'Kill, kill' for they are murdered too
As set upon by Silence and quite killed.
'Speak, speak to us' they cry, 'I would be spoke to'
But oh the friends speak not, they have too much to do.

At School

*a Paolo and Francesca situation but more hopeful,
say in Purgatory*

At school I always walk with Elwyn
Walk with Elwyn all the day
Oh my darling darling Elwyn
We shall never go away.

This school is a most curious place
Everything happens faintly
And the other boys and girls who are here
We cannot see distinctly.

All the day I walk with Elwyn
And sometimes we also ride
Both of us would really always
Rather be outside.

Most I like to ride with Elwyn
In the early morning sky
Under the solitary mosses
That hang from the trees awry.

*The wind blows cold then
And the wind comes to the dawn
And we ride silently
And kiss as we ride down.*

Oh my darling darling Elwyn
Oh what a sloppy love is ours

Oh how this sloppy love sustains me
When we come back to the school bars.

There are bars round this school
And inside the lights are always burning bright
And yet there are shadows
That belong rather to the night than to the light.

Oh my darling darling Elwyn
Why is there this dusty heat in this closed school?
All the radiators must be turned full on
Surely that is against the rules?

Hold my hand as we run down the long corridors
Arched over with tombs
We are underground now a long way
Look out, we are getting close to the boiler room.

We are not driven harshly to the lessons you know
That go on under the electric lights
That go on persistently, patiently you might say,
They do not mind if we are not very bright.

Open this door quick, Elwyn, it is break-time
And if we ride quickly we can come to the sea-pool
And swim; will not that be a nice thing to do?
Oh my darling do not look so sorrowful.

Oh why do we cry so much
Why do we not go to some place that is nice?
Why do we only stand close
And lick the tears from each other's eyes?

Darling, my darling
You are with me in the school and in the dead trees' glade
If you were not with me
I should be afraid.

Fear not the ragged dawn skies
Fear not the heat of the boiler room
Fear not the sky where it flies
The jagged clouds in their rusty colour.

Do not tell me not to cry my love
The tears run down your face too
There is still half an hour left
Can we not think of something to do?

There goes the beastly bell
Tolling us to lessons
If I do not like this place much
That bell is the chief reason.

Oh darling Elwyn love
Our tears fall down together
It is because of the place we're in
And because of the weather.

Can it Be?

Can it be, can it be
That beasts are of various bravery,
Some brave by nature, some not at all,
Some trying to be against a fall?

I saw a cat. Beside a lily tank,
Paved level with the grass, she stood, this cat,
Considering her leap.
Three times she backed for jumping, gathered tight
(So tight, thought landed her already over)
And did not jump. And then,
After a pause, as scolding humanly
'Not nervy, eh? We'll see.'
She jumped. And what a jump that was!
Quite twice as long
And high
As it need be,
Now why
Did this cat jump at all, so force herself?
There was a path around the tank,
She could have walked.

Can it be, can it be
That beasts are of various bravery,
Some simply brave, some not, some taking thought
(Most curiously) to cast themselves aloft?

The Old Sweet Dove of Wiveton

'Twas the voice of the sweet dove
I heard him move
I heard him cry
Love, love.

High in the chestnut tree
In the nest of the old dove
And there he sits solitary
Crying, Love, love.

The gray of this heavy day
Makes the green of the trees' leaves and the grass
　brighter
And the flowers of the chestnut tree whiter
And whiter the flowers of the high cow-parsley.

So still is the air
So heavy the sky
You can hear the splash
Of the water falling from the green grass
As Red and Honey push by,
The old dogs,
Gone away, gone hunting by the marsh bogs.

Happy the retriever dogs in their pursuit
Happy in bog-mud the busy foot.

Now all is silent, it is silent again
In the sombre day and the beginning soft rain
It is a silence made more actual
By the moan from the high tree that is occasional,

Where in his nest above
Still sits the old dove,
Murmuring solitary
Crying for pain,
Crying most melancholy
Again and again.

The Past

People who are always praising the past
And especially the times of faith as best
Ought to go and live in the Middle Ages
And be burnt at the stake as witches and sages.

The Singing Cat

It was a little captive cat
 Upon a crowded train
His mistress takes him from his box
 To ease his fretful pain.

She holds him tight upon her knee
 The graceful animal
And all the people look at him
 He is so beautiful.

But oh he pricks and oh he prods
 And turns upon her knee
Then lifteth up his innocent voice
 In plaintive melody.

He lifteth up his innocent voice
 He lifteth up, he singeth
And to each human countenance
 A smile of grace he bringeth.

He lifteth up his innocent paw
 Upon her breast he clingeth
And everybody cries, Behold
 The cat, the cat that singeth.

He lifteth up his innocent voice
 He lifteth up, he singeth
And all the people arm themselves
 In the love his beauty bringeth.

Longing for Death
because of Feebleness

Oh would that I were a reliable spirit careering around
Congenially employed and no longer by *feebleness* bound
Oh who would not leave the flesh to become a reliable spirit
Possibly travelling far and acquiring merit.

My Heart Goes Out

My heart goes out to my Creator in love
Who gave me Death as end and remedy.
All living creatures come to quiet Death
For him to eat up their activity
And give them nothing. Which is what they want, although
When they are living they do not think so.

Look!

I am becalmed in a deep sea
And give signals, but they are not answered
And yet I see ships in the distance
And give signals, but they do not answer.

Am I a pariah ship, or a leper
To be shunned reasonably?
Or did I commit a crime long ago
And have forgotten, but they remember?

Into the dark night to darker I move
And the lights of the ships are not seen now
But instead there is a phosphorescence from the water.
That light shines, and now I see

Low down, as I bend my hand in the water
A fish so transparent in his inner organs
That I know he comes from the earthquake bed
Five miles below where I sail, I sail.

All his viscera are transparent, his eyes globule on stalks,
Is he dead? Or alive and only languid? Now
Into my hand he comes, the travelling creature,
Not from the sea-bed only but from the generations,
Faint because of the lighter pressure,
Fainting, a long fish, stretched out.

So we meet, and for a moment
I forget my solitariness
But then I should like to show him,
And who shall I show him to?

Who is this Who Howls and Mutters?

Who is this that howls and mutters?
It is the Muse, each word she utters
Is thrown against a shuttered door
And very soon she'll speak no more.

Cry louder, Muse, make much more noise
The world is full of rattling toys
I thought she'd say, Why should I then?
I have spoke low to better men
But oh she did not speak at all but went away
And now I search for her by night and day.

Night and day I seek my Muse
Seek the one I did abuse
She had so sweet a face, so sweet a voice
But oh she did not make sufficient noise.

False plea. I did not listen then
That listen now and listen now in vain.

And still the tale of talent murdered
Untimely and untimely buried
Works in my soul. Forgive me, Lord, I cry
Who only makest Muses howl and sigh
Thou, Lord, repent and give her back to me
Weeping uncomforted, Lord have pity.

He did repent. I have her now again
Howling much worse, and oh the door is open.

Oh What is the Thing He Done?

Oh what is the terrible thing he has done
You are always going on about
My pitiful cousin, my darling one,
That will shut him out from the grace of the sun
Oh what is the thing he done?

Oh is it such a thing as the crocodile
Would shake in each sensitive coil
Oh is it such as thing as would make the blood
Of an adder and his young ones boil
Oh it is a thing as the Prince of Hell
Would plainly declare it was not well.

But what is the thing, oh what is it, pray?
My lips shall never be sullied to say,
Go forth with your cousin, you wretched woman,
And dwell with him in the dark of the sun.

Magna est Veritas

With my looks I am bound to look simple or fast I would rather
 look simple
So I wear a tall hat on the back of my head that is rather a temple
And I walk rather queerly and comb my long hair
And people say, Don't bother about her.
So in my time I have picked up a good many facts,
Rather more than the people do who wear smart hats
And I do not deceive because I am rather simple too
And although I collect facts I do not always know what they
 amount to.
I regard them as a contribution to almighty Truth, magna est
 veritas et praevalebit,
Agreeing with that Latin writer, Great is Truth and will prevail
 in a bit.

The Light of Life

Put out that Light,
Put out that bright Light,
Let darkness fall.

Put out that Day,
It is the time for nightfall.

In the Park

Walking one day in the park in winter
I heard two silvered gentlemen talking,
Two old friends, elderly, walking, talking
There by the silver lake mid-pooled black in winter.

'Pray for the Mute who have no word to say,'
Cried the one old gentleman, 'Not because they are dumb,
But they are weak. And the weak thoughts beating in the brain
Generate a sort of heat, yet cannot speak.
Thoughts that are bound without sound
In the tomb of the brain's room, wound. Pray for the Mute.'

'But' (said his friend), 'see how they swim
Free in the element best loved, so wet; yet breathe
As a visitor to the air come; plunge then, rejoicing more,
Having left it briefly for the visited shore, to come
Home to the wet
Windings that are yet
Best loved though familiar; and oh so right the wet
Stream and the wave; he is their pet.'

Finished, the mild friend
Smiled, put aside his well-tuned hearing instrument
And it seemed
The happiness he spoke of
Irradiated all his members, and his heart
Barked with delight to stress
So much another's happiness.

But which other's? The sombre first
Speaker reversed
The happy moment; cried again
(Mousing for pain) 'Pray for the Mute' (a tear drops)
'They are like the brute.'

Struck by the shout
That he may not know what it's about
The deaf friend again
Up-ends his hearing instrument to relieve the strain.
What? Oh shock, ' "Pray for the Mute"?
I thought you said the newt.'

Now which is Christianer pray, of these old friends, the one
 who will say
For pain's sake pray, pray; or the deaf other that rejoices
So much that the cool amphibian
Shall have his happiness, all things rejoicing with him?

But wait: the first speaker now, the old sombre one,
Is penetrated quite by his friend's sun

And, 'Oh blessed you,' he cries, 'to show
So in simplicity what is true.'
All his face is suffused with happy tears and as he weeps he
 sings a happy song,
Happier even than his friend's song was, righting the wrong.
So two, better than one, finally strike truth in his happy song:

'Praise,' cries the weeping softened one,
 'Not pray, praise, all men,
Praise is the best prayer, the least
 self's there, that least's release.'

Evangelie
or
The Figure of Literary Corruption, seeking Glory not Truth

Wicked and corrupt
Was Evangelie
And the corruption came out of her
On to me.

Corruptest and most wicked
Of creatures,
Can I forget a word she said
Or her features?

Lord, cleanse me of the corruption
Of Evangelie,
And of my feelings for her,
That I may wear again the garment of whiteness,
And the fair crown in my hair.

Jumbo

Jumbo, Jumbo, Jumbo darling, Jumbo come to Mother.
But Jumbo wouldn't, he was a dog who simply wouldn't bother
An ugly beast he was with drooping guts and filthy skin,
It was quite wonderful how 'mother' loved the ugly thing.

The Choosers

Who shall we send to fetch him away
This young-man Author of the Month of May?
We will send Mr Puff to fetch him away,
We are the Choosers and stand in the way.

Oh we are the Choosers, what we say goes.
Does Puff know this? Yes, Puff knows.
Hey ho what a merry game,
It is as if we were still in Pop, it is the same.

With a hey-ho and a yah
No, we will not have So-and-So
Because we do not like his hat or his Ma.

Outside of this eclectic and up-to-date circle
Slink the sleek Great Ones, and you know
They may go and not care a particle
Because the Angel of Posterity has chosen them
And the Choosers will not be known then,
All the same it a shame to treat them so.

Let Posterity-Time come
Quick and Choosers be dumb.

Oh why does England cherish her arts in this
 wise,
Picking inferiorly with grafted eyes?
It is because it is like the school they never forget,
So-and-so must be the driven out one, this the pet.

The Occasional Yarrow

It was a mile of greenest grass
Whereon a little stream did pass,
 The Occasional Yarrow

Only in every seventh year
Did this pretty stream appear,
 The Occasional Yarrow

Wading and warbling in its beds
Of grass decked out with daisy heads,
 The Occasional Yarrow

There in my seventh year, and this sweet stream's,
I wandered happily (as happy gleams
 The Occasional Yarrow).

Though now to memory alone
I can call up thy lovely form,
 Occasional Yarrow.

I still do bless thy Seventh days
Bless thy sweet name and all who praise
 The Occasional Yarrow.

The Sorrowful Girl

Muriel, Muriel, marry me Muriel,
And I will comfort you as well
And bring life to your pale hair
And your languid air.

Ah then I shall not be I, for I am here
With my languid air and lifeless hair
And I do not feel cold or heat
I am imprisoned and do not need to be freed
My prison is my sorrowful mind
And I do not wish to leave it behind
Wake me not, leave me here, leave me alone
I am as God made me, a sorrowful one.

And singing she sang, I am sorrowful, sorrowful
And because I am sorrowful I am beautiful.

Her lover has left her and gone angrily off
He speaks of her only to laugh and to scoff
Pretending he only wanted to marry her for her money
Intending to prove his thoughts were not moony
With love, or any such stuff,
That he is not such a fool as to have had a rebuff.

A pale light-moon-white lily romantic girl-of-a-lover
With nothing to her name but two thousand pounds in Old
 Consols, who will have her?
Is the burden of the anger of this churl and of his troubles.

But ever here came from far away
Growing fainter with the passing day
The sorrowful song on the sorrowful air
Of the languid girl with the lifeless hair
Singing: Oh I am sorrowful, sorrowful, sorrowful
And because I am sorrowful I am beautiful.

The Starling

I will never leave you darling
To be eaten by the starling
For I love you more than ever
In the wet and stormy weather.

Thus to the husband sang the wife
That loved him more than his own life
Oh at these words the husband felt
Each hair rise separate upon his icy pelt.

He let himself down from out his room
He went upon the ancient mountain
And there he quite forgot his gloom
As he trod the torrent's icy fountain.

Cold, cold, icy cold,
Cold, cold, cold I am,
Cold has no place in my wife's warm thought
There she will have me cradled and wraught.
Oh nothing, nothing, nothing I
He cried, that in her thinking does not lie.

Then he doffed his clothes and quickly froze
In the ice of the ancient mountain-side
And there in an icy happy doze
He doth for evermore abide.

Down in the valley waits the wife
That loved him more than his own life

And still she sings, in hope to lure
Him to her side again, Be very sure

I will never leave you darling
To be eaten by the starling
For I love you more than ever
In the wet and stormy weather.

Die Lorelei

An antique story comes to me
And fills me with anxiety,
I wonder why I fear so much
What surely has no modern touch?

It is of Germany it speaks,
One evening time; the mountain peaks
Are in the sun, but the old Rhine
Flows secretly and does not shine.

There, on a rock majestical,
A girl with smile equivocal,
Painted, young and damned and fair,
Sits and combs her yellow hair.

With a yellow comb she combs it,
Sings a song, and sometimes moans it,
That has a most peculiar turn,
It makes the heart and belly burn.

The sailor sailing, hearing it
Falls at once into a fit,
He does not see the rocky race,
His eyes are looking for a face.

The boat strikes hard, as she must do,
And down she goes, and he goes too.
This story brings me so much grief
I know not how to find relief.

Lurks there some meaning underneath?

Farewell

Farewell dear friends
I loved you so much
But now I must leave you
And spread over me the dust

Fare life fare well
Fare never ill
Far I go now
And say, Farewell.

Farewell dear world
With the waters around you curled
And the grass on your breast
I loved you best.

Farewell fish and insect
Bird, animal, swift mover
Grim reptile as well
I was your approver.

Wide sky, farewell,
Sun, moon, stars in places
Farewell all fair universes
In far places.

Ding dong, ding dong
As a bell is rung,
Sing ding dong farewell
As a sweet bell.

SELECTED POEMS (1962)

Thoughts about the Person from Porlock

Coleridge received the Person from Porlock
And ever after called him a curse
Then why did he hurry to let him in? –
He could have hid in the house.

It was not right of Coleridge in fact it was wrong
(But often we all do wrong)
As the truth is I think he was already stuck
With Kubla Khan.

He was weeping and wailing, I am finished, finished,
I shall never write another word of it
When along comes the Person from Porlock
And takes the blame for it.

It was not right, it was wrong,
But often we all do wrong.

*

May we enquire the name of the Person from Porlock?
Why, Porson, didn't you know?
He lived at the bottom of Porlock Hill
So had a long way to go

He wasn't much in the social sense
Though his grandmother was a Warlock,
One of the Rutlandshire ones I fancy
And nothing to do with Porlock

And he lived at the bottom of the hill as I said
And had a cat named Flo,
And had a cat named Flo.

Thoughts about the Person from Porlock (cont.)

I long for the Person from Porlock
To bring my thoughts to an end,
I am becoming impatient to see him
I think of him as a friend

Often I look out of the window
Often I run to the gate
I think, He will come tomorrow
I think it is rather late.

I am hungry to be interrupted
For ever and ever amen
Oh Person from Porlock come quickly
And bring my thoughts to an end.

*

I felicitate the people who have a Person from Porlock
To break up everything and throw it away
Because then there will be nothing to keep them
And they need not stay.

*

Why do they grumble so much?
He comes like a benison
They should be glad he has not forgotten them
They might have had to go on.

*

These thoughts are depressing I know. They are depressing,
I wish I was more cheerful, it is more pleasant,
Also it is a duty, we should smile as well as submitting
To the purpose of One Above who is experimenting
With various mixtures of human character which goes best.
All is interesting for him it is exciting, but not for us.
There I go again. Smile, smile and get some work to do
Then you will be practically unconscious without positively
 having to go.

Thoughts about the Christian Doctrine
of Eternal Hell

Is it not interesting to see
How the Christians continually
Try to separate themselves in vain
From the doctrine of eternal pain.

They cannot do it,
They are committed to it,
Their Lord said it,
They must believe it.

So the vulnerable body is stretched without pity
On flames for ever. Is this not pretty?

The religion of Christianity
Is mixed of sweetness and cruelty
Reject this Sweetness, for she wears
A smoky dress out of hell fires.

Who makes a God? Who shows him thus?
It is the Christian religion does,
Oh, oh, have none of it
Blow it away, have done with it.

This god the Christians show
Out with him, out with him, let him go.

Recognition not Enough

Sin recognised – but that – may keep us humble,
But oh, it keeps us nasty.

Was He Married?

Was he married, did he try
To support as he grew less fond of them
Wife and family?

No,
He never suffered such a blow.

Did he feel pointless, feeble and distrait,
Unwanted by everyone and in the way?

From his cradle he was purposeful,
His bent strong and his mind full.

Did he love people very much
Yet find them die one day?

He did not love in the human way.

Did he ask how long it would go on,
Wonder if Death could be counted on for an end?

He did not feel like this,
He had a future of bliss.

Did he never feel strong
Pain for being wrong?

He was not wrong, he was right,
He suffered from others', not his own, spite.

But there *is* no suffering like having made a mistake
Because of being of an inferior make.

He was not inferior,
He was superior.

He knew then that power corrupts but some must govern?

His thoughts were different.

Did he lack friends? Worse,
Think it was for his fault, not theirs?

He did not lack friends,
He had disciples he moulded to his ends.

Did he feel over-handicapped sometimes, yet must draw even?

How could he feel like this? He was the King of Heaven.

. . . find a sudden brightness one day in everything
Because a mood had been conquered, or a sin?

I tell you, he did not sin.

Do only human beings suffer from the irritation
I have mentioned? learn too that being comical
Does not ameliorate the desperation?

Only human beings feel this,
It is because they are so mixed.

All human beings should have a medal,
A god cannot carry it, he is not able.

A god is Man's doll, you ass,
He makes him up like this on purpose.

He might have made him up worse.

He often has, in the past.

To choose a god of love, as he did and does,
Is a little move then?

Yes, it is.

A larger one will be when men
Love love and hate hate but do not deify them?

It will be a larger one.

Was it not curious?

Was it not curious of Aúgustin
Saint Aúgustin, Saint Aúgustin,
When he saw the beautiful British children
To say such a curious thing?

He said he must send the gospel, the gospel,
At once to them over the waves
He never said he thought it was wicked
To steal them away for slaves

To steal the children away
To buy and have slavery at all
Oh no, oh no, it was not a thing
That caused him any appal.

Was it not curious of *Gregory*
Rather more than of Aúgustin?
It was not curious so much
As it was wicked of them.

The Frozen Lake

To a mere
Sir Bedevere
Consigned Excalibur

White and silent is the snowflake
Falling, falling, and it will make
Soon all flat and like a white lake
In a white and silent state
Beaming flat and vacant.

Underneath the frozen water
Steps the Lord of Ullan's daughter
She is a witch of endless might
And rules the borders of the night.

So however white and silent
Seems the lake, it is not vacant
But contains Lord Ullan's daughter
Walking as her Uncle taught her.

Her Uncle is a greater sage
At witchcraft than the lady is
But he has gone, one knows not where
And so his niece only is here.

No, this water is not vacant
But is full of deep intent
Of deep intent and management
Contrived by Ullan's daughter
To what end I know not.

And to my mind the lake is brighter
For the lady's presence; whiter
Though its coat of winter make it
It is for Ullan's daughter's sake it
Beams to me so brightly.

Often as I gaze upon it
Tread upon the ice upon it
I can feel the water shiver
As the lady with a slither
Comes to tap the ice, to tear it,
Yes, I think that I can hear it
Tapped and tickled with her fingers
Where a floe in splinter lingers
Where I cannot come.
But I swear I hear her, seem to
See her face that seems to beam to
Me that hovers half-enchanted
Yes I hover half-enchanted
Wondering if I am wanted
Beckoned by her smile or threatened,
And as always, so today
As I stand and wonder, Ullan's daughter
Goes away.

To a mere
Sir Bedevere
Consigned Excalibur
And who is this who now comes here?
It *is* Sir Bedevere.

This afternoon Sir Bedevere
Found me hesitating by

The icy lake, and he said: 'Sir,
Where lies the sword Excalibur?'
I answered with a lie:
'It must be in some other mere.'
And then I said, 'I truly love her,
Love the Lord of Ullan's daughter.'
And so I answered with a lie
As I can only think of her.
'Oh shall I go beneath the water
Where she walks, or wait for her?
Tell me, Sir Bedevere,
Shall I wait here for her?'
He looked at me, but did not say
A word, then he too went away.

And so they go. I am alone,
The white lake beams beneath the moon,
O dear white lake, O dearest love
That will not show yourself above
The bitter ice, but leave me here
To be annoyed by Bedevere,
I come, I come. And then I dived
Into the lake, but through my side
As I went down to seek for her
There passed the sword Excalibur,
In cold and silence seek for her,
The sword sunk in the mere,

And so I died, and the lake-water
That holds the form of Ullan's daughter
With all my blood is dyed,
Is dyed,
With all my love is dyed.

Poor Soul, poor Girl!

a débutante

I cannot imagine anything nicer
Than to be struck by lightning and killed suddenly crossing a
 field
As if somebody cared.
Nobody cares whether I am alive or dead.

From the French (1)

Indolent youth,
Drawn by everything in turn,
By not being decided enough
I lost my life.

Admire Cranmer!

Admire the old man, admire him, admire him,
Mocked by the old priests of Mary Tudor, given to the flames,
Flinching and overcoming the flinching, Cranmer.

Admire the martyrs of Bloody Mary's reign,
In the shocking arithmetic of cruel average, ninety
A year, three-hundred; admire them.

But still I cry: Admire the Archbishop,
The old man, the scholar, admire him.
Not simply, for flinching and overcoming simply,
But for his genius, admire him,
His delicate feelings of genius, admire him,

That wrote the Prayer Book
(Admire him!)
And made the flames burn crueller. Admire Cranmer!

Votaries of Both Sexes Cry First to Venus

Crying for pleasure,
Crying for pain,
Longing to see you
Again and again.

But one stood up and said: I love
The love that comes in the dark fields,
In the late night, in the hot breathless dark night;
In the moony forest, when there is a moon,
In the moony rides of the dark forest.

I love this love; it is eerie if there is not
My love in *my* arms then. It is an excitement
In the arms of a person. It is exciting then,
It is such an excitement as is on the approach
Of Death: it is *my* love in *my* arms, and then
The trees and the dark trees and the soft grass and the moon
Are not arrogant, as they are if I am alone,
Not a measure, a great measure of indifference, not arrogant
Or in their way exciting either in a way that is too much.

Here this person standing up before Venus wept
And wept, and the tears of this person were warm
And this person then said: There is no love in my arms
No sweet person I love in my arms, and the tears
And the soft strong feelings I parade underneath the trees,
I lay them down; on the soft dark green grass I lay down
My strong feelings. They are for you to eat up, Venus,
But you do not care for them much. Then they are
For the god who created me. Let him have them.

Then this person began to laugh and dance
And Venus was offended; but behind Venus there came
First a little light, then some laughter, then a hand
That took up the great feelings, and then a blessing fell
Like the moon, and there was not any Venus any longer
But the votaries were not abashed, they were blessed.

> Crying for pleasure,
> Crying for pain,
> Longing to see you
> Again and again.

Yes this time when they sang their song they were blessed.

From the French (2)

'We shall never be one mummy only
Beneath the antique deserts and the happy palms.'

I Was so Full . . .

I was so full of love and joy
There was not enough people to love,
So I said: Let there be God,
Then there was God above.

I was so full of anger and hate
To be hated was not enough people,
So I said: Let there be a Devil to hate,
Then down below was the Devil.

These persons have worked very much in my mind
And by being not true, have made me unkind,
So now I say: Away with them, away; we should
Not believe fairy stories if we wish to be good.

Think of them as persons from the fairy wood.

From the Italian

an old superstition

A woolly dog,
A red-haired man,
Better dead
Than to have met 'em.

God Speaks

I made Man with too many flaws. Yet I love him.
And if he wishes, I have a home above for him.
I should like him to be happy. I am genial.
He should not paint me as if I were abominable.
As for instance, that I had a son and gave him for their
 salvation.
This is one of the faults I meant. It leads to nervous prostration.
All the same, there is a difficulty. I should like him to be happy
 in heaven here,
But he cannot come by wishing. Only by being already at home
 here.

Edmonton, thy cemetery . . .

Edmonton, thy cemetery
In which I love to tread
Has roused in me a dreary thought
For all the countless dead,
Ah me, the countless dead.

Yet I believe that one is one
And shall for ever be,
And while I hold to this belief
I walk, oh cemetery,
Thy footpaths happily.

And I believe that two and two
Are but an earthly sum
Whose totalling has no part at all
In heavenly kingdom-come,
I love the dead, I cry, I love
Each happy happy one.

Till Doubt returns with a dreary face
And fills my heart with dread
For all the tens and tens and tens
That must make up a hundred,
And I begin to sing with him
As if Belief has never been
Ah me, the countless dead, ah me
The countless countless dead.

My Muse

My Muse sits forlorn
She wishes she had not been born
She sits in the cold
No word she says is ever told.

Why does my Muse only speak when she is unhappy?
She does not, I only listen when I am unhappy
When I am happy I live and despise writing
For my Muse this cannot be but dispiriting.

THE FROG PRINCE AND OTHER POEMS (1966)

The Frog Prince

I am a frog
I live under a spell
I live at the bottom
Of a green well

And here I must wait
Until a maiden places me
On her royal pillow
And kisses me
In her father's palace.

The story is familiar
Everybody knows it well
But do other enchanted people feel as nervous
As I do? The stories do not tell,

Ask if they will be happier
When the changes come
As already they are fairly happy
In a frog's doom?

I have been a frog now
For a hundred years
And in all this time
I have not shed many tears,

I am happy, I like the life,
Can swim for many a mile
(When I have hopped to the river)
And am for ever agile.

And the quietness,
Yes, I like to be quiet
I am habituated
To a quiet life,

But always when I think these thoughts
As I sit in my well
Another thought comes to me and says:
It is part of the spell

To be happy
To work up contentment
To make much of being a frog
To fear disenchantment

Says, It will be *heavenly*
To be set free,
Cries, *Heavenly* the girl who disenchants
And the royal times, *heavenly*,
And I think it will be.

Come then, royal girl and royal times,
Come quickly,
I can be happy until you come
But I cannot be heavenly,
Only disenchanted people
Can be heavenly.

Tenuous and Precarious

Tenuous and Precarious
Were my guardians,
Precarious and Tenuous,
Two Romans.

My father was Hazardous,
Hazardous,
Dear old man,
Three Romans.

There was my brother Spurious,
Spurious Posthumous,
Spurious was spurious
Was four Romans.

My husband was Perfidious,
He was perfidious,
Five Romans.

Surreptitious, our son,
Was surreptitious,
He was six Romans.

Our cat Tedious
Still lives,
Count not Tedious
Yet.

My name is Finis,
Finis, Finis,
I am Finis,
Six, five, four, three, two,
One Roman,
Finis.

A House of Mercy

It was a house of female habitation,
Two ladies fair inhabited the house,
And they were brave. For although Fear knocked loud
Upon the door, and said he must come in,
They did not let him in.

There were also two feeble babes, two girls,
That Mrs S. had by her husband had,
He soon left them and went away to sea,
Nor sent them money, nor came home again
Except to borrow back
Her Naval Officer's Wife's Allowance from Mrs S.
Who gave it him at once, she thought she should.

There was also the ladies' aunt
And babes' great aunt, a Mrs Martha Hearn Clode,
And she was elderly.
These ladies put their money all together
And so we lived.

I was the younger of the feeble babes
And when I was a child my mother died
And later Great Aunt Martha Hearn Clode died
And later still my sister went away.

Now I am old I tend my mother's sister
The noble aunt who so long tended us,
Faithful and True her name is. Tranquil.
Also Sardonic. And I tend the house.

It is a house of female habitation
A house expecting strength as it is strong
A house of aristocratic mould that looks apart

When tears fall; counts despair
Derisory. Yet it has kept us well. For all its faults,
If they are faults, of sternness and reserve,
It is a Being of warmth I think; at heart
A house of mercy.

The Best Beast of the Fat-Stock Show at Earls Court

in monosyllables

The Best Beast of the Show
Is fat,
He goes by the lift –
They all do that.

This lift, large as a room,
(Yet the beasts bunch),
Goes up with a groan,
They have not oiled the winch.

Not yet to the lift
Goes the Best Beast,
He has to walk on the floor to make a show
First.

Great are his horns,
Long his fur,
The Beast came from the North
To walk here.

Is he not fat?
Is he not fit?
Now in a crown he walks
To the lift.

When he lay in his pen,
In the close heat,
His head lolled, his eyes
Were not shut for sleep.

Slam the lift door,
Push it up with a groan,
Will they kill the Beast now?
Where has he gone?

When he lay in the straw
His heart beat so fast
His sides heaved, I touched his side
As I walked past.

I touched his side,
I touched the root of his horns;
The breath of the Beast
Came in low moans.

Exeat

I remember the Roman Emperor, one of the cruellest of them,
Who used to visit for pleasure his poor prisoners cramped in
 dungeons,
So then they would beg him for death, and then he would say:
Oh no, oh no, we are not yet friends enough.
He meant they were not yet friends enough for him to give them
 death.
So I fancy my Muse says, when I wish to die:
Oh no, Oh no, we are not yet friends enough,

And Virtue also says:
We are not yet friends enough.

How can poet commit suicide
When he is still not listening properly to his Muse,
Or a lover of Virtue when
He is always putting her off until tomorrow?

Yet a time may come when a poet or any person
Having a long life behind him, pleasure and sorrow,
But feeble now and expensive to his country
And on the point of no longer being able to make a decision
May fancy Life comes to him with love and says:
We are friends enough now for me to give you death;
Then he may commit suicide, then
He may go.

Easy

Easy in their ugly skins
Claudius and Gertrude were,
They liked as well as loving each other,
They were a humdrum pair.

Of all the people in that bloodstained play
They are the only ones
Who might have been living today.

Hamlet dimly perceived
They were not entirely of his times.
Their witless freedom of the ages
Irked him sometimes.

He, a man of two times –
His Yesterday, *his* Today –
Could not stretch
To their timelessness,
He was too much on edge.

Banausic, he called them, banausic,
A villainous banausic couple.
He turned to blow on his love for his father
And found it rubble.

Mouthing at Yesterday's ghostly manifestation
A sentence or two from Wittenberg, likely at least
To put a ghost in its place,

He discovered no satisfaction,
And no sense.

Sadly his heart heaved. Where was there a shield for him
Against banausic couples in their ugly skin
Easy, easy? There was never any ease for him.

Oh Christianity, Christianity

Oh Christianity, Christianity,
Why do you not answer our difficulties?
If He was God He was not like us,
He could not lose.

Can Perfection be less than perfection?
Can the creator of the Devil be bested by him?
What can the temptation to possess the earth have meant to Him
Who made and possessed it? What do you mean?

And Sin, how could He take our sins upon Him? What does
 it mean?
To take sin upon one is not the same
As to have sin inside one and feel guilty.

It is horrible to feel guilty,
We feel guilty because we are.
Was He horrible? Did He feel guilty?

You say He was born humble – but He was not,
He was born God –
Taking our nature upon Him. But then you say,
He was Perfect Man. Do you mean
Perfectly Man, meaning wholly; or Man without sin? Ah
Perfect Man without sin is not what we are.

Do you mean He did not know that He was God,
Did not know He was the Second Person of the Trinity?
(Oh, if He knew this, and was,
It was a source of strength for Him we do not have)
But this theology of 'emptying' you preach sometimes –
That He emptied Himself of knowing He was God – seems
A theology of false appearances
To mock your facts, as He was God, whether He knew He was
 or not.

Oh what do you mean, what do you mean?
You never answer our difficulties.

You say, Christianity, you say
That Trinity is unchanging from eternity
But then you say
At the incarnation He took
Our Manhood into the Godhead,
That did not have it before,
So it must have altered it,
Having it.

Oh what do you mean, what do you mean?
You never answer our questions.

Why do you rage?

Why do you rage so much against Christ, against Him
Before Whom angel brightness grows dark, heaven dim?
Is He not wonderful, beautiful? Is He not Love?
Did He not come to call you from Heaven above?
Say, Yes; yes, He did; say, Yes; call Him this:
Truth, Beauty, Love, Wonder, Holiness.

Say, Yes. Do not always say, No.

Oh I would if I thought it were so,
Oh I know that you think it is so.

The True Tyrant
or
The Spirit of Duty Rebuked

Oh my darling Goosey-Gander
Why do you always wish to wander
Evermore, evermore?

Now I have you safe at home
I will never let you roam
Ever more.

Then cried the lady from her kitchen
Standing in her chains of grass:
It is not Duty, it is Love
That will not let me pass
Evermore, evermore
Through the grass-enchainèd door, the grassy door.

Under Wrong Trees . . .
or
Freeing the Colonial Peoples

Under wrong trees
Walked the zombies

They were told to walk under oaks, you know,
But they preferred willows.

It was the first time they had been old
Enough not to do as they were told

They thus became
Not zombies
But *splendide*

Until one day they fell in
The river the willows were weeping in

Which was *stupide*
Of them, people said, and showed they were
 not old
Enough yet not to do as they were told.

But really I think this tale of wrong trees
Shows that they never were zombies

But men, women and men.

So why should we notice them?

I had a dream . . .

I had a dream I was Helen of Troy
In looks, age and circumstances,
But otherwise I was myself.

It was the ninth year of the siege
And I did not love anybody very much
Except perhaps Cassandra,
It was those peculiar eyes she had
As if she were short-sighted
That made me feel I could talk to her,
I would have loved anybody I could talk to.
I suppose you know how it's going to end, I
 said,
As well as I do? Dreams, dreams? They aren't
 dreams
You know. Do you know?

I used to walk on the walls
And look towards the Grecian tents . . .
It's odd, I said (to Cassandra, of course) how
Everything one has ever read about Troy
As they have always been such splendid writers who were
 writing
Naturally gets into one's conversation . . .
Where Cressid lay that night, except they did not say
How beastly Scamander looks under this sort of sky,
And the black Greek ships piled up on the seashore beyond
Like prison hulks, like slugs. So there we were
On the walls of Troy. But what I did not know,
And I could not get Cassandra to say either,

Was which of the Helen legends I was,
The phantom, with the real Helen in Egypt,
Or the flesh-and-blood one here
That Menelaus would take back to Sparta.
Remembering this, that there was still some uncertainty,
Raised my spirits, I must say
Dispiritedness was what we were all sunk in,
And though the Royal Family may have seemed spectral
Their dispiritedness was substantial enough, and I dare say
The Greeks were in much the same case, dispirited;
Well, nine years that had been of it, and now
The heavy weather, and the smells
From the battlefield, when the wind was in that direction,
And the spirit of the men, too, on both sides,
This was substantial enough; it seemed to me
Like the spirit of all armies, on all plains, in all wars, the men
No longer thinking why they were there
Or caring, but going on; like the song the English used to sing
In the first world war: We're here because, we're here because,
We're here because, we're here. This was the only time
I heard Cassandra laugh, when I sung this to her. I said:
There you are, you laugh; that shows you are not nearly so
Religious as you think. That's blasphemous, that laugh,
Sets you free. But then she got frightened. All right, I said,
Don't be free, go along and finish up on Clytemnestra's sword-
 point,
Pinked like a good girl. I used to get so cross.
Paris was stupid, it was impossible to talk to him.
Hector might have been different, at least he understood enough
To be offended – fear of the gods again, I suppose – because
When I said: Well, you know what the Trojan Women
Are going to say about the sack of Troy and being led away
Into captivity, they are going to say: If these things

Had not happened to us we should not be remembered. I hope that
Will be a comfort to you. He was angry and said
I should bring ill luck to Troy by my impiety, so I laughed
But I felt more like crying. I went into our palace then
And into my own room. But the heaviness of the sky
Still oppressed me, and the sad colours of rust and blood
I saw everywhere, as Cassandra saw too. Oh, I thought,
It is an ominous eternal moment I am captive in, it is always
This heavy weather, these colours, and the smell of the dead
 men.
It is curious to be caught in a moment of pause like this,
As a river pauses before it plunges in a great waterfall.
I was at home with these people at least in this, that we wished
It was over and done with. But oh, Cassandra, I said, catching
 hold of her,
For she was running away, I shall never make
That mischievous laughing Helen, who goes home with
 Menelaus
And over her needlework, in the quiet palace,
 laughs,
Telling her story, and cries: Oh shameful me.
 I am only at home
In this moment of pause, where feelings,
 colours and spirits are substantial,
But people are ghosts. When the pause finishes
I shall wake.

Dear Child of God

Dear child of God
With the tears on your face
And your hands clasped in anger
What is the matter with your race?

In the beginning, Father,
You made the terms of our survival
That we should use our intelligence
To kill every rival.

The poison of this ferocity
Runs in our nature,
And O lord thou knowest
How it nourishes thy creatures.

Oh what a lively poison it was
To bring us to full growth,
Is then becoming loving
As much as our life is worth?

It is a price I would pay
To grow loving and kind,
The price of my life
And the life of human kind.

Father in heaven
Dear Father of peacefulness
Is it not often we remember
You put this poison in us,

Generally we stand
With the tears on our face
And our hands clasped in anger,
Faithful but unfortunate.

The Wedding Photograph

Goodbye Harry I must have you by me for a time
But once in the jungle you must go off to a higher clime
The old lion on his slow toe
Will eat you up, that is the way you will go.

Oh how I shall like to be along on the jungle path
But you are all right now for the photograph
So smile Harry smile and I will smile too
Thinking what is going to happen to you,
It is the death wish lights my beautiful eyes
But people think you are lucky to go off with such a pretty prize.

Ah feeble me that only wished alone to roam
Yet dares not without marrying leave home
Ah woe, burn fire, burn in eyes' sheathing
Fan bright fear, fan fire in Harry's breathing.

Phèdre

I wonder why Proust should have thought
The lines from Racine's Phèdre
 Depuis que sur ces bords les dieux ont envoyé
 La fille de Minos et de Pasiphaé to be
Entirely devoid of meaning,
To me they seem
As lucid as they are alarming.

I wonder why
The actresses I have seen
Playing Phèdre
Always indulge
In such mature agonizing.
Phèdre was young,
(This is as clear in Racine as Euripides)
She was young,
A girl caught in a trap, a girl
Under the enforcement
Of a goddess.
I dare say Phèdre
In fact I'm sure of it
Was by nature
As prim as Hippolytus,
Poor girl, poor girl, what could she do
But be ashamed and hang herself,
Poor girl.

How awful the French actress
Marie Bell
Made her appear.

Poor Phèdre,
Not only to be shamed by her own behaviour,
Enforced by that disgusting goddess,
Ancient enemy
Of her family,
But nowadays to have to be played
By an actress like Marie Bell
In awful ancient agonizing, something painful.

Now if I
Had been writing this story
I should have arranged for Theseus
To die,
(Well, *he* was old)
And then I should have let
Phèdre and Hippolytus
Find Aricie out
In some small meanness,
Say
Eating up somebody else's chocolates,
Half a pound of them, soft centred.
Secretly in bed at night, alone,
One after another,
Positively wolfing them down.
This would have put Hip. off,
And Phædra would be there too
And he would turn and see
That she was pretty disgusted, too,
So then they would have got married
And everything would have been respectable,
And the wretched Venus could have lumped it,
Lumped, I mean, Phèdre
Being the only respectable member

Of her awful family,
And being happy.

I should have liked one member
Of that awful family
To be happy,
What with Ariadne auf Naxos,
And Pasiphaé and that awful animal,
And Minos sitting judging the Dead
In those awful dark halls.
Yes, I should like poor simple honourable sweet prim Phèdre
To be happy. One would have to be pretty simple
To be happy with a prig like Hippolytus,
But she was simple.
I think it might have been a go,
If I were writing the story
I should have made it a go.

Everything is Swimming

Everything is swimming in a wonderful wisdom
She said everything was swimming in a wonderful wisdom
Silly ass
What a silly woman
Perhaps she is drunk
No I think it is mescalin
Silly woman
What a silly woman
Yes perhaps it is mescalin
It must be something
Her father, they say . . .
And that funny man William . . .
Silly ass
What a silly woman

Elle continua de rire comme une hyène.

'The Persian'

The gas fire
Seemed quite a friend
Such a funny little humming noise it made
And it had a name, too, carved on it you know,
'The Persian'. The Persian!
Ha ha ha; ha ha.

Now Agnes, pull yourself together.
You and your friends.

Emily writes such a good letter

Mabel was married last week
So now only Tom left

The doctor didn't like Arthur's cough
I have been in bed since Easter

A touch of the old trouble

I am downstairs today
As I write this
I can hear Arthur roaming overhead

He loves to roam
Thank heavens he has plenty of space to roam in

We have seven bedrooms
And an annexe

Which leaves a flat for the chauffeur and his wife

We have much to be thankful for

The new vicar came yesterday
People say he brings a breath of fresh air

He leaves me cold
I do not think he is a gentleman

Yes, I remember Maurice very well
Fancy getting married at his age
She must be a fool

You knew May had moved?
Since Edward died she had been much alone

It was cancer

No, I know nothing of Maud
I never wish to hear her name again
In my opinion Maud
Is an evil woman

Our char has left
And a good riddance too
Wages are very high in Tonbridge

Write and tell me how you are, dear,
And the girls,
Phoebe and Rose
They must be a great comfort to you
Phoebe and Rose.

November

In the dawn of a sumptuous November
I left my house in the park
I went for a walk in the park.

The mists had been grey and ephemeral
The mists they were damp and ephemeral
As they clung to the trees in the park
And swayed o'er the grass of the park,
They swayed o'er the grass of the park.

But the sun rose up red in a sumptuous glow
And made the mists rosy where'er they did blow
And all the great park in a rosiness lay
In that sumptuous dawn of a sumptuous day.

What made all spectacular, especially spectacular
Was the black of the trees as they stood, a particular
Blackness so damp, so bare and so dark,
As they stood 'gainst the sun in the sumptuous park,
As they stood 'gainst the sun in the park.

Monsieur Pussy-Cat, blackmailer

C'est un grand Monsieur Pussy-Cat
Who lives on the mat
Devant un feu énorme
And that is why he is so fat,
En effet il sait quelque chose
Et fait chanter son hôte,
Raison de plus pourquoi
He has such a glossy coat.
Ah ha, Monsieur Pussy-Cat
Si grand et si gras,
Take care you don't *pousser trop*
The one who gives you such *jolis plats.*

Si peu séduisante

Il était une petite fille de dix ans,
Si peu séduisante,
Qui entra dans le wagon-restaurant
Pour retrouver ses parents.
Elle portait son school uniform,
Si peu séduisante,
And a perfectly frightful little pair of shoes,
Mais ses yeux, malgré des lunettes hideuses,
Etaient si pleins de bonté et de franchise
Que tout autre aspect of this little schoolgirl,
Si peu séduisante,
Really only made one like her more.

To Carry the Child

To carry the child into adult life
Is good? I say it is not,
To carry the child into adult life
Is to be handicapped.

The child in adult life is defenceless
And if he is grown-up, knows it,
And the grown-up looks at the childish part
And despises it.

The child, too, despises the clever grown-up,
The man-of-the-world, the frozen,
For the child has the tears alive on the cheek
And the man has none of them.

As the child has colours, and the man sees no
Colours or anything,
Being easy only in things of the mind,
The child is easy in feeling.

Easy in feeling, easily excessive
And in excess powerful,
For instance, if you do not speak to the child
He will make trouble.

You would say a man had the upper hand
Of the child, if a child survive,
I say the child has fingers of strength
To strangle the man alive.

Oh it is not happy, it is never happy,
To carry the child into adulthood,
Let children lie down before full growth
And die in their infanthood
And be guilty of no one's blood.

But oh the poor child, the poor child, what can he do,
Trapped in a grown-up carapace,
But peer outside of his prison room
With the eye of an anarchist?

Mutchmore and Not-So

The big family
In our parts
Are the Likelies
(A cousin of mine married one of them)
They have a large house called Mutchmore
Standing in well-wooded grounds,
A beautiful place, dating
In the front hall and lower part of the fire-place
From the days of Henry the Eighth.
In this house
Now alone since his wife died
And the girls married
Lives Sefton the head of the family.
We always called him Mutchmore Likely
To distinguish him from Gerald.
Gerald Likely is the son
Of old Sir Sefton's younger brother
(Nobody thought much of *him*).
Gerald is not on speaking terms with his Uncle
Ever since he changed the name of *his* house

Such a pretty little Georgian house
Fronting on the High Street
As you come into Mutch village
Opposite the church yard
(You cannot see the church because
Of the left-hand turn to the mill house)
Changed the name of *his* house
From Parkins to Not-So.
Gerald has such a *peculiar* sense of humour;
Why should that old rascal Sefton,
He used to say,
Preen himself, the unlovable old character,
On what he fondly imagines to be
The lovable nickname of Mutchmore?
So you see, he, Gerald, thought he would
Take away from the pleasure his uncle took in his
 nickname,
Spite him, really, by calling his own house Not-So.
Mutchmore Likely and now Not-So Likely!
Oh course we had to laugh,
But it made the whole thing ridiculous,
Which is what Gerald wanted.
The old man may have his faults
But Gerald is really too ill-natured.

The Last Turn of the Screw

I am Miles, I did not die
I only turned, as on shut eye
To feel again the silken dress
Of my lovely governess.

Yes, it was warm, poetical and cosy,
I never saw the other fellow when
I lolled on Lady's lap (I called her Lady)
But there were two of us all right. And both were men.

Yes, there's the oddest part. She made me feel
A hundred years more old than I was, than she was,
She'd had a sheltered life, of course – a vicarage,
Some bustling younger children, a father pious, I'm sure he
 was.

But two of us? Of me? I'll be explicit,
A soft boy, knowing rather more than boys should, lolling,
No harm in that, on Lady's lap; the other,
Source of my knowledge, half myself by now, but calling . . .

Some children are born innocent, some achieve it,
You scowl; that doesn't fit with your philosophy?
Can you by choosing alter Nature, you inquire?
Yes, my dear sir, you can; I found it fairly easy.

But calling (to go back a step) but calling? –
That proved he was not yet quite One of Us,
The vulgar little beast, the fellow Quint.
It was at first my lordly feelings held him off
That dapper knowingness of his for instance,
The clothes right, being my uncle's, but worn wrong,
The accent careful, well he must be careful,
I dare say he had thumbed a book about it . . .
To spend ten minutes with a Thing like this
Would be too long.
So snobbery made the breach, religion followed . . .
Ten minutes? No, Eternity, with Quint
That Quint, whose seedy sickness in my blood
I could detect (in time?) running to flood,
The sickliness of sin,
Oh yes, I saw quite plain by now
What was going in.
How did I fob him off? (now we know why)
When half my heart
Was panting for him and what he could teach
Reaching for shame, and retching too
(It was, as I have said, this squeamishness I had
First judged him bad).

Oh there was still some rotting to go on
In my own heart
Before I was quite ready to cry 'Out!'
And see him off, though half my blood went with him.
I grow a shade dramatic here, none went at all,
My sinews have remained the same, my blood, my heart
Have not, as I'm aware, taken a taint,
I was not and I am not now a saint,
But I loved Virtue, and I love her still,
Especially as I see her in the dress
Of my sweetly fatheaded governess . . .
Well, let's be plain, I fobbed Quint off
By simply failing to be clever enough.
By taking nothing in, not looking and not noticing
I made myself as dull to the persuading
Of all that shabby innuendo as
The plainest ten-year schoolboy ever was,
And so I have remained and by intent
Quite dull. And shall remain
Sooner than chance such entering again.
I did not die, but bought my innocence
At the high price of an indifference
Where once I knew the most engaging love
That first through squeamishness made virtue move,
The love, now lost of my sweet governess
Who cannot bear I should be so much less
The Miles she knew, or rather did not know.
Yes, I have lost my interestingness for Lady who,
I fear, like other innocent ladies do,
Hankered for something shady,
Well, say, dramatic, not what I am now,
An empty antic Clumsy, a mere boy.
She'll never know

The strength I have employed and do employ
To make it sure
I shall be this
And nothing more.
I am Miles, I did not die,
I only turn, as on shut eye
To feel again the silken dress
Of my lost and lovely governess,
And sigh and think it strange
That being dull I should feel so much pain.

Company

Rise from your bed of languor
Rise from your bed of dismay
Your friends will not come tomorrow
As they did not come today

You must rely on yourself, they said,
You must rely on yourself,
Oh but I find this pill so bitter said the poor man
As he took it from the shelf

Crying, Oh sweet Death come to me
Come to me for company,
Sweet Death it is only you I can
Constrain for company.

Saffron

Underneath the ice
Lies the frozen spirit of Bice

Green are her eyes, green her hair,
The spirit of Bice is winter's prisoner.

When spring comes Pale is her name, and her hair
And eyes are pale blue, and she is freer.

In summertime she is called Saffron,
Yellow are eyes and hair then. I welcome

Bice, Pale and Saffron but I love best
Beautiful summer Saffron, running fast.

Because this beautiful spirit should not be frozen
And is furthest from it when she is saffron.

Avondale

How sweet the birds of Avondale
Of Avondale, of Avondale,
How sweet the birds of Avondale
Do swoop and swing and call.

The children too of Avondale,
Of Avondale, of Avondale,
The boys and girls of Avondale
Do swoop and swing and call,

And all the little cats and dogs,
Of Avondale, of Avondale,
In their own way in Avondale
Do swoop and swing and call,

And oh it is a pleasant sight
It is a very pleasant sight
To see the creatures so delight
To swoop and swing and call,
In Avondale, in Avondale,
To see them swoop and call.

Avondall

I had a dream I was a bird
A bird of Avondall
Sitting with birds upon a roof
To swoop and swing and call
I was athirst with other birds
To swoop and swing and call
But no bird turned to me in love
All were inimical,
They were inimical.

Valuable

All these illegitimate babies . . .
Oh girls, girls,
Silly little cheap things,
Why do you not put some value on yourselves,
Learn to say, No?
Did nobody teach you?
Nobody teaches anybody to say No nowadays,
People should teach people to say No.

Oh poor panther,
Oh you poor black animal,
At large for a few moments in a school for young children in
 Paris,
Now in your cage again,
How your great eyes bulge with bewilderment,
There is something there that accuses us,
In your angry and innocent eyes,
Something that says:
I am too valuable to be kept in a cage.

Oh these illegitimate babies!
Oh girls, girls,
Silly little valuable things,
You should have said, No, I am valuable,
And again, It is because I am valuable
I say, No.

Nobody teaches anybody they are valuable nowadays.

Girls, you are valuable,
And you, Panther, you are valuable,
But the girls say: I shall be alone
If I say 'I am valuable' and other people do not say it of me,
I shall be alone, there is no comfort there.
No, it is not comforting but it is valuable,
And if everybody says it in the end
It will be comforting. And for the panther too,
If everybody says he is valuable
It will be comforting for him.

I Wish

Oh I wish that there were some wing, some wing,
Under which I could hide my head,
A soft grey wing, a beautiful thing,
Oh I wish that there were such a wing,

And then I should suddenly be quite sure
As I never was before,
And fly far away, and be gay instead
Of being hesitating and filled with dread,
Oh I wish I could find a wing.

But today as I walk on the pavement I see
Where a car is parked, where a car is parked,
In the wheel's bright chromium hub I see
A world stretching out that is like but unlike
The world that encloses me.

And I wish to pass through the shining hub
And go far away, far away,
As far as I might on the wings of the dove
That first I thought would succour me
And carry me far away,
Oh the hub is my love far more than the dove
That first I thought would succour me.

And now the shining beautiful hub
Opens its door to me,
I enter, I enter, through the hub I have entered
The world that shines so bright,
The road stretches there in ochre; and blue

Is the sky I am walking into; and white
Is the beach I perceive of a heavenly sea
A-roll in the realms of light,
It rolls in the realms of light.

The Listener

Listening one day on the radio
To 'An Encounter with mosquitoes in New Guinea' by Miss
 Cheeseman,
I fell to thinking of the animal kingdom
And experienced at once a relief of nervous tension.
For I thought, Their battles are as ours, as ours,
They are no different from our own,
Then rose up a Spirit from the ether that touched my eyelids
And cast me in a deep swoon.

Hymn to the Seal

to the tune 'Soldiers of Christ arise!'
(Hymns Ancient and Modern)

Creature of God, thy coat
That lies all black and fine
I do admire, as on a sunny
Rock to see thee climb.

When thou wast young thy coat
Was pale with spots upon it,
But now in single black it lies
And thou, Seal, liest on it.

What bliss abounds to view
God's creatures in their prime
Climb in full coat upon a rock
To breathe and to recline.

Fish Fish

Look, man, look,
Underneath the brook
Sits the fish fish
On a hook.

What, man, what?
Let him off?
No fear fear
I'm going to look.

Yes, now I think I will go down to him,
To have a look at him,
In the depths
Of the perishable brook.

So go now man, pray go,
No more say
Loose the fish fish from the hook
To swim away.

Underneath the brook dim
Sits the fish,
He sits *on* the hook
It is not *in* him.

He is waiting for me
To carry me to the sea
I shall be happy then
In the watery company of his kingdom.

Goodbye, man dear,
Goodbye quickly,
I go to the fish fish
Impatiently.

Venus When Young Choosing Death

I stood knee-deep in the sea
I saw gods coming towards me
All came and kissed, all kissed
It was for friendship.

It was a hot day
The sea
Lapped to my knees
And kissed me.

All the gods were old friends
I knew them from long ago
They kissed me each after each and went
In friendship.

Kissed me on the lips
Held me to them

Set me again in the knee-deep sea
And went, in friendship.

Then came out drawing a boat after him
He set me in the boat
He set me on his knees in the boat, kissing me.
It was not for friendship.

Oh how happy this day was
All day in his arms I was,
But not for friendship.

A little breeze drew now from the land
Bringing a smell of poppies
And on his head, was poppies
And in his hand, poppies
And on his lips when he kissed me
A taste of poppies.

Sleep or Death, Sleep or Death kissed me,
Not for friendship.

You do not kiss one for friendship?
No, for welcome,
To welcome one home.

Lord Say-and-Seal

Lord Say-and-Seal, Lord Say-and-Seal
Why not for once say and *reveal*
All the dark thoughts your words go over
To make a pretty bog-hole cover.

The Days of Yore

What pleased him more
Than anything else
Was the resemblance he bore
To the Prince of Wales,

To the Prince of Wales
And more and more
As the Prince of Wales was
In the days of yore.

Pearl

to an American lady poet committing suicide
because of not being appreciated enough

Then cried the American poet where she lay supine:
'My name is Purrel; I was caast before swine.'

Yes, I know

The pale face stretches across the centuries
It is so subtle and yielding; yet innocent,
Her name is Lucretia Borgia.

Yes, I know. I knew her brother Cesare
Once. But only for a short time.

Widowhood

or

The Home-Coming of Lady Ross

her husband, the Lord of the Isles, is dead,
and she lives alone by the sea

Nobody hears me, nobody sees me,
My father, the General, used to say
He had only to come into a room
For everybody else to go out for it.

('Ach, wie schrecklich, so alt zu sein,
Und diese schrecklichen Tränensäcke,
Als wenn sie viel geweint hätte!'
Said the young girl to her friend,
In her hotel at Baden.)

My heart is a frozen lump,
I look forward to nothing but Death,
I am glad Harold is not here
To see me now.

('Oh how awful, to be so old,
And those awful tear-tracks on her cheeks,
As if she had cried a lot!'
Said the young girl to her friend
In the hotel at Cheltenham.)

Harold loved the hotel at Baden and the hotel at Cheltenham
He loved staying in hotels, he loved staying in 'em.

Now I live alone by the sea
And I am happy as never I used to be,
Harold, can you forgive me?
My family were never much good in company.

That's what you used to say, dear, do you remember, when I
 stayed in my room
In the hotel at Baden, or wherever it might be, Up you would
 come
Rushing, and kiss me and cry: Rhoda, your family,
I must say, are not much good in company.

Oh Harold, our house looks so beautiful today,
Why did you always want to go away?

Voice from the Tomb (1)

nightmare, after reading the Parable of the Talents

Here lies a poet who would not write
His soul runs screaming through the night
Oh give me paper, give me pen,
And I will very soon begin.

Poor Soul, keep silent; in Death's clime
There's no pen, paper, notion,
And no Time.

Voice from the Tomb (2)

to the tune 'From Greenland's icy mountains'
(Hymns Ancient and Modern)

I trod a foreign path, dears,
The silence was extreme
And so it came about, dears,
That I fell into dream,

That I feel into my dream, my dear,
And feelings beyond cause,
And tears without a reason
And so was lost.

Voice from the Tomb (3)

Such evidence I have of indifference
Were surely enough to break the coldest heart,
But this heart is not cold, it never has been cold,
It never, never, never has been cold.

Voice from the Tomb (4)

I died for lack of company
Did my dear friends not know?
Oh why would they not speak to me
Yet said they loved me so?

Voice from the Tomb (5)

*a Soul earthbound by the grievance
of never having been important*

You never heard of me, I dare
Say. Well, I'm here.

The Dedicated Dancing Bull and the Water Maid

*Beethoven's Sonata in F, Op. 17, for Horn and Piano,
played by Dennis Brain and Denis Matthews*

Hop hop, thump thump,
Oh I am holy, oh I am plump,
A young bull dancing on the baked grass glade,
And beside me dances the Water Maid.
She says I must dance with her,
Why should I? I loathe her,
She has such a stupid way of singing
It does not amount to anything,
But she thinks it does, oh yes
She does not suppose she is spurious.
I wish I could be rid of the Water Maid
Or hid from her. Does she think she can make me afraid?
Ho ho, thump thump,
Oh I am elegant, oh I am plump,
As I wave my head my feet go thud
On the baked grass. Oh I am good.

Now night comes and I go into the wood shades
And the moon comes up and lights them as the day fades.
Hop hop, faster faster,
Thump thump, but the Maid comes after,
She is teasing me by singing with a stupid sound
That does not go at all well with my bound,
Oh how I should like to tread her in the ground.
But I must think only about my feet
And remember to bring them down on the beat.
Hoo hoo, now I sing through my nose,
Hoo hoo, and off the Maid goes
A little way in an affected flutter
Pretending to be startled by the hoo of my deep mutter.
Hoo, then, hoo, with a hop and a jump
Who is this beautiful young animal who is so plump?
Why is it our famous dedicated dancing bull,
Did you notice how delicately he goes?
Was that a hoof somewhere in those silver toes?
With nonsense
The Water Maid makes off into the distance.
The night is mine now and I come to the forest pool
 And drink and do not think I am a fool.

Night Thoughts

There were thoughts that came to Phil
And Oh they made him feel quite ill,

They were so envious and bitter,
He wished he could have something sweeter,

But still he felt it was all right
As long as they only came by night.

He thought about his job . . . so dull
And poorly paid; all that was awful,

And then his girl, he loved her very much,
Only she did not seem to love him quite so much.

As for friends – Phil groaned aloud,
His thoughts drove in like a night-cloud,

But still it *was* night, and so he felt
It was just something that could not be helped.

The thoughts however by now were single-minded,
They did not fuss or beat around it,

They simply tried to find a way
To make it seem they came by day.

When at last they succeeded in doing this
Poor Phil adopted a most peculiar neurosis,

He summoned up a picture of shallow sea-water
And in it he paddled, he was a sea-walker.

On an empty beach, in full sun,
He paddled for miles and did not see anyone,

And as he walked, the salty smell and the air
Of the beautiful place, *worked*; he did not remember.

That beach, as a matter of fact, shelves to deep water,
He must be careful to remain always a coastal-walker.

Happy Phil in his solitude. I am glad
He has this retreat. But it is not good.

Piggy to Joey

Piggy to Joey,
Piggy to Joe,
Yes, that's what I was –
Piggy to Joe.

Will he come back again?
Oh no, no, no.
Oh how I wish I hadn't been
Piggy to Joe.

Pretty

Why is the word pretty so underrated?
In November the leaf is pretty when it falls
The stream grows deep in the woods after rain
And in the pretty pool the pike stalks

He stalks his prey, and this is pretty too,
The prey escapes with an underwater flash
But not for long, the great fish has him now
The pike is a fish who always has his prey

And this is pretty. The water rat is pretty
His paws are not webbed, he cannot shut his nostrils
As the otter can and the beaver, he is torn between
The land and water. Not 'torn', he does not mind.

The owl hunts in the evening and it is pretty
The lake water below him rustles with ice
There is frost coming from the ground, in the air mist
All this is pretty, it could not be prettier.

Yes, it could always be prettier, the eye abashes
It is becoming an eye that cannot see enough,
Out of the wood the eye climbs. This is prettier
A field in the evening, tilting up.

The field tilts to the sky. Though it is late
The sky is lighter than the hill field
All this looks easy but really it is extraordinary
Well, it is extraordinary to be so pretty.

And it is careless, and that is always pretty
This field, this owl, this pike, this pool are careless,
As Nature is always careless and indifferent
Who sees, who steps, means nothing, and this is pretty.

So a person can come along like a thief – pretty! –
Stealing a look, pinching the sound and feel,
Lick the icicle broken from the bank
And still say nothing at all, only cry pretty.

Cry pretty, pretty, pretty and you'll be able
Very soon not even to cry pretty
And so be delivered entirely from humanity
This is prettiest of all, it is very pretty.

The Small Lady

In front of the mighty washing machine
The small lady stood in a beautiful dream,
'That these clothes so clean (oh what a relief)
 Must still be ironed, is my only grief.'

But then came a great witch passing on the air
Who said, 'What is it you still wish for, my pretty dear?
Would you like to be a duck on a northern lake,
A milky white duck with a yellow beak?'
'Aroint thee, false witch!' cried the lady with a brave face,
'Human inventions help properly, magic is a disgrace.'
The witch flew off cackling for the harm was done,
'I smell water,' cried the lady and followed her into the setting sun.
And now in a false shape, on the wind-driven black pelt
Of that far northern lake, she is without help:
Crying, Away, away,
Come, ray of the setting sun,
Over the lake
Spread thy red streak,
Light my kingdom.

Heart of my heart, it is a mournful song,
Never will this poor lady come home.

Animula, vagula, blandula

the Emperor Hadrian to his soul

Little soul so sleek and smiling
Flesh's friend and guest also
Where departing will you wander
Growing paler now and languid
And not joking as you used to?

Friends of the River Trent

(*at their Annual Dinner*)

A dwindling body of ageing fish
Is all we can present
Because of water pollution
In the River Trent
Because of water pollution, my boys,
And a lack of concerted action,
These fish of what they used to be
Is only a measly fraction
A-swimming about most roomily
Where they shoved each other before,
Yet not beefing about being solitary
Or the sparseness of the fare.
Then three cheers for the ageing fish, my boys,
Content in polluted depths
To grub up enough food, my boys,
To carry 'em to a natural death,
And may we do the same, my boys,
And carry us to a natural death.

Is it Happy?

Is it happy for me, is it happy
That my father, Lord Beale, was so famous
And I am a ne'er-do-weel? Is it happy?

And what of my mother – 'the lady'
We called her, because she was so high-minded, born Plaidy –
Was it happy for her
That Father was never there?
Was it happy?

And Rory, Rory my brother
Who knew neither father nor brother
Being adopted in infancy by Uncle Pym
Whose name he took, was it happy for him?

Thorwald, our spaniel, gun-trained,
Died of a fatty heart;
Well, Father was never at home,
And I didn't shoot.
Was it happy for Thorwald?

. . . all that money paid for a worthless scrip
That might have been mine today
If Papa had stuck to Gilt Edged or Blue Chip.
Is that happy?

My father died in his fame
Saving his country and me
From the people over the sea.

How does it feel being Beale,
Lord Beale and a ne'er-do-weel?

I've brought Mother home to the little house,
Having let the grand one for a commando course,
Telling 'em to look out for the pictures, of course.

All my life I have tried not to be envious
Of Father, or take it out by being nefarious,
Truly I loved him, revere
The memory of this great soldier,
Field Marshall Lord B. he was when he died,
(Happy, for me?)

Mother says I should bring home a bride,
Greatness skips a generation, she says, and he,
My son, need not be a nonentity.

I'll do it, why not?
Play the part out,
Find a sort of happiness in it too I dare say, slyly
Being as it were all this quite so entirely,
Blithely calling the saviour of my country, Father,
(Happy for me)
Blithely begetting sons to carry it farther,
(Will that be?)

I'll ask Cynthia tonight, she'll say yes,
When I've got the Commandos out she'll love the place.

It's occurred to me also once or twice of late
To join the True Church, something Father would hate,

Not the Anglicans of course, they're too humdrum,
It would have to be the Roman Communion.
Well, I've read Father Gerard and about the recusants quite a lot
And can prove: *As they suffered*, there cannot have been a
 Catholic Plot.

Is it happy for me, driving Mother mad?
Does she wish I was bad?
Think Rory might have been better than me?
Well, if she does, she don't let me see.

Happy, is it happy?

Watchful

a Tale of Psyche

When Watchful came to me he said
As he never said before,
Wait, wait, I will see you
On Northumberland Moor.

I played with my brothers
In Northumberland House
And we laughed as we skipped and ran
And made a great noise,

And I looked through the window
And saw the sea run white
Against Northumberland,
Country of my delight.

When Watchful spoke,
As he never used to speak,
I drew apart from my brothers,
I scowled to hear Watchful speak,

Come to me, come to me,
Upon Northumberland Moor, hurry!
I will not come yet
But I will come some day.

First I must play with my brothers
And make some money
On the Stock Exchange. It was funny
How we made so much money
Because we did not want it in the old
Tall house in Northumberland,
In fact we did not want it much at all.

Often we gave parties
In London
For Senior Civil Servants
And barristers
And Junior Members
Of the Government.

I said to my brother Tommy,
It is funny
How they come
When we do not want them very much.

Tommy said, It is funny
Like the money,
We do not want
It or them very much,
Yet they come.

It is funny, Tommy, too, I said,
How the warmth of the parties

Fascinates me, and the wild laughing eyes
Of the people hold me.

You would not have thought
That the people we had
At our parties would have
These wild laughing eyes, but they had.

Watch out, said Tommy, the word is Watchful,
Then
We were in Northumberland again.

The window of our schoolroom was open
And in the group of my brothers in the room was one, quickly
Who was not a brother, coming to me.

I climbed down from the window in the high moonlight
Along the high brick wall of the kitchen garden
I crawled. But the wall was higher
Than I remembered it was. So when I went to drop
Off the high wall, where we used to by the mulberry tree,
It was suddenly too high, I hung by my fingers above a
 precipice,
But I could not hang long, I let go, I fell, fell far, fell,
Was caught. I stiffened in the arms that held me, slipped down
 and ran free.

Over the saltings I ran. The midnight high wind
Pulled my straight hair in streaks behind me, and I ran and ran
And did not care, as I ran by the sea shore
If Watchful ran behind or waited for me
On Northumberland Moor.

Oh how strongly the wind drew. When day broke
The waves leapt and their crests ran gold
In the morning sun, the gold sun was in their crests.

Turn away, turn away
From the high crests of the golden sea,
It was funny
How easily I turned away from the high crests, as easily
As from the parties
And the money.

I was running in a wood now, a wood of pine trees,
Very dark it was and silent, I ran on a brown pine needles
Silently, and came to a gamekeeper's gallows. The mournful
 birds
Hanging there cried: We are not Watchful, and an old badger
Crawling to his sett to die said: I am not Watchful. But the
 wind
Cried: Hurry! and drove great snowflakes against my face.
Then I came to a dark house and the door swung and I went in,
Oh Watchful, my darling, you have led me such a dance.

He lay on a truckle bed, cold, cold; his eyes shut.

First I made a fire from the wood stacked and the pine cones,
Then I came back to him, Oh Watchful, you are so cold,
So I lay on him to warm him, and by and by
He opened his eyes and laughed to see me cry.

We need not dance any more
He said, Only the fire dances on Northumberland Moor,
The fire you have lighted for me dances
On Northumberland Moor.

Then winter blew away, a sweet sea ran pretty
And in this new world everything was happy.

How Cruel is the Story of Eve

How cruel is the story of Eve
What responsibility
It has in history
For cruelty.

Touch, where the feeling is most vulnerable,
Unblameworthy – ah reckless – desiring children,
Touch them with a touch of pain?
Abominable.

Ah what cruelty,
In history
What misery.

Put up to barter
The tender feelings
Buy her a husband to rule her

Fool her to marry a master
She must or rue it
The Lord said it.

And man, poor man,
Is he fit to rule,
Pushed to it?
How can he carry it, the governance,
And not suffer for it
Insuffisance?
He must make woman lower then
So he can be higher then.

Oh what cruelty,
In history what misery.

Soon woman grows cunning
Masks her wisdom,
How otherwise will he
Bring food and shelter, kill enemies?
If he did not feel superior
It would be worse for her
And for the tender children
Worse for them.

Oh what cruelty,
In history what misery
Oh falsity.

It is only a legend
You say? But what
Is the meaning of the legend
If not

To give blame to women most
And most punishment?

This is the meaning of a legend that colours
All human thought; it is not found among animals.

How cruel is the story of Eve,
What responsibility it has
In history
For misery.

Yet there is this to be said still:
Life would be over long ago
If men and woman had not loved each other
Naturally, naturally,
Forgetting their mythology
They would have died of it else
Long ago, long ago,
And all would be emptiness now
And silence.

Oh dread Nature, for your purpose,
To have made them love so.

The Story I Have Told

I saw the ghostly lady fleeting
In imperial purple clad
Through the trees of Lost Oleela
By the slopes of Morgenstad,

Where a carven pillar stood up,
White as bone, as white as bone,
Paused the lady, weeping paused she,
Laid her hand upon the stone,
There with fixèd mien awhile
She stood, and vanished with a moan.

Then spake a voice within my bosom
Answering what I had not asked:
You have seen the lady Fausta
Who in life was overtasked

Overtasked to seek a daughter,
Seek the lovely Eulalie,

Daily comes she, daily pauses,
Seeking Eulalie.

Eulalie beloved daughter,
A fair child and lost,
Close were they to one another
In misfortune crossed,

It was the Emperor Eelogab
Who sent them both away,
A daughter fair, a virtuous wife,
A deed to darken day,
He sent them forth to live or die
For all it happened had,
Beside the trees of Lost Oleel'
And the slopes of Morgenstad,
In castle grim and sad.

Often through the groves at midnight
Eulalie alone
Gathered moonflowers to her breast
And tarried by the stone.

In a white dress tarried she,
Sashed with violet,
In a white dress sashed with violet
Tarried Eulalie.

Until one night a sullen storm,
A storm of deep intent,
Caught her up and carried her
And never home she went.

Never home went Eulalie
In her dress of white
And the lady Fausta waited
For her this and every night,
Waited for her, weeping for her,
This and every night.

The lady Fausta long is dead
Though she may weep and crave,
But Eulalie, fair Eulalie,
She lies not in the grave.

Ah me, what changèd voice is this
That was so soft and sad,
That now cries: Fear Oleela's grove
And the slopes of Morgenstad,
That bids me flee Oleela's grove
And the slopes of Morgenstad.

There is no place in all the world
Where I shall not behold
The lady Fausta weeping, pause
As she paused in days of old,
Beside the stone whose sides are carved
With the story I have told,

Of Fausta and of Eulalie,
The story I have told.

Fairy Story

I went into the wood one day
And there I walked and lost my way

When it was so dark I could not see
A little creature came to me

He said if I would sing a song
The time would not be very long

But first I must let him hold my hand tight
Or else the wood would give me a fright

I sang a song, he let me go
But now I am home again there is nobody I know.

Angel Face

Angel face so close above me
In the snowflake glowing smugly
Sweet Angel, love me, love me.

White and silent is the snowflake
Falling, falling, and it will make
Soon all flat and like a white lake
In a white and silent state
Beaming flat and vacant.

But thy face will beckon, beckon,
Saying to me, Come soon, come soon,
As is thy snowy custom
It is thy snowy custom

When at night the flakes are falling
Of the midnight snowstorm falling

To be so appealing, teasing
Smiling, teasing and appealing,
In thy white and silent way
Saying only, Come away.

If I doubt thee, if I think thee
But a figment of my fancy,
Sweet Angel, love me, love me,
In thy bosom cover me.

The Grange

Oh there hasn't been much change
At the Grange,

Of course the blackberries growing closer
Make getting in a bit of a poser,
But there hasn't been much change
At the Grange.

Old Sir Prior died,
They say on the point of leaving for the seaside,
They never found the body, which seemed odd to some
(Not me, seeing as what I seen the butler done.)

Oh there hasn't been much change
At the Grange.

The governess 'as got it now,
Miss Ursy 'aving moved down to the Green Cow –
Proper done out of 'er rights, she was, a b. shame,
And what's that the governess pushes round at night in the old
 pram?

Oh there hasn't been much change
At the Grange.

The shops leave supplies at the gate now, meat, groceries,
Mostly old tinned stuff you know from McInnes's,
They wouldn't go up to the door,
Not after what happened to Fred's pa.

Oh there hasn't been much change
At the Grange.

Parssing there early this morning, cor lummy,
I 'ears a whistling sound coming from the old chimney,
Whistling it was fit to bust and not a note wrong,
The old pot, whistling The Death of Nelson.

No there hasn't been much change
At the Grange,

But few goes that way somehow,
Not now.

'I believe.' 'I do not.'

Mrs Arbuthnot

Mrs Arbuthnot was a poet
A poet of high degree,
But her talent left her;
Now she lives at home by the sea.

In the morning she washes up,
In the afternoon she sleeps,
Only in the evenings sometimes
For her lost talent she weeps,

Crying: I should write a poem,
Can I look a wave in the face
If I do not write a poem about a sea-wave,
Putting the words in place.

Mrs Arbuthnot has died,
She has gone to heaven,
She is one with the heavenly combers now
And need not write about them.

Cry: She is a heavenly comber,
She runs with a comb of fire,
Nobody writes or wishes to
Who is one with their desire.

Magnificent Words

*'Ye shall be a blessing; fear not, but
let your hands be strong.'*
ZECH. VIII, 13

These magnificent words that I read today
Are what the Daily Telegraph had chosen, to display
From the bible.

Who is it who chooses at the Daily Telegraph each day
Magnificent words out of all of them, to display
From the bible?

This unknown person's hand is strong, he is a blessing,
Everyday
He chooses magnificent words in the Daily Telegraph, to
 display
From the bible.

So can anger . . .

They do not come separately
They are never alone
They come all together
Or they stay at home

I liked one of them,
I asked one,
But he laughed and said; You forget
Our name is Legion.

All right, stay away then,
If I have to have the others as well.

So can anger sometimes
Save us from hell.

On Walking Slowly After an Accident

I used to walk quickly
But now I walk slow
I see the sunshine on each leaf
And the spider below.

I know the spider
I know his trick
I see the web shake
As he gives a kick

And I see that the fly he goes for
Is not a fly but a dandelion seed,
He harvests with chagrin
What cannot feed.

I turn to the sunny leaf
From the chagrin below
Knowing never a spider, poor spider,
Could so,

Nor a quick walker either
For he would have seen neither
Leaf nor spider, leaf nor spider,

Ni le chagrin de dandelion seed.

I am a girl who loves to shoot

I am a girl who loves to shoot,
I love the feathered fowl and brute,
I love them with a love as strong
As ever there came from heaven down.

Why should I not love them living as dead?
As I shoot, as I shoot, and as my fine dog Tray
Brings the shot one to hand, he is I, I am they.
Oh why do my friends think this love is so questionable?
They say they love animals but they do not love them as I am able,

Seeing them run and fly and letting them run, fly and die,
I love them to distraction as the wild wind goes by,
As the rain and the storm on this wide upper hill,
Oh no one loves the animals as I do or so well.
If I am not hungry I let them run free,
And if I am hungry they are my darling passionate delicacy.

Into the wild woods I go over the high mountains to the valley low,
And the animals are safe; if I am not hungry they may run and go,
And I bless their beautiful appearance and their fleetness,
And I feel no contradiction or contriteness.
I love them living and I love them dead with a quick blood spurt
And I may put them in the pot and eat them up with a loving
 heart.

I am a girl who loves to shoot,
I love the feathered fowl and brute,
I love them with as great a love
As ever came down from heaven above.

I love . . .

I love the English country scene
But sometimes think there's too much Hooker's green,
Especially in August, when the flowers that might have lent a
Lightness, don't; being gamboge or magenta.

Cœur Simple

Where is the sky hurrying to
Over my head,
Mother, is the sky hurrying
To bed?

Where is the sky hurrying to
Over my head?
Where it will be hurrying to
When you are dead.

Nodding

Tizdal my beautiful cat
Lies on the old rag mat
In front of the kitchen fire.
Outside the night is black.

The great fat cat
Lies with his paws under him
His whiskers twitch in a dream,
He is slumbering.

The clock on the mantelpiece
Ticks unevenly, tic toc, tic-toc,

Good heavens what is the matter
With the kitchen clock?

Outside an owl hunts,
Hee hee hee hee,
Hunting in the Old Park
From his snowy tree.
What on earth can he find in the park tonight,
It is so wintry?

Now the fire burns suddenly too hot
Tizdal gets up to move,
Why should such an animal
Provoke our love?

The twigs from the elder bush
Are tapping on the window pane
As the wind sets them tapping,
Now the tapping begins again.

One laughs on a night like this
In a room half firelight half dark
With a great lump of a cat
Moving on the hearth,
And the twigs tapping quick,
And the owl in an absolute fit
One laughs supposing creation
Pays for its long plodding
Simply by coming to this –
Cat, night, fire – and a girl nodding.

v.

Adela is such a silly woman
Tom says Adela is going off her head

Adela is staying down in the country
She is v. happy

Dr Not is v. nice

Such a jolly old place quite like home

Dr Not is v. nice
Adela is v. happy

Adela is Not is
v. v. happy

With extensive grounds.

A British Song

It was a slender British bird
Stood on the drinking bath
But another came and nipped him there
Before he could have a bath.

Then came a great British starling, nipped the nipper and drove
 him away
And sat down in the bath, and sat down in the bath. And there
 did stay.

When the wind . . .

When the wind is in the East
I give a feast

When the wind is in the West
I rest

When the wind is in the South
There is a taste of sugar in my mouth

When the wind is North
I go not forth.

By the spread Arabian table
Sit the friends whom I am able
To arouse. They come to me
Across the pink Arabian sea.

I like to sleep beneath my canopy
The sun reaches to me
By the silent sea on the sands
The tropical evening sun reaches to me.

Heavy the scent of bees, heavy the sun
Heavy the taste of sugar on my tongue
Heavy the days, will they never pass?
Heavy my sleep, will it come at last?

It is winter now: the wind howls
The snowy fox and the snowy owls
Hunt in the night. I stay within.
Outside my house I hear the storms begin.

Which winds did I like best?
Why, the East and the West,
They brought me tranquillity
The others, anxiety.

Northumberland House

I was always a thoughtful youngster,
Said the lady on the omnibus,
I remember Father used to say:
You are more thoughtful than us.

I was sensitive too, the least thing
Upset me so much,
I used to cry if a fly
Stuck in the hatch.

Mother always said:
Elsie is too good,

There'll never be another like Elsie,
Touch wood.

I liked to be alone
Sitting on the garden path,
My brother said he'd never seen a
Picture more like Faith in the Arena.

They were kindly people, my people,
I could not help being different,
And I think it was good for me
Mixing in a different element.

The poor lady now burst out crying
And I saw her friend was not a friend but a nurse
For she said, Cheer up duckie the next stop is ours,
They got off at Northumberland House.

This great House of the Percys
Is now a lunatic asylum,
But over the gate there still stands
The great Northumberland Lion.

This family animal's tail
Is peculiar in that is it absolutely straight,
And straight as a bar it stood out to drop after them
As they went through the gate.

The Crown of Gold

an English Writer in Search
of an Established English Publisher

Mother procure for me a golden crown
Said the child, That the fire may not burn me nor the seas drown.

She took the child and ran for three years in the wilderness with
 him.
And beside them ran a German-Jewish man
And he loved the child and protected him,
Crying: Remember Jerusalem.
And he crowned the child with a crown of affection.

But the child said
Mother, it is not a crown of affection I want
It is a crown of gold.

And the child and his mother ran more quickly in the wilderness
And more quickly beside them ran the German-Jewish man
Crying: Remember Jerusalem.
And he said, Nobody has loved your child as I have loved him.

And the child said, Mother procure for me a crown of gold
You are not required to think about anything else.

And the German-Jewish man kissed the crowned child's hand as
 he ran
Crying: Remember Jerusalem.

And the child stood in the path
And he took from his head the crown of affection
And threw it at the feet of the German-Jewish man
Crying: Remember Jerusalem.

And they left the German-Jewish man and left the wilderness
And she procured for her child a crown of gold
And they sat in a pleasant garden in a fine city.

And the child said, Mother, gold is the right material for a crown
Is it only in the wilderness that crowns of affection are worn,
And she said, Not it is not and began to weep and wring her
 hands,
Do not be foolish Mother, he said, I am no longer young.
And she said, Remember Jerusalem.

And the wind blew strong and rattled the leaves of the poplar trees
And the child did not hear, or heard and laughed, he did not care
But the strong wind took the words and carried them to the
 wilderness
Where they fell to the ground in a dry place.

And the mother of the child stopped crying and was resigned to
the golden crown
And she said, Now may the fire not burn my child nor the seas
drown.

Why do I . . .

Why do I think of Death as a friend?
It is because he is a scatterer
He scatters the human frame
The nerviness and the great pain
Throws it on the fresh fresh air
And now it is nowhere
Only sweet Death does this
Sweet Death, kind Death,
Of all the gods you are best.

Some Are Born

Some are born to peace and joy
And some are born to sorrow
But only for a day as we
Shall not be here tomorrow.

'*My beauty was unnoticed.*'

'It was I!'

SCORPION AND OTHER POEMS (1972)

Scorpion

'This night shall thy soul be required of thee'
My soul is never required of *me*
It always has to be somebody else of course
Will my soul be required of me tonight perhaps?

(I often wonder what it will be like
To have one's soul required of one
But all I can think of is the Out-Patients' Department –
'Are you Mrs Briggs, dear?'
No, I am Scorpion.)

I should like my soul to be required of me, so as
To waft over grass till it comes to the blue sea
I am very fond of grass, I always have been, but there must
Be no cow, person or house to be seen.

Sea and *grass* must be quite empty
Other *souls* can find somewhere *else*.

O Lord God please come
And require the soul of thy Scorpion

Scorpion so wishes to be gone.

Seymour and Chantelle

or

Un peu de vice

in memory of A. Swinburne and Mary Gordon

Pull my arm back, Seymour,
Like the boys do,
Oh Seymour, the pain, the pain,
Still more then, do.
I am thy schoolboy friend, now I
Am not Chantelle any more but mi.
Say 'sweet mi', 'my sweet mi.' Oh the pain, the pain,
Kiss me and I will kiss you again.

Tell me, Seymour, when they . . . when . . .
Does it hurt as much as this
And this and this? Ah what pain,
When I do so I feel
How very painful it is for you,
No I will, so, again and again,
Now stuff the dockleaves in your mouth
And bite the pain.

Seymour, when you hold me so tight it hurts
I feel my ribs break and the blood spurt,
Oh what heaven, what bliss,
Will you kiss me, if I give you this
Kiss, and this and this? Like this?

Seymour, this morning Nanny swished me so hard
(Because I told her she had the face
Of an antediluvian animal that had
Become extinct because of being so wet)
She broke her hair-brush. What bliss.
No, don't stop me now with a kiss, oh God it was pain-
Ful, I could not stop crying.

Oh darling, what heaven, how did you think
Of doing that? You are my sweetest angel of a
Little cousin, and your tears
Are as nice as the sea, as icy and salt as it is.

How do you see?

How do you see the Holy Spirit of God?
I see him as the holy spirit of good,
But I do not think we should talk about spirits, I think
We should call good, good.

But it is a beautiful idea, is it not?
And productive of good?

Yes, that is the problem, it is productive of good,
As Christianity now is productive of good,
So that a person who does not believe the Christian faith
Feels he must keep silent in case good suffers,
In case what good there is in the world diminishes.

But must we allow good to be hitched to a lie,
A beautiful cruel lie, a beautiful fairy story,
A beautiful idea, made up in a loving moment?

Yes, it is a beautiful idea, one of the most
Beautiful ideas Christianity has ever had,
This idea of the Spirit of God, the Holy Ghost,
My heart goes out to this beautiful Holy Ghost,
He is so beautifully inhuman, he is like the fresh air.
They represent him as a bird, I dislike that,
A bird is parochial to our world, rooted as we are
In pain and cruelty. Better the fresh air.

But before we take a Christian idea to alter it
We should look what the idea is, we should read in their books

Of holy instruction what the Christians say. What do they say
Of the beautiful Holy Ghost? They say

That the beautiful Holy Ghost brooded on chaos
And chaos gave birth to form. As this we cannot know
It can only be beautiful if told as a fairy story,
Told as a fact it is harmful, for it is not a fact.

But it is a beautiful fairy story. I feel so much
The pleasure of the bird on the dark and powerful waters,
And here I like to think of him as a bird, I like to feel
The masterful bird's great pleasure in his breast
Touching the water. Like! Like! What else do they say?

Oh I know we must put away the beautiful fairy stories
And learn to be good in a dull way without enchantment,
Yes, we must. What else do they say? They say

That the beautiful Holy Spirit burning intensely,
Alright as never was anything in this world alight,
Inspired the scriptures. But they are wrong,
Often the scriptures are wrong. For I see the Pope
Has forbidden the verse in Mark ever to be discussed again
And I see a doctor of Catholic divinity saying
That some verses in the New Testament are pious forgeries
Interpolated by eager clerks avid for good.

Ah good, what is good, is it good
To leave in scripture the spurious verses and not print
A footnote to say they are spurious, an erratum slip?

And the penal sentences of Christ: He that believeth
And is baptized shall be saved, he that believeth not
Shall be damned. Depart from me ye cursed into everlasting fire
Preparing for the devil and his angels. And then
Saddest of all the words in the scripture, the words,
They went away into everlasting punishment. Is this good?

Yes, nowadays certainly it is very necessary before we take
The ideas of Christianity, the words of our Lord,
To make them good, when often they are not very good,
To see what the ideas are and the words; to look at them.

Does the beautiful Holy Ghost endorse the doctrine of eternal hell?
Love cruelty, enjoin the sweet comforts of religion?
Oh yes, Christianity, yes, he must do this
For he is your God, and in your books

You say he informs, gives form, gives life, instructs.
Instructs, that is the bitterest part. For what does he instruct
As to the dreadful bargain, that God would take and offer
The death of his Son to buy our faults away,
The faults of the faulty creatures of the Trinity?
Oh Christianity, instructed by the Holy Ghost,
What do you mean? As to Christ, what do you mean?

It was a child of Europe who cried this cry,
Oh Holy Ghost what do you mean as to Christ?
I heard him cry. Ah me, the poor child,
Tearing away his heart to be good
Without enchantment. I heard him cry:

Oh Christianity, Christianity,
Why do you not answer our difficulties?
If He was God He was not like us
He could not lose.

Can Perfection be less than perfection?
Can the creator of the Devil be bested by him?
What can the temptation to possess the earth have meant to
 Him
Who made and possessed it? What do you mean?

And Sin, how could He take our sins upon Him? What does it
 mean?
To take sin upon one is not the same
As to have sin inside one and feel guilty.

It is horrible to feel guilty,
We feel guilty because we are.
Was He horrible? Did He feel guilty?

You say he was born humble – but he was not,
He was born God –

Taking our nature upon Him. But then you say
He was perfect Man. Do you mean
Perfect Man, meaning wholly? Or Man without sin? Ah
Perfect Man without sin is not what we are.

Do you mean He did not know that He was God,
Did not know He was the Second Person of the Trinity?
(Oh if he knew this and was,
It was a source of strength for Him we do not have)
But this theology of emptying you preach sometimes –
That He emptied Himself of knowing He was God – seems
A theology of false appearances
To mock your facts, as He was God whether He knew it
 or not.

Oh what do you mean, what do you mean?
You never answer our difficulties.

You say, Christianity, you say
That the Trinity is unchanging from eternity,
But then you say
At the incarnation He took
Our Manhood into the Godhead
That did not have it before
So it must have altered it, having it.

Oh what do you mean, what do you mean?
You never answer our questions.

So I heard the child of Europe cry,
Tearing his heart away

To be good without enchantment,
Going away bleeding.

Oh how sad it is to give up the Holy Ghost
He is so beautiful, but not when you look close,
And the consolations of religion are so beautiful,
But not when you look close.
Is it beautiful, for instance, is it productive of good
That the Roman Catholic hierarchy should be endlessly
 discussing at this moment
Their shifty theology of birth control, the Vatican
Claiming the inspiration of the Holy Spirit? No it is not good,
Or productive of good. It is productive of
Contempt and disgust. Yet
On the whole I suppose Christianity is kinder than it was,
Helped to it, I fear, by the power of the Civil Arm.

Oh Christianity, Christianity,
That has grown kinder now, as in the political world
The colonial system grows kinder before it vanishes, are you
 vanishing?
Is it not time for you to vanish?

I do not think we will be able to bear much longer the dishonesty
Of clinging for comfort to beliefs we do not believe in,
For comfort, and to be comfortably free of the fear
Of diminishing good, as if truth were a convenience.
I think if we do not learn quickly, and learn to teach children,
To be good without enchantment, without the help
Of beautiful painted fairy stories pretending to be true,
Then I think it will be too much for us, the dishonesty,
And, armed as we are now, we shall kill everybody
It will be too much for us, we shall kill everybody.

The Ass

In the wood of Wallow
Mash, walked Eugenia, a callow
girl, they said she was,
An Ass.

Beyond the wood there lay a soppy mórass
But the path across was firm, was
Not a-wash.

Three years in the wood Eugenia stayed
By briar and bramble and lost ways she was delayed,
And in a witch's house within a thicket of yew trees
Was put to work, but seemed so happy that the witch
Finding no pleasure in her tyranny
Gave her release.
She is an ass, she cried, let her pass.
And perish in the soppy mórass.

Eugenia was as happy in the change
To be free to roam and range
As she had been happy and not sad or sorry
At her labours in the witch's bothy.
The sun fell hot upon the causeway
That was not very wide
And the mórass sopped and shuffled
Either side.

And the little beetles ran
About, and all the gnats and the mosquitoes sang

And the mórass was as sweet a green
As Eugenia had ever seen.

She sang: Baa-baa-ba-bay
And seven happy years spent on the way.

Once there came a fiend
Who tempted her to go upon the green
Mórass: Come, ass, and go
Upon the green. But she said, No.
She was not such an ass to try the green,
It would deliver her below.

Heigh-ho, heigh-ho
Never was such a happy idle ass
Since idleness ran glad in Paradise
As Eugenia was.
Paradise. Paradise.

Now the seven years have passed,
The causeway's ended, the soppy mórass
Has sucked its last; the ass
Comes to a sandy pass
Between low sandhills that are tufted over with esparto grass.
Beyond, the great seas splash
And roll in pleasure to be so a-wash,
Their white crests coming at a dash
To fetch the ass.

Oh my poor ass
To run so quickly as if coming home
To where the great waves crash.

Now she is gone. I thought
Into her tomb.

Yet often as I walk that sandy shore
And think the seas
Have long since combed her out that lies
Beneath, I hear the sweet ass singing still with joy as if
She had won some great prize, as if
All her best wish had come to pass.

A Soldier Dear to Us

It was the War
I was a child
They came from the trenches
To our suburb mild.

Our suburb then was more a country place
They came to our house for release.

In the convalescent Army hospital
That was once a great house and landed estate
Lay Basil, wounded on the Somme,
But his pain was not now so great

That he could not be fetched in a bath-chair
Or hobble on crutches to find in our house there
My mother and aunt, his friends on leave, myself (I was twelve)
And a hearth rug to lie down in front of the fire on and rest
 himself.

It was a November golden and wet
As there had been little wind that year and the leaves were yet
Yellow on the great trees, on the oak trees and elms
Of our beautiful suburb, as it was then.

When Basil woke up he liked to talk and laugh
He was a sweet-tempered laughing man, he said:
'My dear, listen to this' then he read
From The Church Times, how angry the Bishop was because
Of the Reserved Sacrament in the church
Of St Alban's, Holborn. 'Now, my dear' he said, 'for a treat
Next Sunday I will take you to All Saints, Margaret Street; only
You will have to sit on the ladies' side, though you are not yet
 one really.'

Basil never spoke of the trenches, but I
Saw them always, saw the mud, heard the guns, saw the
 duckboards,
Saw the men and the horses slipping in the great mud, saw
The rain falling and never stop, saw the gaunt
Trees and the rusty frame
Of the abandoned gun carriages. Because it was the same
As the poem 'Childe Roland to the Dark Tower Came'
I was reading at school.

Basil and Tommy and Joey Porteous who came to our house
Were too brave even to ask *themselves* if there was any hope
So I laughed as they laughed, as they laughed when Basil said:
What will Ronny do now (it was Ronny Knox) will he pope?

And later, when he had poped, Tommy gave me his book for a
 present,
'The Spiritual Aeneid' and I read of the great torment

Ronny had to decide, Which way, this or that?
But I thought Basil and Tommy and Joey Porteous were more
 brave than that.

Coming to our house
Were the brave ones. And I could not look at them,
For my strong feelings, except
Slantingly, from the hearth rug, look at them.

Oh Basil, Basil, you had such a merry heart
But you taught me a secret you did not perhaps mean to impart,
That one must speak lightly, and use fair names like the ladies
They used to call
The Eumenides.

Oh Basil
I was a child at school,
My school lessons coloured
My thoughts of you.

Envoi

Tommy and Joey Porteous were killed in France. Now fifty
 years later
Basil has died of the shots he got in the shell crater
The shrapnel has worked round at last to his merry heart, I
 write this
For a memorial of the soldier dear to us he was.

The Forlorn Sea

Our Princess married
A fairy King,
It was a sensational
Wedding.

Now they live in a palace
Of porphyry,
Far, far away,
By the fòrlorn sea.

Sometimes people visit them,
Last week they invited me
That is how I can tell you
They live by a fòrlorn sea.

(They said: Here's a magic carpet,
Come on this,
And when you arrive
We will give you a big kiss.)

I play in the palace garden,
I climb the sycamore tree,
Sometimes I swim
In the fòrlorn sea.

The King and the Princess were shadowy,
Yet beautiful,
They are waited on by white cats,
Who are dutiful.

It is like a dream
When they kiss and cuddle me,
But I like it, I like it,
I do not wish to break free.

So I eat all they give me
Because I have read
If you eat fairy food
You will never wake up in your own bed.

But will go on living,
As has happened to me,
Far, far away
By a fòrlorn sea.

Angel Boley

There was a wicked woman called Malady Festing
Who lived with her son-in-law, Hark Boley,
And her daughter Angel,
In a house on the high moorlands
Of the West Riding of Yorkshire
In the middle of the last century.

One day Angel
Overheard her mother, Malady, talking to Hark, her husband.
Hark, said Malady, it is time
To take another couple of children
Into our kitchen.
Hark laughed, for he too was wicked and he knew
For what purpose the little children
Were required.

But Angel, who was not happy and so
Lived out her life in a dream of absentmindedness,
In order not to be too much aware
Of her horrible relatives, and what it was
That happened every now and then
In the kitchen; and why the children who came
Were never seen again, this time
When she heard what her husband and mother said,
Came out of her absentmindedness and paid attention.
I know now, she said, and all the time I have known
What I did not want to know, that they kill all children
They lure to this house; and that is why, when I pass in the
 village,
The people look askance at me, and they whisper –
But not so that I cannot hear –
There goes the daughter of Mother Lure. And the stranger says:
Who is Mother Lure? And they answer: Mrs Festing and
 they make the sign
That is to protect them from evil. Selfish wretches, said
 Angel,
They do not mind about the children, that evil is not kept
 from *them*.
Angel wandered into the woods and she said: No more children
Are going to be murdered, and before they are murdered,
 tormented
And corrupted; no more children are going to be the
 victims
Of Mother Lure and my husband, Hark. Dark was the
 look then
On Angel's face, and she said: I am the Angel of Death.

Mrs Festing and Boley
Always left the cooking to Angel, they despised Angel but Angel

Could cook, and that they thought was all she was fit for,
To cook and keep house. And they realized
It was far from being to their disadvantage that Angel was,
As they thought, half-witted, and never knew
Or wanted to know, what was going on around her.

As soon as Angel
Said to herself: I am the Angel of Death
She became at once very practical and went out into the woods
 and fields
And gathered some A. Phalloides, commonly called the 'white'
 or deadly
Amanita, a mushroom of high toxicity. These poisonous fungi
She put into a soup, and this soup she gave
To Hark, and her mother, Malady, for supper, so that they died.

Angel then went to the police and said:
I have done evil, but I have saved many children.

The Judge said: Why did you not tell the police
That children were being destroyed? There was no proof, said
 Angel,
Because there were no bodies. I never could find out
What they did with the children after they had killed them.

So then the police searched hard, the wells, the rivers and the
 woodlands,
But never could find out where
The children lay. Nor had the parents of the children
At any time done anything but weep. For they thought their
 children

Had been bewitched and done away with, and that
If they told their fears of Mother Lure and her wickedness
To the police, they would not believe them, and more children
 than ever
Would disappear.

From then onwards in the trial, Angel spoke
No words more, except to say: I am the Angel of Death.
So they put her in a lunatic asylum, and soon she died
Of an outbreak of typhoid fever. The people of the village
Now loved Angel, because she had delivered them from the fear

Of Mother Lure and Hark Boley, and had saved their
Little children from being tormented and slain by these wicked
 people.
So they wrote on her tombstone: 'She did evil that good
Might come'. But the Vicar said it was better not to put this but
Just her name and age, which was sixteen.
So he had the words
The villagers had written taken off the tombstone. But the next
 day
The words were again on the tombstone; so again the Vicar had
 them
Removed. And this time a watch was set on the grave,
A police constable and the village sexton watched there that
 night.

And no man came again to write on the tombstone
The forbidden words. Yet when morning came,
Again the words were on the tombstone.
So the Vicar said: It is the hand of the Lord.

And now in that graveyard, at that grave's head beneath the yew
 trees,
Still stands today the tombstone of Angel, with the words writ
 on it:
'She did evil that good might come'. May God be merciful.

The Donkey

It was such a pretty little donkey
It had such pretty ears
And it used to gallop round the field so briskly
Though well down in years.

It was a retired donkey,
After a life-time of working
Between the shafts of regular employment
It was now free to go merrymaking.

Oh in its eyes was such a gleam
As is usually associated with youth
But it was not a youthful gleam really,
But full of mature truth.

And of the hilarity that goes with age,
As if to tell us sardonically
No hedged track lay before this donkey longer
But the sweet prairies of anarchy.

But the sweet prairies of anarchy
And the thought that keeps my heart up
That at last, in Death's odder anarchy,
Our patterns will be broken all up.
Though precious we are momentarily, donkey,
I aspire to be broken up.

Cock-A-Doo

I love to hear the cock crow in
The middle of the day
It is an eerie sound in
The middle of the day
Sometimes it is a very hot day
Heavy for coming thunder
And the grass I tread on is dusty
And burnt yellow. Away
Over the river Bean which naturally
(It having been hot now for so long)
Runs shallow, stand up
The great yellow cornfields, but
Walking closely by the farm track
Not lifting my head, but foot by
Foot slowly, tired after a long
Walk, I see only the blue
And gray of the flint path, and
Each one of the particles of
Yellow dust on it. And this
Seeing, because of tiredness, becomes
A transfixion of seeing, more sharp
Than mirages are. Now comes the cry
Of the cock at midday
An eerie sound – cock-a-doooo – it
Sharpens a second time
The transfixion. If there were
A third sharpener
Coming this hot day with a butcher's edge
It would spell death.

Francesca in Winter

O love sweet love
I feel this love
It burns me so
It comes not from above

It burns me so
The flames run close
Can you not see
How the flames toss

Our souls like paper
On the air?
Our souls are white
As ashes are

O love sweet love
Will our love burn
Love till our love
To ashes turn?

I wish hellfire
Played fire's part
And burnt to end
Flesh soul and heart

Then we could sit beside our fire
With quiet love
Not fear to look in flames and see
A shadow move.

Ah me, only
In heaven's permission
Are creatures quiet
In their condition.

So to fatness come

Poor human race that must
Feed on pain, or choose another dish
And hunger worse.

There is also a cup of pain, for
You all to drink all up, or,
Setting it aside for sweeter drink,
Thirst evermore.

I am thy friend. I wish
You to sup full of the dish
I give you and the drink,
And so to fatness come more than you think
In health of opened heart, and know peace.

Grief spake these words to me in a dream. I thought
He spoke no more than grace allowed
And no less than truth.

The Sallow Bird

A sallow bird sat on a tree
Yclad in black from head to hee'
And oh he wept sae piteously.

Why sitst thou there and a' so blackit?
Why sitst thou there in thy black jacket,
With feathers furled?

Ah me, ah me,
Come now, tell me.

Then spake the bird in accents sar'
'Something human's dearer far
To me than wealth of a' the world,
And I lack it, and I lack it, I lack it.'

He never seyd a word again
(Nor went away). Yet oft in pain
He'll hauk that crik as if he spak it:
'I lack it, I lack it, I lack it.'

When Walking

A talented old gentleman painting a hedge
Came suddenly upon my mind's eye when walking;
Forgive me for my sins
And bring me to everlasting life to be with thee in happiness for
 ever,
I wanted to say. But I could not.
My heart leaps, I said. I am filled with joy
For your hedge. Nodding, he vanishèd.

Her-zie

a troll and his wife speak of the human child they stole

What's wrong with you-zie?
Nothing with me-zie,
Then what with who-zie?
Only with Her-zie,
So what with Her-zie?
A hearse for her-zie
A hearse for her-zie
Came for her.

What colour was it then?
Golden, golden,
Was there anyone in it?
A pale king was in it.
That was not a hearse for Her-zie, husband,
It was her marriage carriage.
It was a hearse for me, then,
My heart went with them and died then.

Husband, ah me-zie,
Your heart has died for Her-zie,
Without it you cannot be easy.

The Word

My heart leaps up with streams of joy,
My lips tell of drouth;
Why should my heart be full of joy
And not my mouth?

I fear the Word, to speak or write it down,
I fear all that is brought to birth and born;
This fear has turned my joy into a frown.

Nor We of Her to Him

He said no word of her to us
Nor we of her to him,
But oh it saddened us to see
How wan he grew and thin.
We said: She eats him day and night
And draws the blood from him,
We did not know but said we thought
This was why he grew thin.

One day we called and rang the bell,
No answer came within,
We said: She must have took him off
To the forest old and grim,
It has fell out, we said, that she
Eats him in forest grim,
And how can we help him being eaten
Up in forests grim?

It is a restless time we spend,
We have no help for him,
We walk about and go to bed,
It is no help to him.
Sometimes we shake our heads and say
It might have better been
If he had spoke to us of her
Or we of her to him.
Which makes us feel helpful, until
The silence comes again.

Mrs Blow and Her Animals

There was a dog called Clanworthy
Who lives with his friend the cat Hopdance
In the house of Mrs Blow, a widow,
Upon a glade in Cluny.

Hey, Hopdance,
How is Mrs Blow?
So-so, said Hopdance,
Bow, said the dog.

Mrs Blow
Loved her animals very much
She often said:
I do not know what I should do
Without Hopdance and
Clanworthy.

They loved her too.

Hey, Hopdance,
How is Mrs Blow?
So-so, said Hopdance,
She is not very well, said the dog.

Hopdance fetched her a fish
Which she cooked by the fire.
That will do her good,
Said Hopdance; but, said the dog,
She must have wine as well as food.

Clanworthy, brave Clanworthy,
Clanworthy for aye
Through fire and water brought wine
That Mrs Blow might not die.

Mrs Blow has now become their only thought
And care,
All the other animals

In the forest of Cluny
Say there is no talking to them now
Because their only thought is Mrs Blow.
Hey Hopdance,
How is Mrs Blow?
Oh, very well now.
She is quite recovered, said the dog.

But a woodcutter has opined
It was the spirit of Mrs Blow he saw dancing one night
When a full moon fell on the glade of Cluny
With her animals, and that
Clanworthy and Hopdance
Stood upright upon their hind legs
Holding the hand of Mrs Blow the widow
As if she was a child.
If it was Mrs Blow
But he said he thought it was the ghost
Of Mrs Blow, her spirit; and that
The animals, too, did not look like animals; he said
It was three spirits playing ring-a-ring
With crowns on their head.

So everyone remembered then
That a long time ago
The King and Queen had lost their little children
As
A great witch had changed the boys into animals
And the girl into Mrs Blow the widow

Crying: Hopdance, go Hopdance; Clanworthy go,
For a hundred and seven years
Be the animals of Mrs Blow.

Everyone was glad it had come right
And that the princes and the princess
Were dancing in the night.

Oh grateful colours, bright looks!

The grass is green
The tulip is red
A ginger cat walks over
The pink almond petals on the flower bed.
Enough has been said to show
It is life we are talking about. Oh
Grateful colours, bright looks! Well, to go
On. Fabricated things too – front doors and gates,
Bricks, slates, paving stones – are coloured
And as it has been raining and is sunny now
They shine. Only that puddle
Which, reflecting the height of the sky
Quite gives one a feeling of vertigo, shows
No colour, is a negative. Men!
Seize colours quick, heap them up while you can.
But perhaps it is a false tale that says
The landscape of the dead
Is colourless.

O Pug!

to the Brownes' pug dog, on my lap, in their car,
coming home from Norfolk

O Pug, some people do not like you,
But I like you,
Some people say you do not breathe, you snore,
I don't mind,
One person says he is always conscious of your behind,
Is that your fault?

Your own people love you,
All the people in the family that owns you
Love you: Good pug, they cry, Happy pug,
Pug-come-for-a-walk.

You are an old dog now
And in all your life
You have never had cause for a moment's anxiety,
Yet,
In those great eyes of yours,
Those liquid and protuberant orbs,
Lies the shadow of immense insecurity. There
Panic walks.

Yes, yes, I know,
When your mistress is with you,
When your master
Takes you upon his lap,
Just then, for a moment,
Almost you are not frightened.

But at heart you are frightened, you always have been.

O Pug, obstinate old nervous breakdown,
In the midst of *so* much love,
And such comfort,
Still to feel unsafe and be afraid,

How one's heart goes out to you!

Archie and Tina

Archie and Tina
Where are you now,
Playmates of my childhood,
Brother and sister?

When we stayed in the same place
With Archie and Tina
At the seaside,
We used

To paddle the samphire beds, fish
Crabs from the sea-pool, poke
The anemones, run,
Trailing the ribbon seaweed across the sand to the sea's edge
To throw it in as far as we could. We dug
White bones of dead animals from the sandhills, found
The jaw-bones of a fox with some teeth in it, a stoat's skull,
The hind leg of a hare.

Oh, if only; oh if only!

Archie and Tina
Had a dog called Bam. The silver-sand
Got in his long hair. He had
To be taken home.

Oh, if only . . . !

One day when the wind blew strong
Our dog, Boy, got earache. He had
To be taken home in a jersey.

Oh what pleasure, what pleasure!
There never were so many poppies as there were then,
So much yellow corn, so many fine days,
Such sharp bright air, such seas.

Was it necessary that
Archie and Tina, Bam and Boy,
Should have been there too?
Yes, then it was. But to say now:

Where are you today
Archie and Tina,
Playmates of my childhood,
Brother and sister? Is no more than
 to say:

I remember
Such pleasure, so much pleasure.

The Poet Hin

The foolish poet wonders
Why so much honour
Is given to other poets
But to him
No honour is given.

I am much condescended to, said the poet Hin,
By my inferiors. And, said the poet Hin,
On my tombstone I will have inscribed:
'He was much condescended to by his inferiors.'
Then, said the poet Hin,
I shall be properly remembered.

Hin – wiping his tears away, I cried –
Your words tell me
You know the correct use of *shall* and *will*.
That, Hin, is something we may think about,
May, may, may, man.

Well yes, true, said Hin, stopping crying then,
Well yes, but true only in part,
Well, your wiping my tears away
Was a part.

But ah me, ah me,
So much vanity, said he, is in my heart.
Yet not light always is the pain
That roots in levity. Or without fruit wholly
As from this levity's
Flowering pang of melancholy

May grow what is weighty,
May come beauty.

True too, Hin, true too. Well, as now: You have gone on
Differently from what you begun.
Yet both truths have validity,
The one meanly begot, the other nobly,
And as each alone glosses over
What the other says, so only together
Have they a full thought to uncover.

The House of Over-Dew

Over-dew
Became a dread name for Cynthia
In 1937
It was then that Mr Minnim first began to talk openly
About his dear wish.
How dear it was to be
For all of them!

Mr and Mrs Minnim had two sons
Who had done well at school
And won scholarships to Oxford.
Their boyhood was a happy time for all. Then
The elder son married Helen,
A fellow-student at the university,
And, coming down, found a good post with sufficient money.
His wife also
Had money of her own, they were doing well.

The young son, Georgie,
Was engaged to Cynthia. But that did not go so well.
He took a First in Greats, but then
The difficulties began. He could not find a job.
He did nothing, tried again; no good.
He grew sulky. It seemed hopeless.

It was now that the dread name of Over-Dew
Was spoken,
And a scheme bruited. It was this:
The Minnims were sincere and practising Christians, to
 Mr Minnim

Anyone who was not a Christian
Was a half-educated person.
It was, for instance, suggested
That his daughter-in-law should write a Life of St Benedict,
There was no good life of St Benedict, said Mr Minnim.
So Cynthia suggested that Helen should write it,
Because Helen was a Mediaeval History student,

Whereas Cynthia herself was a Latinist,
So why not Helen, with her special knowledge?
But Helen was not a Christian,
So, 'No', said Mr Minnim, she was a half-educated person.

The Over-Dew scheme was orthodox Christian.
When Mr Minnim retired from his accountancy work
He said that they should move from the suburb where they
 lived
And buy the house of Over-Dew, which was

A retreat for missionaries to have
On their leave-holidays in England.
And now it was being run, he said, in a fantastical fashion.

When they bought it
Everything would be better,
And different.
Where was the money to come from? No matter,
They had their savings, also they had the faith
Of Mr and Mrs Minnim.

Mrs Minnim loved her husband
And was pleased to follow him to the end of the earth, and
 certainly
Over-Dew was not that.

But oh when Cynthia heard that word
It was the knell
Of all her life and love. This, she said,
Is the end of happy days, and the beginning
Of calamity. Over-Dew, she thought,
Shall be the death of my love and the death of life.
For to that tune, she thought,
Shall come up a European war and personal defeat.

The Georgie situation
Was already sad. What could she do there? Nothing,
But see him and be silent and so enrage,
Or see him and speak, and the more enrage.

The wise and affectionate Cynthia
Must break the engagement and give back the ring.
There is nothing but this that she can do.

She takes up a post at London University
And in lecturing and study passes the days.
No more of that.

She had read a paper to her pupils
And fellow-dons, the subject is
The development of Latin from the first early growth
Upon the Grecian models. The study entrances,
She finds and reads a Latin prayer:
'I devote to Hades and Destruction'. It is a prayer
For time of battle, the thought is this:
I dedicate the enemy to Hades and Destruction. And perhaps
One or two of the praying Romans
Will devote also themselves
To Hades and Destruction. Rushing then into battle,
These 'devoted' people hope they may be killed. If not,
They are held for dead,
They are stateless, and in religion
Have no part at all. The gods have not accepted them,
They are alive, but yet they are destroyed.

In Cynthia's life, this sad year
Was twice as long as all the happy years before. She must
 now
Withdraw from Georgie and see him miserable.

She is at work and fast within her family,
The happy careless laughter
Of the brothers and sisters
Rings her round,
She has the home tasks, too,
And thinks of Georgie.

At the end of the year, in the bitter snow that fell that Christmas
The phrenzied Minnims
Moved from their life-long-suburb.

The house of Over-Dew
Lay buried half in snow,
It stood five miles from any town upon a hillside.
Very bleak it was, and all the pipes were froze.
Mrs Minnim worked hard,
They had a girl to help them then she left.

Mrs Minnim had courage and was cheerful
But she was by now an old lady. Suddenly
There was the gift of a little money. Mr Minnim
Bought chasubles for visiting priests. But at first
There were no visitors at all, but only
The old cold house, and the lavatories frozen up
And wood kindling to be chopped and dried.
The work was bitter hard.
Mr Minnim, released suddenly
From the routine of his accountancy
Suffered in his head a strange numbness,
He moved about in a dream, would take no hand with the
 dishes. Even
When five-and-twenty missionaries came for a conference
He would do nothing.
He paced the garden plots, 'And here' he said,
'I will build twelve lavatories. And in this room
We will have a consecration and build an altar.'

The thaw came and turned all to mud and slush,
There was still no post for Georgie, he came down from Oxford
And washed the dishes for his mother,

And chopped the wood and moved also in a daze,
The immense learning
Lay off from him, the crude work of the house
Was an excuse from study.

But now Mrs Minim was not happy, like a sad animal
She roamed the rooms of Over-Dew. This woman
Who had been so boisterous and so loving
With many friends, but still her own best thoughts
For Mr Minnim and their sons,
Was like a sad animal that cannot know a reason

Georgie, with the guilt of the excuse upon his heart,
Grew savage with her. The moody silences
Were shot with cruel words
It was so bitter cold within the house
Though now without the snow was melted and turned
 to slush.

The money situation preyed upon the mind of
 Mrs Minnim.

But her husband
Spoke of faith.

In the suburb where they once lived friends said:
How are the Minnims? Did you hear
That Mr Minnim has bought chasubles?
And then the foolish, unkind laughter: Chasubles!
It will be
The ruin of them, the end.

There was one hope that Mrs Minnim had, it was this,
That they might return at last to their house in the suburb,
She had refused to let her husband
Sell this house. No, that she would not allow. No,
That must be for a return.
But now, out of this refusal was made

The bitterness of their life at Over-Dew. For, said her husband,
You kept back the seven hundred and fifty pounds
We might have had for selling the house.

In London
The girl who should have been Georgie's wife
Hears all; understands; loves Georgie; is helpless; reads to her
 class
The Latin prayer: I devote to Hades and Destruction.
She rules the harsh thoughts that run; cries;
'Come, love of God.'

Oblivion

It was a human face in my oblivion
A human being and a human voice
That cried to me, Come back, come back, come back.
But I would not, I said I would not come back.

It was so sweet in my oblivion
There was a sweet mist wrapped round about
And I trod in a sweet and milky sea, knee deep,
That was so pretty and so beautiful, growing deeper.

But still the voice cried out, Come back, come back,
Come back to me from sweet oblivion!
It was a human and related voice
That cried to me in pain. So I turned back.

I cannot help but like Oblivion better
Than being a human heart and human creature,
But I can wait for her, her gentle mist
And those sweet seas that deepen are my destiny
And must come even if not soon.

The Galloping Cat

Oh I am a cat that likes to
Gallop about doing good
So
One day when I was
Galloping about doing good, I saw
A Figure in the path; I said:
Get off! (Because
I am a cat that likes to
Gallop about doing good)
But he did not move, instead
He raised his hand as if
To land me a cuff
So I made to dodge so as to
Prevent him bringing it orf,
Un-for-tune-ately I slid
On a banana skin
Some Ass had left instead
Of putting in the bin. So
His hand caught me on the cheek
I tried
To lay his arm open from wrist to elbow
With my sharp teeth
Because I am
A cat that likes to gallop about doing good.
Would you believe it?
He wasn't there
My teeth met nothing but air,
But a Voice said: Poor Cat
(Meaning me) and a soft stroke

Came on me head
Since when
I have been bald
I regard myself as
A martyr to doing good.
Also I heard a swoosh,
As of wings, and saw
A halo shining at the height of
Mrs Gubbins's backyard fence,
So I thought: What's the good
Of galloping about doing good
When angels stand in the path
And do not do as they should
Such as having an arm to be bitten off
All the same I
Intend to go on being
A cat that likes to
Gallop about doing good
So
Now with my bald head I go,
Chopping the untidy flowers down, to
 and fro,
An' scooping up the grass to show
Underneath
The cinder path of wrath
Ha ha ha ha, ho,
Angels aren't the only ones who do
 not know
What's what and that
Galloping about doing good
Is a full-time job
That needs
An experienced eye of earthly

Sharpness, worth I dare say
(If you'll forgive a personal note)
A good deal more
Than all that skyey stuff
Of angels that make so bold as
To pity a cat like me that
Gallops about doing good.

Hippy-Mo

I had a sweet bird
Called Hippy-Mo
But he did not wish to stay
With me, he wished to go.
Hippy-Mo, Hippy-Mo.

I hugged him tight, I said:
You shall not go,
You shall stay here with me
Hippy-Mo.

Then he grew tall as a house,
Hippy-Mo,
Took me in his claws and would
Not let me go,
Hippy-Mo.

His eyes were black as the night
Through which we flew,
And the lightnings flashed from his eyes
As we flew through,
Hippy-Mo what are
You going to do
With me?

Hippy-Mo, Hippy-Mo,
Brought me to a sunny land.
Put me in a cage
Wherein I rage

And when I rage he holds
My hand
So tight I cannot move
From him.

Hippy-Mo
Let me go,
Do you wish me
To die?

He was so mean he did not condescend
To reply. Even
Yes or no.

Hendecasyllables

It is the very bewitching hour of eight
Which is the moment when my new day begins,
I love to hear the pretty clock striking eight
I love to get up out of my bed quickly.
Why is this? Because morning air is so cold?
Or because of new strength that seems to come then?
Both. And also because waking up ends dreams.

Black March

I have a friend
At the end
Of the world.
His name is a breath

Of fresh air.
He is dressed in
Grey chiffon. At least
I think it is chiffon.
It has a
Peculiar look, like smoke.

It wraps him round
It blows out of place
It conceals him
I have not seen his face.

But I have seen his eyes, they are
As pretty and bright
As raindrops on black twigs
In March, and heard him say:

I am a breath
Of fresh air for you, a change
By and by.

Black March I call him
Because of his eyes
Being like March raindrops
On black twigs.

(Such a pretty time when the sky
Behind black twigs can be seen
Stretched out in one
Uninterrupted
Cambridge blue as cold as snow.)

But this friend
Whatever new names I give him
Is an old friend. He says:

Whatever names you give me
I am
A breath of fresh air,
A change for you.

Grave by a Holm-Oak

You lie there, Anna,
In your grave now,
Under a snow-sky,
You lie there now.

Where have the dead gone?
Where do they live now?
Not in the grave, they say,
Then where now?

Tell me, tell me,
Is it where I may go?
Ask not, cries the holm-oak,
Weep, says snow.

The Sea-widow

How fares it with you, Mrs Cooper my bride?
Long are the years since you lay by my side.
Do you wish I was back? Do you speak of me dearest?
I wish you were back for me to hold nearest.
Who then lies nearer, Mrs Cooper my bride?
A black man comes in with the evening tide.
What is his name? Tell me! How does he dare?
He comes uninvited. His name is Despair.

The Stroke

for M.

I was a beautiful plant
I stood in the garden supreme
Till there came a blight that fell on each leaf
How I wish this had not been
Oh I wish this had not been.

I can feel the sun, and my blighted leaves
In an elderly way grow glad
But oh in my depths I bleed, I bleed,
From a heart that is youthful and sad
From a heart that is piercèd and sad.

Come, Death (2)

I feel ill. What can the matter be?
I'd ask God to have pity on me,
But I turn to the one I know, and say:
Come, Death, and carry me away.

Ah me, sweet Death, you are the only god
Who comes as a servant when he is called, you know,
Listen then to this sound I make, it is sharp,
Come Death. Do not be slow.

APPENDIX I – UNCOLLECTED POEMS

'Casmilus'

Casmilus, whose great name I steal,
Whose name a greater doth conceal,
Indulgence, pray,
And, if I may,
The winged tuft from either heel.

'As falls the gravelled grouse'

As falls the gravelled grouse
From clear sky,
Or as the clear eyed hawk,
Sighting through skyey spaces,
Some lesser creature, formed and nurtured
By the dear gods for his peculiar pleasure,
Down plunges through the empyrean blue
And takes what is his own,
What rightly,
Time, place, circumstance harmonious,
Does, with the ageing of a weary world,
Escheat to him.

Henry Wilberforce

Henry Wilberforce as a child
Was much addicted to the pleasures of the wild;
He observed Nature, saw, remembered,
And was by a natural lion dismembered.

From the Latin

Be mine, sweet child, let not the blush departing
From thy soft cheek declare it was in vain
The signal flashed, the message to engage departing
Ah, not in vain, dear girl; ah, not in vain.

Portrait of a Fool

Is she not a stupid girl? Just see,
With heaving beating heart she stands
And likes to be in bed at love and twists her hands,
And never laughs at all but only censures or approves
In pompous hesitating sixth form syllables.
Yes, she's rather like a prefect,
In an adult I always think a de-fect:
She has a pompous hesitating soul,
Well, there's the portrait of a fool.

Souvenir de Jacky Vandenbroeck

Very *louche* is this dog, very *louche*
And that is why he is looking this way;
For the dog that is *louche* by the night-time
Can never be smiling by day
Oh, he prefers to be *louche* by the night-time
To smiling and nodding by day.

'The grief of an unquiet mind is a thing accursed'

The grief of an unquiet mind is a thing accursed,
It layeth a violent hand upon the flesh;
But the soul is its enemy and the flesh is torn
That the soul may be taken and driven untimely forth.

Unhappy the soul that is linked with an unquiet mind,
 The fight may be long or short but the end is one,
And the mark of the fight is set on the brow of
 the flesh
That men may see and be warned and hurry away.

Marriage I Think

Marriage I Think
For women
Is the best of opiates.
It kills the thoughts
That think about the thoughts,
It is the best of opiates.
So said Maria.
But too long in solitude she'd dwelt,
And too long her thoughts had felt
Their strength. So when the man drew near,
Out popped her thoughts and covered him with fear.
Poor Maria!
Better that she had kept her thoughts on a chain,
For now she's alone again and all in pain;
She sighs for the man that went and the thoughts that stay
To trouble her dreams by night and her dreams by day.

Lulu

I do not care for Nature,
 She does not care for me;
You can be alone with a person,
 You can't be alone with a tree.

Death of Cold

Often in her bath, ah cold,
A thought would come to give her pause;
And she would stand and only stare
Upon a sudden cause.
And this matured her mind so that the gravestone bold
Declared she died too young to be so old.

Via Media Via Dolorosa

There's so much to be said on either side,
I'll be dumb.
There's so much to be said on either side,
I'll hold my tongue.
For years and years I never said a word,
Now I have lost the art: my voice is never heard,
For my apprehension
Snaps beneath the tension
Of what is to be said on either side.

Sigh No More

Sigh no more ladies nor gentleman at all,
Whatever fate attend or woe befall;
Sigh no more, shed no bitter tear,
Another hundred years you won't be here.

Salon d'Automne

One thousand and one naked ladies
With a *naïveté*
At once pedantic and sympathetic
Deck the walls
Of the Salon d'Automne.
This is the Slap school of art,
It would be nice
To smack them
Slap, slap, slap,
That would be nice.
It is possible
One might tire of smacking them
In time
But not so soon
As once tires of seeing them.
We too
Have our pedantic and unsympathetic
School,
It used to show
A feeling for animals.

The English are splendid with animals,
There was The Stag at Bay
And Faithful unto Death,
And Man's Best Friend the horse this time
Usually under gunfire,
The English are splendid with animals.
That older school
Was perhaps
Of an intellectual level
With the Salon d'Automne.
Nowadays, of course,
We are more advanced:
The bad modern painter
Has lost the *naïveté*
Of that earlier school
And in its place
Has developed a talent
For making the work of his betters
Seem stale
By unspirited
Imitation.
Really
This is more tiring
Than the thousand and one
Naked ladies.

Sterilization

Carve delinquency away,
Said the great Professor Clay.

A surgical operation is just the thing
To make everybody as happy as a king.

But the great Dostoievsky the Epileptic
Turned on his side and looked rather sceptic.

And the homosexual Mr Wilde
Sat in the sunshine and smiled and smiled.

And a similarly inclined older ghost in a ruff
Stopped reading his sonnets aloud and said 'Stuff!'

And the certainly eccentric Swift, Crashawe and Donne,
Silently shook hands and thanked God they had gone.

But the egregious Professor Clay
Called on Theopompous and won the day.

And soon all our minds will be flat as a pancake,
With no room for genius, exaltation or heartache.

And our children and theirs will preen, smirk and chatter,
With not even the sense to ask what is the matter.

The Word

Oh where is the word
Said sweet Sally Soo
Oh! where is the word I seek
It cannot be true
There is no word from you

To put in my velvet cheek
But the echoes ran
And the silence came
And alone in the cold
She is much the same
Oh! where is the word oh! where is it pray
Don't keep me waiting all night and day.

Landrecie

What shall I say to the gentlemen, mother,
They stand in the doorway to hear what is said,
Waiting and watching and listening and laughing,
Is there no word that will send them away?

What shall I say to the gentlemen, mother,
What shall I say to them, must I say nothing?
If I say nothing, then will they not harm us,
Will they not harm us and shall we not suffer?

What shall I say to the gentlemen, mother?
See, they are waiting, and will not depart.
Closed are your eyelids, your lips closed in silence
Cannot instruct me, oh what shall I answer?

This Baronet

This Baronet is very funny
And I do so hope he makes some money

He deserves to for not being a pompous ass
Like the Bishop of Bye and Mrs Grampus.

Swift to Depart

Swift
to depart
As falling leaves in autumn
is your
Love.

The Horror of the Midnight

Little children in the sunlight
Please be happy while you may
For the horror of the midnight
It shall never pass away
Not though darkness yield to daylight
Shall it wholly pass away
Then be happy and let laughter
Bearing gifts to fortune's feet
Cry aloud above the echoes
We are sure that life is sweet
Swear again as swore the Danaans
Oh, life could not be more sweet.

The Angel

Underneath the speckled leaves
Of the speckled laurel-tree
Sits an angel fawningly
Looking on the greenery.

But his eye is very cold
Bright as night and starry old
Though he sits so fawningly
Looking on the greenery.

O forbear enquiry.

Revenge

Revenge, Timotheus cries, and in that shout
There's all there is about it and about
Between this man and men, whate'er befall
There is no word more to be said at all.

Lift Thy Sad Heart

Lift thy sad heart
Oh lift thy eyes
Lift thy sad heart.

Never more lifted
My heart shall be
Dead is my heart
Of misery.
Never more lifted
My eyes at all
From a low place
Of funeral.

Flounder

(Part of an Acrostic)

Rather a fishy thing to do –
And yet this is not wholly true.

The Pupil

Je ne peux le verstehen
Je ne peux pas le verstehen
Je ne peux pas le comprendre
Ich kann es nicht verstehen.

Portrait

Stupid and self-satisfied
Stupid is the word
He sits and claps his own applause
Isn't he absurd?

Isn't he a darling baby
Crowing in the sun
Cockadoodle on the dunghill
Lots of happy fun?

Isn't he a little monster –
Thirty-two? My God
I should have said that he was two
Without the thirty. Odd.

Left, Right

Left, right;
Be bright.

Ichabod

Oh Ichabod, the glory is departed,
Those antique deserts and those happy palms
Bloom not for me, alone and broken hearted,
Stir but the sails of thought that grief becalms.

[672]

On Coming Late to Parnassus

Upon his loneliness and pain
Fame broke
Too strong a wave for him
And slew.

A Portrait

I never know what to say
When I'm in company
I feel quite tonguetied and shy,
I'm a perfect misery.
It really is tantalising,
And after the Education I've had
Surprising.
There's nothing I'd rather say
Than something Edifying and Unusual.

The Horrible Man

He is a most horrible man,
Why look?
He is a horrible man

He has done something at which the crocodile
Grew wan

He has never done anything at all – no, not by chance,
At which the crocodile kept
Countenance

He is a most horrible man

The Octopus

Darling little Tom and Harry,
When time comes for you to marry,
Lullaby,
Mother will be close at hand,
Close at hand

Little girlies, you who marry
Darling Tom and darling Harry
By and by,
Understand
Mother will be close at hand,
Close at hand

As Sways

As sways the gentle sycamore
Beneath the winds of heaven,
So sways my inconsistent heart, dear love,
When you are far away;

So sways my inconstant heart, dear love,
And shall for ever sway.
No use for you to say:
'Better the oak by tempest riven
Than nodding sycamore beneath the winds of heaven'

Portrait

Mr Petty-Pie
Keeps his masterpieces in his head,
He is a better tactician than I.

Silent, silent thought.
Never to be brought
To the printed page,
Weave a subtle shade.
O'er the facey-fie
Of little Petty-Pie;
And may its lineaments continue to suggest
A wisdom too profound to be expressed.

Two Friends

I only asked my friends to be friendly and polite,
I found them indifferent and censorious;
The one I left to silence, the other to reproach:
God send me over all such friends victorious

'When I Awake'

When I awake
The whole returning flood of consciousness
Is hateful to me
And Death, too often on my lips,
Becomes my shadower.

O Death, Death, Death,
Deceitful friend,
Come pounce,
And take,
And make
An end at once.

'O Silent Visitation'

O silent visitation
In negation of all presences
O felicity of the imagination
O merit
Of integrity in solitude
Where was born the desolation
Of this night sky that lightly lightly
Treads upon the desert
In patience lost beyond cognizance
O desolate night sky
O profundity of patience
Bearing lightly lightly

Upon the desert of the time track
O behold in silence
The shapes of the prevision
That dance and turn again
From comprehension
I am waiting for you.

I Forgive You

I forgive you, Maria,
Things can never be the same,
But I forgive you, Maria,
Though I think you were to blame.
I forgive you, Maria,
I can never forget,
But I forgive you, Maria,
Kindly remember that.

'The Midwife'

The midwife guards the mother's health
But she herself is on the shelf
She cannot have a little child
And that is why she looks so wild.

The Royal Dane

Now is come the horrible mome,
When I to my sulphurous home,
Must go 'ome, must go 'ome.

O Lord!

from 2nd Messenger's Speech to King Pentheus, Bacchae

This god then, O lord whoever he is do receive into the city
For not only is he great but also as I have heard
He gave the pain-killing vine to men.
Take away drink, where's Love?
Any pleasure come to that, O lord there is nothing left.

The English

The English are our friends of course
And on we love them worse and worse
We like to see England looking shabby and poor
And to know that she will not be our rival any more.

You look a little pale? Is anything amiss?
Do you not like our beautiful peace-kiss?

Beautiful

Man thinks he was not born to die
But that's no proof he wasn't,
And those who would not have it so
Are very glad it isn't.

Why should man wish to live for ever?
His term is merciful,
He riseth like a beaming plant
And fades most beautiful,

And his rising and his fading
Is most beautiful.

No, not the one without the other,
But always the two together,
Rising fading, fading rising,
It is really not surprising
To find this beautiful.

Why d'You Believe?

Why d'you believe that God is cruel
And life a hazard of eternity
Spent in a dim cage of cruel punishment?

Oh say not so, why say when you don't know? –
That life beyond the grave and God are such,

Why not believe in something sweeter, oh
Why call Belief what is no more than Hope?

Each man when he believes, when there's no ground for't
But hopes, men don't believe what's only rumour'd.

Write that word right, say 'hope', don't say 'belief',
Then plainly it's absurd to hope for pain beyond relief.

Or does it give some drama when the dull
Pulse of the daily beats a shade too full?

Oh from men's nerves, from the beginning, came
Such aggravation, he'll believe in pain,
Long for it too, or else he'll 'hope', and cry:
Things wrong in this world must be righted by and by.

All this is reasonable, in a man's own sort
Of reason, it explains, but don't excuse,
We learn the cause of man's most savage heart,
Poor wretch, 'tis grounded in a nerve's abuse,

Squirming, he gave us God in his own imagery,
A notion future centuries did well to query,
It really will not do for our own Tom and Mary,

Yes, in these later days I think we might
Contented, leave obscure what is obscure,
Rejoicing that beyond the grave is Night
Impenetrable, glad we can't be sure,

Or sure, if sure at all, but sure of this,
Where speculation's vain it's also slothful,

No time is idler spent than on theologies,
Though there's a luxury in it one supposes,
Softening and puffing up the human creature
To make him the empyrean's chief feature,
There is no end to what mere man can worship, come to that,
The leopard and the egg, black stone, old Egypt's kitty-cat,

And much as witchcraft was a child's endeavour
To side-step learning Nature's hard behaviour,
So nowadays, truth being hard still and quite impersonal,
You'll find men plump for Holy Ghost and Saviour,
Fancy fulfilling and full-flattering more
Than Fact, the image of themselves they adore,
(Armed cap-a-pie, of course,
To make us all agree, lest worse
Befall.)

But oh it is a sorry sort of business,
One can't but sicken at the racks and bloodshed,
The centuries' abuse, the social veto,
The tears forbidden that the people would shed.
Best sicken at what brought 'em, the neglect
Of simple Fact, prime food of Intellect,
Of which foul fancies are as much the enemies
As any dolled-up tramp in idle arms our bodies' is.

O Church of Christ, O Bride of mien ferocious,
In fancy frantic and in deed atrocious,
What though thy scowl leans nowadays on a simper
We're not deceived it means a better temper,
'Tis but a tribute to those Powers whose civil laws,
In countries protestant at least, have clipped your claws,
There's little doubt,
Left to it, what you would be still about.

And it is natural. Crowning his own fancies
A man can scarce allow equivocation,
The matter's without proof? then without mercy
He'll call a fellow-creature's fancies heresy,

(From which the proposition plainly runs:
A man may be far worse employed than doing sums.)
Not that I'd have imagination smothered,
It is a part of knowledge after all,
It draws us on. If recognised
For what it is, it does no harm at all.
If recognised? But then it often isn't,
But wears a crown and puts us all in prison.

Beware, beware, authority sits ill
On Fancy. Ill? It is the devil,
To pull our nerves until they break
And say it's done for true religion's sake.

Know thy world, Man; through Art or Science, dote on it,
But do not build a fairy tale upon it.

The Vision

These before the worlds in congress
Stood to sing their songs in song-dress,
Never one was in a wrong dress
Never one was out of tune.

Oh it filled my heart with pity
Ah, so serious and pretty,

Stood my Race to sing its ditty,
Unsolicited.

The worlds were quite indifferent
As to how the singing went,
If the Race were elegant
They did not care.

But still the people stood and chanted
For to chant was all they wanted,
So their bravery was vaunted
Emptily, emptily.

Yet I was proud to see their singing,
Proud the human race was flinging
Such a song at such a ceiling
Gustily,

Then it vanished all away,
Worlds and singers went away;
Nothing now is left to say
But this: it was a vision.

Heartless

My little dog is called
Heartless,
His nature is
Heartless,
Yet when he barks he cries

'Heartless, heartless',
And this is a complaint,

So perhaps he will improve,
. . . one day learn to love?

'Heartless!', I call,
But he barks again
'Heartless, heartless'
Only to complain.

I hope he finds where it is love is lacking,
And stops barking.

Silence

Why do people abuse so much our busy age?
They can withdraw into themselves and not rage
It is better to do this and live in one's own kingdom
Than by raging add to the rage of our busy time.

This is a time when there are too many words,
Silent, silent, silent the waters lie
And the beautiful grass lies silent and this is beautiful,
Why can men then not withdraw and be silent and happy?

It is better to see the grass than write about it
Better to see the water than write a water-song,
Yet both may be painted and a person be happy in the painting,
Can it be that the tongue is cursed, to go so wrong?

The Old Poet

There was an old poet lay dying
And as he lay dying, said he (said he)
I'd've done much better as a literurry editor
Than a-writing of poetry
Hey ho, hey ho,
A-writing of poetry.

A literurry editor has great sensibility
Cried the old poet, cried he,
Why sometimes the creature's even written a poem
God help us all, said he,
And got it published, and got it published, and got it published
Coincidentally
Hey ho, hey ho,
Coincidentally.

Then the poor old poet turned on his side
And to save putting another shilling in the gas meter
Died,
Hey ho, hey ho,
Died.

I walked in the graveyard . . .

I walked in the graveyard
The ghosts came to me:
'Give us a saucer of blood!'
You will get no blood from me.

Then they took me and tore and drank
And called me by name
And drank my bright blood
As it ran in a stain.

It was for pity I fed them,
For pity stood still
In the land of the Shades
Now I dwell.

La Robe Chemise

Disarmed off-guard *tendre et soumise*
How foolish of women to abandon *la Robe Chemise*,
Especially Englishwomen with their long backs and bend
 serpentine –
Such figures look best without a waistline.
But of course the Americans would not have it, in that women-
 dominated place
All girls must be bright and brittle and have a tight waist.

Oh under the old trees of Europe, on the soft grass
I sigh for the tender ungirt dress,
Oh bring it back, bring it back, *douce et soumise*,
Bring back to my arms again *la Robe Chemise*.

If you will not allow the implication of this dress's story
Say at least it is comfortable and be hypocritical,
For you cannot, unless you are stupid, not know it is irresistible
To be so off-guard gay tender and vulnerable.

From the French

I have plunged in a poem of the sea.
Alight with stars at first and growing milky
It ate the pretty blues and greens as I went down
And turned quite dark. There,
Like piece of flotsam torn about and stained,
A pensive corpse came floating to my side.
It was at this great depth I was aware
Of crimson flowing in the cold dark sea
All crimson, all bright red. I thought it was
As if our human love lay bleeding there,
Bleeding in anger, bleeding yet alive;
And I was glad, although I was not happy,
Because it was alive. The rest was dead.

The Holiday

The time is passing now
And will soon come
When you will be able
To go home.

The malice and the misunderstanding
The loneliness and the pain
Need not in this case, if you are careful,
Come again.

Say goodbye to the holiday, then.
To the peace you did not know,
And to the friends who had power over you,
Say goodbye and go.

When One

When one torments another without cease
It cannot but seem
It cannot but seem
That Death is the only release.

When two torment each other in this way
The one by being tormented easily
The other by tormenting actively
It cannot but seem
It cannot but seem
That Death, as he must come happily,
Should not delay.

Ah this unhappy Two
It seems as if
They never could leave off
Tormenting. And so nervily
All is done,
Death, quieten them.

Why do I think of Death
As a friend?
It is because he is a scatterer,

He scatters the human frame
The nerviness and the great pain,
Throws it on the fresh fresh air
And now it is nowhere.
Only sweet Death does this,
Sweet Death, kind Death,
Of all the gods you are best.

Miss Snooks, Poetess

Miss Snooks was really awfully nice
And never wrote a poem
That was not really awfully nice
And fitted to a woman,

She therefore made no enemies
And gave no sad surprises
But went on being awfully nice
And took a lot of prizes.

Saint Foam and the Holy Child

A Christmas Legend

On a black horse
A long time ago in a northern forest
Rode Rothga the heathen child.

Rothga, where are you riding?
Said a great witch.
I am not riding to see you,
Said Rothga.

Then came a bear who stood upright
Upon his hind legs: Where are you riding, Rothga,
Not that I mind? Well, not to see you.
And she rode more quickly. Because, she said,
There is not much time.

On, on they went,
The heathen child and her black horse,
Until the forest broke –
And they came to a sea-shore where the great waves
Threw their froth and foam beneath the lights
Of a northern sky.

Rothga left her black horse and ran
Down to the sea's edge. I am in time,
She said, and laughed to see
Riding the greatest of the sea-waves
A Child of Light who cried:
I am new born tonight, in the city of Bethlehem.
Rothga, be sure I am.

I am sure, said Rothga. You must bless me.

I bless you Rothga, said the Child. I am come to save
All people from the malign witch,
From the indifferent bear
And from the dark forest.
Rothga, take this foam-curd for a token,
It shall never grow dull or grow less.

Rothga went home and said:
Father, mother, we have been blessed by a sea-child
Who gave me this for a token.

Thus it was there came to be built
As it stands today, the Great Church
Of St Foam and the Holy Child
On a northern shore.

B.B.C. Feature Programme on Prostitution

How hypocritical this dear old fellow is
Mr Something who runs the Nude Theatre,
He tells us it lifts the mind and is artistic
And does no harm in fact it does good
(And makes money. Beg pardon no that he did not say.)

And then he said, My girls don't do so much
Harm as those stunted spinsters who write poison letters
And a good many other of your goody people who fancy
 themselves
Et cetera. Et cetera. And how artistic it is.

In the end you'd hardly have got this fine old creature to admit
Some girls off the streets are just as good as those on it.

The girls themselves said, Chaps
Often came behind the scenes afterwards and said, Ten
Fifteen or twenty pounds, and yes it was tempting.

After that in this interesting radio feature
The prostitutes spoke with an interviewing clergyman.
What do you think sin is? he asked 'Judy',
Judy said it was doing something for nothing,
No, she said, prostitution wasn't wrong

It didn't nearly do so much harm as
Stunted spinsters writing poison letters et cetera
But she wouldn't go to church all the same
As long as she was doing it.

And all of them said it was dangerous
And not really very enjoyable
As often they got carved up or beaten or killed
But there you are, it was twenty pounds a week untaxed
(And a good deal more)
Compared with five in a job, subject to taxation.

So they all admitted money was the thing
(Being plainer than Mr Something, or stupider)
And money, money, not with the old alternative
Of nothing at all, but with not enough for the telly,
And not getting up to catch a bus to the office,

And having pink lampshades, and ultimately
Getting out of it with the money you had invested
And buying a place of your own and being respected.

So you see it's money all the time and how to get it
And not caring about money is what is wicked
And idiots who think like this are always generous
When it comes to paying the price for money. Only
The wise look twice at that price and are parsimonious. Only
The clergyman in this radio programme seemed not stupid, not
 half an idiot.

Pretty Baby

Sweet baby, pretty baby, I bless thee,
Thou liest so snug and lookst so prettily,
And yet I think you also look imperially.

Why shouldst thou not? If it is Deity
Couches in mother's lap, prettily, prettily,
Then thou art God and canst not sin or feel guilty,

And we can do, for we have our sins innerly,
Sweet baby. Now I think there is a fee
That you must pay for looking happily.

And that is: not to know what being free
From sins means, being sinless. Only we
Can bless and measure that felicity.

But let the angels sing a song for thy birth sweetly,
And we will try to sing songs too, but differently,
For we are earth-born and the song is heavenly.

Our Doggy

First he sat, and then he lay,
And then he said: I've come to stay.
And that is how we acquired our doggy Pontz.
He is all right as dogs go, but not quite what one wants.

Because he talks. He talks like you and me.
And he is not you and me, he is made differently.
You think it is nice to have a talking animal?
It is not nice. It is unnatural.

My Tortoise

I had a sweet tortoise called Pye
Wabbit.
He ate dandelions, it was
His habit.
Pye Wabbit, Pye Wy-et,
It was more than a habit, it was
His diet.
All the hot summer days, Pye
Wy-et, Pye Wiked-it,
Ate dandelions. I lay on the grass flat to see
How much he liked it.
In the autumn when it got cold, Pye Wiked-it, Pye
Wy-bernator
Went to sleep till next spring. He was
A hibernator.
First he made a secret bed for the winter,
To lie there.
We loved him far too much ever
To spy where.
Why does his second name change every time?
Why, to make the rhyme.
Pye our dear tortoise
Is dead and gone.

He lies in the tomb we built for him, called
'Pye's Home'.
Pye, our dear tortoise,
We loved him so much.
Is he as dear to you now
As he was to us?

Have Done, Gudrun

Sir, –

 Have done, Gudrun,
 Self-appointed scourge
 Of our kingdom,

 No truth lies
 In your foolish words, but
 As much vanity
 As there is in Germany,
 Yours faithfully,
 Stevie Smith

William the Dog

William the Dog
When he comes to tea
Always asks to sit next to me.

William the Dog
Behaves very well

He sits up straight
And wags his tail.

When tea is over
He sings a song
And then he says
'I must be gone'.

Yes, he must be gone
For he lives on the moon,
'Good-bye, William,
Come back soon.'

'Good-bye, good-bye,'
'Good-bye, good-bye,'
William the Dog
Runs up to the sky.

He runs up the sky
Till he gets to the moon,
'Good-bye, good-bye,
I will come back soon.'

Sapphic

(in mixed speech)

The mune ha gien her loicht an' gan
The stardies eek are flee
Upon ma bett in durchet nich'
Ah lane ah lee.

The Hound Puss

I have a cat: I call him Pumpkin,
A great fat furry purry lumpkin.
Hi-dee-diddle hi-diddle dumpkin.

He sleeps within my bed at night,
His eyes are Mephistopheles-bright:
I dare not look upon their blight.

He stalks me like my angry God,
His gaze is like a fiery rod:
He dines exclusively on cod.

Avaunt, you creeping saviour-devil,
Away with thy angelical evil!

APPENDIX II – UNPUBLISHED POEMS

Northumberland Park

Northumberland Park Northumberland Park
In the month of November is very dark
The children run happily in the streets
And the old parrot croaks behind a curtain of beads
The leaves have fallen from the trees in the park
And if it does not rain will make a fine spark
Always in November in the dark there is this idea
That very soon a great fire will start
The smell of this place is of soot and sulphur
And in the darkness lights flare
It may be the naptha
Flares on the street stall
Or the scarlet light runs on the cinema walls
And there are the orange and yellow lights
Of shops and houses and the pale green light

Fussy

Is Fussy coming?
Will Fussy be there?
Oh I do hope Fussy's coming
Fussy is my ideal

Who is Fussy? Fussy Mapham
Fussy is the prettiest girl in Upper Clapham.

Goodnight

Miriam and Horlick spend a great deal of time putting off going
 to bed.
This is the thought that came to me in my bedroom where they
 both were, and she said:
Horlick, look at Tuggers, he is getting quite excited in his head.

Tuggers was the dog. And he was getting excited. So.
Miriam had taken her stockings off and you know
Tuggers was getting excited licking her legs, slow, slow.

It's funny Tuggers should be so enthusiastic, said Horlick nastily,
It must be nice to be able to get so excited about nothing really,
Try a little higher up old chap, you're acting puppily.

I yawned. Miriam and Horlick said Goodnight
And went. It was 2 o'clock and Miriam was quite white
With sorrow. Very well then, Goodnight.

Porgy Georgie

Porgy Georgie
only 4 years old
You eat too much my lad
You are too bold.

Give over overeating
Put off that childish grin
I really think for one so young
You are too old to sin.

Father Damien Doshing

Father Damien Doshing
Used to take in washing
To supplement his stipend which was really rather skinny
This conduct in a man of God
His flock thought very very odd
And to his priestly honour detrimental
They told the Bishop who though transcendental
In his views was seriously shocked
And had poor Fr. Damien unfrocked
So now he edits Pliny
And turns an honest farthing with his pen
As well as laundering his fellow men.

Bed

This is my bed
Hereon I slept
And wept
and slept and wept
and wept and slept and woke to weep again
for the remembered pain
of a fled dream
and just as keen
and secondly remembered pain
of waking life
This is my bed
Hereon I quaffed
the cup of dreamless sleep
Hereon I quaffed

And laughed
and quaffed and laughed
and laughed and quaffed and woke to laugh again
for the forgotten pain
of a fled dream
and just as keen
and secondly forgotten pain
of waking life
This is my bed
When I was wed
Hereon I plied for yokèd sleep
Hereon I Plied
and cried
and plied and cried
and cried and plied and woke to cry again
for the remembered pain
of a yoked dream
and just as keen
and secondly remembered pain
of a yoked life
I slept I laughed I plied
I wept I quaffed I cried
And when the dum-dum years
Had made an end of laughter cries and tears
Hereon I died.
Gainsay me not with braggart boast, Mortality,
Bed is Reality.

My Earliest Love

This is my earliest love, sweet Death,
That was my love from my first breath.

The Ballet of the Twelve Dancing Princesses

Hayes Court, June 1939

The schoolgirls dance on the cold grass
The ballet of the twelve dancing princesses
And the shadows pass

Over their cold feet
Above in the cold summer sky the clouds mass

The icy wind blows across the laurel bushes
The sky is hard blue and gray where a cloud rushes
The sky is icy blue it is like the night blue where a star pushes.

But it is not night
It is daytime on an English lawn.
The scholars dance. The weather is as fresh as dawn.
Dawn and night are the webs of this summer's day
Dawn and night the tempo of the children's play.

Who taught the scholars? Who informed the dance?
Who taught them so innocent to advance
So far in a peculiar study? They seem to be in a trance.

It is a trance in which the cold innocent feet pass
To and fro in a hinted meaning over the grass
The meaning is not more ominous and frivolous than the clouds
 that mass.

There is nothing to my thought more beautiful at this moment
Than a vision of innocence that is bound to do something
 equivocal

I sense something equivocal beneath the veneer of an innocent
 spent
Tale and in the trumpet sound of the icy storm overhead there is
 evocable
The advance of innocence against a mutation that is irrevocable
Only in the imagination of that issue joined for a split second is
 the idea beautiful.

Song in Time of War

God bless the lion, the British animal
His nature to his foes is horrible
He swims the air like a high admiral
And in the fifth year of the war he is entirely hostile.

With steel his claw is armed, his glance is wary
Of bite and slap and pounce he is not chary
God bless the creature, woken from his reverie,
And in the sixth year of the war give him the victory.

In peace, dear animal, thou was too much inclined
To rest thy body and neglect thy mind
Careless of aught save sand and rolling sea
And lay thy head upon a falling tree.

Oh if in peace thou turnst again to sleep
Thine is the world's loss, and our grave deep.

Mrs Midnight

Mrs Midnight
Was rather tight

So she left for home
She thought she would roam

She went into a field where the moon fell
And sat down by a disused well.

Since when
She has not been seen
As a matter of fact
She was not seen then

But her spirit, earthbound by the accident,
Has told everybody how it happened.

They Killed

They killed a poet by neglect
And treating him worse than an insect
They said what he wrote was feeble
And should never be read by serious people

Serious people, serious people,
I should think it was serious to be such people.

Professor Snooks Does His Worst with a Grecian Fragment

'Cassandra'

CHORUS: Oh I am certain he will come again
And lighten our remorse with a religious strain
Or else he'll say
That never never will he go away.

CASS.: Apollo lord of all the lordliest singers
Behold thy mighty priestess where she lingers
Oh pour on her the laurels and the bay
And never never never go away.

CHORUS: Never never never go away.

CASS.: The voices fade I only hear my own
I go towards the House that is my tomb
Where Clytemnestra waits her lover also
I should not now have known that this was so
If Phoebus had not told me long ago
Oh will he come? Or soon or evermore?
Ever ever ever ever ever more?

CHORUS: I am certain he will come again
And lighten our remarks with a religious strain
Or else he'll say
. . . (here a line is missing and the chorus finishes)
Ah ah ah ah ah.

The Lesson

Is it Claudius or Clowdius? my little child Harry said,
Harry with his innocent look on his Latin studies.
Ah my son, my little one, draw near and hear
The Claudian story. First it was Clowdian –
The patrician families always preserved the diphthong,
As nowadays we English do too, speaking Latin, unless it is Eton.
When Claudius went to obtain the vote of the Plebs,
They laughed – his mama, his papa, his relations laughed,
'He is calling it Clodius now, the silly fool, he thinks it will fetch
 'em.'
(The common people were naturally slovenly, it was Clo for them.)
But he wasn't such a silly fool because it did fetch them.
By and by the common pronunciation seeped slowly up
And now is in general use on the Continent.

Call me 'Arry, said the innocent child I was speaking to.
We are not a new family, I said coldly, and I have no vote for you.

On the Dressing gown lent me by my Hostess the Brazilian Consul in Milan, 1958

Dear Daughter of the Southern Cross
Admit your fiery nature and your loss

Your fiery integrity and your intelligence
I admit your high post and its relevance

And I admit, dear Consuelessa, that your dressing gown
Has wrapped me from the offences of the town

From rain in Milan in a peculiar May
From anger at break of day
From heat and cold as I lay

Wrapped me, but not entirely, from the words I must hear
Thrown between you and him, that were not 'dear'.

Oh that him
Was a problem
Consuelessa, your husband.

He and I ran together in the streets, I think
We grew more English with each drink
And we laughed as we ran in the town
Consuelessa, where then was your dressing gown?

The Portuguese and Italian languages
Drew our laughter in stages
Of infantine rages,
This was outrageous.

Yes, I admit your courage, I heard
Heart steel at the word
That found everything absurd,
The English word I spoke and heard.

Tappping at your heels, Consuelessa,
We were children again, your husband and I,
A worthless couple,

Hanging behind, whining, being slow,
'Where is our wife?' we cry. (This you knew.)

'Give us money' we said, 'you have not given us much'.
We were your kiddies, Consuelessa, out for a touch.

Yet I admit your dressing gown
Wrapped me from the offences of the town
But never from my own
Ah Consuelessa, this I own.

From rain in May
From the cold as I lay
When the servant Cesare had stolen
The electric fire, the only one,
From disappointment too I dare say
Consuelessa,
It is your dressing gown I remember today.

A Fiend

Little bird of brightest laugh
Joying on the human hearth
In thy playtime lurks a frown
I do not think you are at home.

Bird of laughter, bird of wrath
Dost thou, dost thou see the path?
The door is ope, the skies are gray,
Up, bird, and run away.

He was a bird of highest mettles,
He left the hearth, he left the people,

They said a fiend had called him off
And how he lives in the sky so rough,

They said, Why should our little Dear
Have left us for the open air?
The skies are gray and the wind blows hard,
He would be better in our yard.

Fools, thy bird flies free and high
His laughter is no longer sly
As on earth it used to be,
Now he laughs as one who is free.

Free, free, I heard him pipe
As the wild winds carried him out of life,
And still they say it was a fiend
That tempted him and not a friend.

Le Paquebot

C'est la, la, la,
Le Paquebot a moi,
Dites-moi Goodbye,
Parce-que je go far.

Voice from the Tomb

Old age is unbecoming, so they say
Yes, it is unbecoming, but in this way,

It is an unbecoming of all we've become
And so is most becoming and most welcome.

To the Brownes' Cat

(on my lap, in their car, coming home from Norfolk)

You can't look out of the window
Because you're not long enough,
If you want to look out of the window
You'll have to grow longer.

To the Brownes' Hamster

(in its cage on Alice's lap in their car coming home from Norfolk)

Hamster
Why do you make so much noise
In your cage?
Are you a cat or a dog
To be loose too, and have
The run of this Daimler?
Or perhaps you would like, Hamster,
To run behind the car, until
You get lost and are eaten
By the puma
That escaped from Lord Sefton's zoo
Not very long ago?

Mort's Cry

Oh, Lamb of God I am
Too sharp, too tired,
Make me more amiable, Oh Lamb,
Less tired,
No longer what I am.

So cried poor Colonel Mort, I heard him cry,
And yet he was a good man and fought energetically,
His men loved him, his country too, and did not find him tearful,
Then what a funny cry for him! I thought it made him
 wonderful.

Change me, Lord Lamb,
Leave me not as I am.

Friend and Neighbour

I go to church because the Rector
Is a friend and neighbour

I lose the war because the general
Is a friend and neighbour

I fix the files for the Treachery
(As he's a friend and neighbour)
In fact in everything I am
A perfect friend and neighbour

The Publisher

There was a careful Wykehamist
(They are quite often rather)
Who after doing this and that
Set up as publisher.

He was an educated chap,
Except in heart and spirit,
And mediocrity for him
Was the essential merit.

Όμισμα, the moneyed mean,
No need to shout about it,
God rest his soul, he's doing well,
Oh very well, without it.

Lord Henry de Bohon

Leave off your singing, Lord Henry de Bohon,
Walk silently by my side
Or we shall have tears by the fall of noon
And tears at eventide.

But still the boy sang, and again and again,
Which drove his poor nurse quite out of her brain
For all the words this young lord sung
Was: Bang bang, trouble come.

The Stream with Two Faces

The nettle and the bog-wort grew
Beside the forest stream,
Toadstools and ground ivy also were there
And the Giant Hemlock everywhere,
It was a sombre sight.

The stream ran black between trees in this dark
 wood.
Soon I began to run too. Because I never could
Stay without feeling peculiar
In places where great woodlands are.
Is not this a peculiar plight?

When I came to the fields beyond the wood, oh then
I dawdled and laughed, and I laughed to see the stream again,
It looked so sweet beneath an open sky,
Pretty stream, I said, I will stay close by
Your smiling face, and forget in woods you turn black as night.

I thank thee, Lord

I thank thee O Lord for my beautiful bed
Have mercy on those who have none
And may all the children still happier lie
When they to thy kingdom come.

[716]

Soupir d'Angleterre

We have given the Welsh a most *awfully*
Nice day out
And now we never want to hear from
 them again
For *years*, and *years*, and *years*,
And never at all
In Welsh.

He preferred . . .

He preferred to be a hearthrug sage
To risk the cold opinion of the world,
Somewhere within him there had been
A lack of courage, a nerve failed.
He was not happy: but then he was not miserable,
He had money. Sometimes he wrote.
You might say his character was cast upon him,
And with it that luck's lot.

Like This (1)

Young Man in an Asylum

It must be some disease I have
To feel so lonely like this,
And not for company I see
The others like this, like this,

It only makes me more isolate
To see another like this,
Oh nobody like this *likes* this.
Or likes another like this.

Like This (2)

Young girl in an Asylum

The greatest love?
The greatest love?
There is no love at all,
What love means is, To Speak to me.
Not leave me in the cold.

How very cold it is out here,
How bitterly the wind blows,
O Love, why did you dedicate me
To the snows?

Telly-me-Do

Telly me do,
Do telly me too!
You have told all the others
Including your mother's
Companion
So telly me too!

But they would not,
I felt quite cut off,
So I thought I would try
To burn their house down to make them die,
But they only laughed and cried:
'Telly me do, Telly me do',
Again and again, to mock me.
Oh what a lot of pain!

Accented

I *love* you, Muse,
In your *arms* I lie,
Speak to me, *feed* me,
I am not your *enemy*.

Cars

Out driving one day in the Merc
With Hassan, a friendly young Turk,
I said, 'Tell me, I pray,
Is the Bosphorus gay,
Or does the whole thing at times rather irk?'

The Bristol makes *everyone* stare
(Or would, if the brute were still there)
Some drivers have wondered
When passed at 200
Why its makers don't stick to the air.

When I drive in my darling Lagonda
I find I grow fonder and fonder
In a vacuum, really,
I love *everyone* dearly
But especially I love my Lagonda.

No matter who rides in my Ford
Nothing happens at all untoward
Because I really will *not*
Have it. Have what?
Oh I don't know . . . well *THAT*. In a Ford!

Surely all souls must rejoice
Whose passage is made by Rolls Royce
So delicious the journey is
Who cares *where* it finishes?
Oh this car should be everyone's choice.

César

The animal that most loved Hans
Was César, his dog-hound
And in the German forests
He walked round and round
Lying snug, beneath a rug.
And in the German State Railways
He never made a sound
Crying César
Bow wow, sir,
Are you there, sir?

Not I, sir.
Oh ho it was a joke.

But when the trees came round
And they left the train
It was not quite the same,
Into the forest César ran faster
And the poor Hans comes pelting after
Crying César,
Bow wow, sir
Come here, sir,
No fear, sir.
Oh ho it was no joke.

What will Hans do?
Round he wanders
And there is no one to hold his hand when he wanders
Where César
Is now,
The wicked César,
Bow wow.
Oh ho it is no joke.

Childhood and Interruption

Now it is time to go for a walk
Perhaps we shall go for a walk in the park
And then it will be time to play until dark
Not quite, when the shadows fall it is time to go home
It is always time to do something I am never torn
With a hesitation of my own

For always everything is arranged punctually
I am guarded entirely from the tension of anxiety
Walk tea-supper bath bed I am a very happy child really
And underneath the pram cover lies my brother Jake
He is not old enough yet to be properly awake
He is alone in his sleep; no arrangement they
 make
For him can touch him at all, he is alone,
For a little while yet, it is as if he had not been born
Rest in infancy, brother Jake; childhood and interruption come
 swiftly on.

Death

There's a great many things I'd rather not be than dead
And this is the thought that runs for ever in my head
When I'm sitting alone or lying on my bed

What's life, friend, that you so much should prize it
Or Death, that you'd think on it to disguise it
Remembering, not go forth to surprise it?

It is the end of life, the end of strife,
A rope, a poisoned cup, a knife.

It is all this and so all this should only be
An end, and at the end, not bear thee company,
Ever at hand and fobbed with an insurance policy

Keep Death where he would be, in his own place,
He has a dusky half familiar face
And waits to do you a last act of grace.

Last, last and ultimate,
Not the thought-fellow of your living state,
Not to be had in mind but only at the end to wait.

Mabel

In her loneliness Mabel
Found the hiss of the unlit gas
Companionable
And in a little time, dying
Sublime.

'Mother Love'

Mother love is a mighty benefaction
The prop of the world and its population
If mother love died the world would rue it
No money would bring the women to it.

None of the Other Birds

None of the other birds seem to like it
It sits alone on the corner edge of the outhouse gutter
They do not even dislike it
Enough to bite it
So it sits alone unbitten
It is always alone.

Oh Thou Pale Intellectual Brow

Oh thou intellectual brow –
The angel said. The boy replied:

The intellect is but a toy
And I a medium-sensual boy
Can hardly hear you now.

This doll that lies against my side
Is easy and agreeable,
And so I like to play with her,
Come, be sensible.

The doll rose up with awful frown
And with the angel fled the town
The boy waits on, and he will play
With anything that comes his way.

He should go up and after them,
Pray heaven he may do so in time,
God send him back his angel friend,

And all the women cried Amen.

Roaming

Far from his home he came, the old person,
Not comely or of much account,

People thought he was a shifty *Eulenspiegel*
Whose nose was out of joint.

Yet how could a man that was shifty
Look so purposeful,
And when he was looking purposeful
Seem beautiful?

He had excellent manners too
And never spoke of Heaven
Only when he came close up
You saw he was driven.

Do I believe in heaven? (he asked)
What is belief?
I only know when I speak of Death
I experience relief.

But since I was sent to roam
And given a place to roam in,
Roam I will with a will of tears.
Was this wise of him?

Yes, he was wise to say it
For being kindly and able to reason
The people saw they could serve him best
By giving him poison.

When he was dead they buried him
And wrote on his tomb:
Eulenspiegel
Who used to roam.

Ruory and Edith

Ruory loved the aged Edith
She lived in kindness with
And ever had done and ever had done
In a sweet domestic kingdom.

And to Aunt Edith the cry went up
From many an uneven stance
For Ruory's soul was pitched awry
And often went unbalanced.

Without that lady's help
Who so firmly behaved
Ruory would not be here at all
But off to the icy glades.

Then God bless Edith's kindness
And her strongmindedness
And Lord God never let Ruory forget
The gracious mercies her path beset.

She got up and went away

She got up and went away
Should she not have? Not have what?
Got up and gone away.

Yes, I think she should have
Because it was getting darker.

Getting what? Darker. Well,
There was still some
Day left when she went away, well,
Enough to see the way.
And it was the last time she would have been able. . .
Able? . . . to get up and go away.
It was the last time the very last time for
After that she could not
Have got up and gone away any more.

The Easter Rose

It was a sweet unnatural rose
That rose at Eastertide,
Its heart seemed hardly warmed at all
By the sun that newly came
And yet its petals burnt so bright
They seemed to burn in flame of unconsuming light.

Why do you come so early, Rose,
Before your time, and burn so bright
That your white petals are more like
A fire than light?

Then spake the rose: You seem to say
I come too soon,
Know then, an afrit planted me
And bade me bloom
And swore and said: All who are drawn
By thy untimely beauty to come near
To see and then to touch

Shall their own hearts on fire for ever clutch
Until God's judgement day.

The speaking rose bowed her head down
I saw a tear fall down
Beware, she said, for that foul afrit watches
and I must perish in his fire if I
Should be seen to warn
And keep thee from his clutches.
How could I heed the afrit evil?
I only thought to save my rose
From peril.

And so I plucked her to my heart
(I heard her groan)
And as I placed her on my heart
I felt it burn
My heart burns now for evermore until the Judgment Day
And all that cools it are the tears
That fall by night and day
From sweet rose whose premature
Sweet flowering has cost us sore
To love and burn and cool in tears
Til the Judgement Day
When God shall wash all afrits and their
Works away.

The Little Birdies

The little birdies
Must get up early

To sing 'Sing-sing' (sing 'Sing-sing')
To the pretty dawning.

But when day time
Is winter time
They get up later
To sing their
Pretty song to
Day's dawning.

Sing 'Sing-sing' (sing 'Sing-sing')
Pretty sing-sing.

The birdies
Would much rather
Get up early
They hate
To be late

Because then their dawning
(Pretty dawning)
Is shared by the morning
People and the noise they make.

All birdies
Would rather
Have the morning
To themselves

To sing 'Sing-sing' (pretty 'Sing-sing')
To sing sing-sing to.

The Old Soul

When all was young the Race began
And life was fair in Eden's span
But oh the way and oh the way
was long that then began.

Oh boys and girls whose laughing curls
The ancient winds well practised toss
I'm very glad the way we tread
is not so long as it once was.
Then dance with me and don't mope
Or ponder or too fondly hope
But oh I hear and oh I see
That oh they will not dance with me.

The Pearl

Weep not my pretty boy, grieve not my girl
Mankind is Nature's pearl
Not so much for his beauty, being beautiful
As in that he's the child of all things irritable.

There is an Old Man

There is an old man
Who sleeps in the park
When he has no light
He sleeps in the dark

When he has no fire
He sleeps in the cold
Oh why do you do this
Old man, so old?

I sleep in the park
And by day I roam
I would rather do this
Than live in a Home
I was put in one once
Where the meth men were
And they stole my money
And kicked me downstair.

So now I sleep
In the lonely park
And I do not mind
If it's cold and dark
As soon as day breaks
I roam up and down
And when night returns
To my park I come.

Oh living like this is much jollier for me
Than anything I've found for the Elderly.

Tom Snooks the Pundit

'Down with creative talent
(I have none)
Down with creative talent,
Kick it down!'

So cried Tom Snooks, a literary pundit,
The tender talent lay where he had stunn'd it,
He kicked the poor thing dead quite easily and then he cried:
'Hats off, my friends, it was a genius died.'
Oh long live Tom, long live his reputation,
(His proper name I'll give on application).

Wife's Lament at Hereford

The beast
At the end of the lane
Has risen again

And spread his slime
On my furniture

Why must the Wye
Rise so high? He is
Such a pretty runner between banks.

Why does the Wild destroy
Peace and joy? the Unhappy
Need tears to make him happy?

APPENDIX III — TABLE OF CONTENTS FOR SELECTED POEMS, THE FROG PRINCE AND OTHER POEMS, AND PENGUIN MODERN POETS 8

Selected Poems (1962) [lists only the previously published
poems chosen by Smith]

Not Waving but Drowning
The Old Sweet Dove of Wiveton
The Blue from Heaven
'Come on, Come back'
Away, Melancholy
In the Park
Fafnir and the Knights
The Airy Christ
Loin de l'Être
The Singing Cat
The Jungle Husband
Longing for Death because of Feebleness
The Starling
I Remember
Songe d'Athalie
Why are the Clergy . . .?
The Fairy Bell
Childe Rolandine
Parents
The Queen and the Young Princess
Harold's Leap
Behind the Knight
My Cats
'Oh stubborn race of Cadmus' seed . . .'
The Ambassador
Thought is Superior
The Deserter
The After-thought
The Warden
Le Singe Qui Swing
The Weak Monk

The Roman Road
The Death Sentence
Le Majeur Ydow
Cool and Plain
The Conventionalist
Pad, pad
The River God (Of the River Mimram in Hertfordshire)
The Wanderer
The Orphan Reformed
La Gretchen de nos Jours (2)
If I lie down
Girls!
Autumn
Conviction (1), (2) and (3)
The Face
Advice to Young Children
The Governess
Ah, will the Saviour . . .?
The Virtuoso
The Heavenly City
Love Me!
Dirge
Study to Deserve Death
Lady 'Rogue' Singleton
The Broken Heart
The Repentance of Lady T
Happiness
The Magic Morning
My Heart was Full
Croft
The Pleasures of Friendship
Après la Politique, la Haine des Bourbons
Lot's Wife
Old Ghosts
Satin-Clad

Unpopular, lonely and loving
Hast Du dich verirrt?
Voices against England in the Night
One of Many
'Ceci est digne de gens sans Dieu'
When the Sparrow Flies
Infelice
Brickenden, Hertfordshire
The Failed Spirit
The Boat
Le Désert de l'Amour
Mother, among the Dustbins
The Deathly Child
The Toll of the Roads
Vater Unser
The Lads of the Village
Nourish me on an Egg
I do not Speak
The Parklands
The Cousin
'I'll have your heart'
Flow, flow, flow
Is it Wise?
Upon a Grave
The Fugitive's Ride
Private Means is Dead
Bereavement
Breughel
Who Killed Lawless Lean?
Portrait
Now Pine-Needles

The Frog Prince and Other Poems (1966) [lists only the prevously published poems chosen by Smith]

St Anthony and the Rose of Life
Anger's Freeing Power
At School
The Occasional Yarrow
Who is this Who Howls and Mutters?
Will Man Ever Face Fact and not Feel Flat?
A Dream of Comparison
A Dream of Nourishment
Oh What is the Thing He Done?
The Choosers
But Murderous
The Castle
Do Take Muriel Out
Touch and Go
The Broken Friendship
Man is a Spirit
I rode with my darling . . .
Mr Over
God and Man
Our Bog is Dood
The Rehearsal
The Hat
Wretched Woman
Lightly Bound
Voices about the Princess Anemone
Human Affection
Murder
Poet!
Quand on n'a pas ce que l'on aime, il faut aimer ce que l'on a –
Dirge
The Wild Dog

Distractions and the Human Crowd
Rencontres Funestes
Be off!
The Film Star
The Bottle of Aspirins
The Devil-my-Wife
The Smile
Forgot!
The White Thought
In the Night
The Fool
The Sliding Mountain
Christmas
The Recluse
Bog-Face
A Man I Am
O Happy Dogs of England
Darling Daughters
Death's Ostracism
Parrot
I Hate this Girl
The Cock and the Hen
A Father for a Fool
Silence and Tears
To a Dead Vole
Noble and Ethereal
Dear Female Heart
La Gretchen de Nos Jours
Dear Muse
Gnädiges Fräulein
'. . . and the clouds return after the rain'
Out of Time
The Children of the Cross
Look, Look
Ceux qui luttent. . .

The Photograph
Little Boy Sick
Egocentric
Alfred the Great
How far can you Press a Poet?
Night-Time in the Cemetery
Alone in the Woods
Es war einmal
Infant
Dream
The Bereaved Swan
Bag-Snatching in Dublin
The River Deben
Never Again
Little Boy Lost
What is the Time? *or* St Hugh of Lincoln
Major Macroo
All Things Pass

Penguin Modern Poets 8 (1966)

Fafnir and the Knights
The Warden
The Fairy Bell
Was He Married?
A Father for a Fool
Louise
The Bereaved Swan
Night-Time in the Cemetery
The Magic Morning
My Cats
Not Waving but Drowning

'Come on, Come back'
Private Means is Dead
The Recluse
Harold's Leap
The Weak Monk
The River God of the River Mimram in Hertfordshire
The Airy Christ
Thoughts about the Person from Porlock
The Wanderer
The Cock and the Hen
Après la Politique, la Haine des Bourbons
Pad, pad
The Jungle Husband
The Blue from Heaven

APPENDIX IV — LIST OF ALTERNATIVE TITLES

Titles given in *Collected Poems and Drawings*	Alternative Titles
Arabella (p. 130)	White and Yellow (*London Mercury*)
Behind the Knight (p. 265)	Post Equitem Sedet Atra (in performances)
Cars (p. 719)	No Matter Who Rides (*MA*)
I had a dream . . . (p. 489)	A Dream (*Ambit*)
'I'll have your heart' (p. 163)	'Tu refuses à obeir à ta mere . . .!' (*TOTO*)
Pretty Baby (p. 693)	Sweet Baby (*Sunday Times*)
Private Means is Dead (p. 77)	Chaps (*AGTWHBA*)
Ruory and Edith (p. 726)	Ruory (*MA*)
The Parklands (p. 38)	Pour Envoyer à Sir Oliver Lodge (*AGTWHBA*)
The Toll of the Roads (p. 103)	Poor Tolly (*London Mercury*)
The River God of the River Mimram in Hertfordshire (p. 273)	The River God (*HL, CP*)
To Dean Inge Lecturing on Origen (p. 264)	Wisdom (*The Holiday Book*)
Vater Unser (p. 152)	Unser Vater (*TOTO, CP*)
Voice from the Tomb (1) (p. 534)	Here lies . . . (*Poetry Review*)
Voice from the Tomb (2) (p. 535)	This Heart is Not Cold (*Time and Tide*)
Untitled illustration (p. 257)	Torquemada (*CP*)

Notes

The following abbreviations are used in these notes.

Works by Smith

NOYP	*Novel on Yellow Paper* (Cape, 1936; Virago, 1980)
AGTWHBA	*A Good Time Was Had By All* (Cape, 1937)
OTF	*Over the Frontier* (Cape, 1938; Virago, 1980)
TOTO	*Tender Only to One* (Cape, 1938)
MWIM	*Mother, What is Man?* (Cape, 1942)
TH	*The Holiday* (Chapman and Hall, 1949; Virago, 1979)
HL	*Harold's Leap* (Chapman and Hall, 1950)
NWBD	*Not Waving but Drowning* (1957)
SAMHTO	*Some Are More Human Than Others: A Sketchbook* (Gabberbochus, 1958)
SP	*Selected Poems* (Longman, 1962)
PMP	*Penguin Modern Poets 8* (Penguin, 1966)
TFP	*The Frog Prince and Other Poems* (Longman, 1966)
TBB	*The Best Beast* (Knopf, 1969)
SAOP	*Scorpion and Other Poems* (Longman, 1972)
CP	*Collected Poems* (Penguin, 1975)
MA	*Me Again: The Uncollected Writings of Stevie Smith* (Penguin, 1981)

Selected Poems (1978) was a selection from *Collected Poems* (1975); all references in the notes to *Selected Poems* are to the 1962 selection by Smith.

Manuscript Collections

UT	The Stevie Smith Collection, McFarlin Library, University of Tulsa
BJ	The Stevie Smith Archive, Brynmor Jones Library, University of Hull

Critical Works

SSAS *Stevie Smith: A Selection* ed. Hermione Lee
 (Faber, 1981)
SABOSS *Stevie: a biography of Stevie Smith* (Heinemann,
 1985)
SSACB *Stevie Smith: A Critical Biography* (Faber,
 1988)

A GOOD TIME WAS HAD BY ALL (1937)

A Good Time Was Had By All was published by Jonathan Cape in April 1937. The cover included the illustrations from 'Suburb', 'Beware the Man', 'Belvoir' and 'Appetite' with the caption 'drawings by the author'. Twenty-seven drawings appear in the original volume; for the poems republished in *SP* and *TFP* Smith added a further seventeen. She included only twenty-six of the seventy-six poems in her 1960s books, but *TFP*, the final poetry book published in her lifetime, ends with 'All Things Pass' (p. 53).

'The Hound of Ulster' (p. 3): the Irish mythological hero Cú Chulainn, popularised by Lady Gregory's *Cuchulain of Muirthemne* (1902).

'On the Death of a German Philosopher' (p. 4): a tribute to Theodor Lessing (1872–1933).

'Egocentric' (p. 7): for final couplet see George Wither, 'Shall I, wasting in despair' (1617), ll.15–16.

'How far can you Press a Poet?' (p. 12): this poem was included at the beginning and end of John Horder's poem-cycle in *Stevie: A Motley Selection of her Poems by John Horder and Chris Saunders* (2002).

'To the Tune of the Coventry Carol' (p. 15): the earliest surviving MS score for this carol is by Thomas Mawdyke (1591); it forms a set of three carols in the *Pageant of the Shearman and Tailors*, a Coventry Mystery Play. The carol follows Matthew 2, which recounts the Massacre of the Innocents.

'The Suburban Classes' (p. 16): cf. the weekend competition Smith set *New Statesman* readers in July 1938 to 'compose, for the friendly use of the German government in England, an *Appeal* to the people of Great Britain and the Empire seriously to consider the voluntary absorption of themselves – a regrettably separate aryan-blood brotherhood – by the Third Reich', *SSACB*, pp. 143–4.

'Spanish School' (p. 17): the paintings described are El Greco's *The Crucifixion with two Donors* (c.1590), Francisco de Goya's 'Y No Hai Remedio' from *The Disasters of War* (c.1810), *Don Andrés del Peral* (c.1798), and *Doña Isabel de Porcel* (c.1805), and Josepe de Ribera's *Jacob with the Flock of Laban* (c.1628); all are held by the National Gallery, London, and Smith references their inventory number for Ribera. For l.24, see Pedro Calderón's play *Life is a Dream* (1635), I.ii.

'Night-Time in the Cemetery' (p. 19): text follows more heavily punctuated version Smith prepared for *PMP*; later version has 'form' for *AGTWHBA*'s 'forms'; illustration substituted for drawing of cat and woman wearing shorts in *TFP*; *CP* misprints 'lie' for 'lies'.

'From the Greek' (p. 22): see the final lines of Pindar's Pythian 12. The first line inspired the sculpture of the same name by artist Brent Green.

'Intimation of Immortality' (p. 24): cf. William Wordsworth, 'Ode: Intimations of Immortality from Recollections of Early Childhood' (1806).

'Infant' (p. 25): earlier version in *NOYP* (p.163) is more heavily punctuated.

'God and the Devil' (p. 26): for final couplet see Samuel Johnson, *The Vanity of Human Wishes* (1749), ll.220–1.

'Es war einmal' (p.27): cf. the eponymous Zemlinsky opera (1902).

'From the County Lunatic Asylum' (p. 32): poet John Clare spent 1841–64 in the Northampton General Lunatic Asylum. The 1920 Lambeth Conference denounced the rise of spiritism.

'Lament of a Slug-a-bed's Wife' (p. 34): cf. Robert Herrick's 'Corinna's Going A-Maying', *Hesperides* (1648), ll.5–6.

'The Bereaved Swan' (p. 35): see Alfred Lord Tennyson, 'The Dying Swan' (1830), Sir John Suckling, 'Why so pale and wan, fond lover?' (1637), Thomas Hood, 'The Two Swans' (1824), and John Keats, 'The Eve of St Agnes' (1820), ll.7–8. Although Smith omitted the poem from *SP*, confessing to her editor at Longman, 'I never really liked that "cake of soap"' (UT, 28 April 1961), it was popular in performance, and was included in the 25-poem selection for *PMP* and in *TFP*: drawings were added for *TFP*. A 1960s performance script of the poem substitutes 'wrapped' for 'hid'.

'The Parklands' (p. 38): retitled from 'Pour Envoyer à Sir Oliver Lodge' for *SP* and *CP*. Sir Oliver Lodge (1851–1940), known for his contributions to wireless telephony, was derided in the 1930s for his spiritualist beliefs. Cf. Wordsworth, 'Alice Fell' (1802) and William Blake, 'The Chimney Sweeper' (1794).

'Eng'. (p. 40): Smith's use of 'ci-devant' ('former') invokes its French source, the post-revolutionary nobility in France who refused to accept the new social order.

'Bag-Snatching in Dublin' (p. 43): this version follows the revised text Smith prepared for the essay 'What Poems Are Made Of' (*Vogue*, 15 March 1969). The murder of the prostitute Lizzie O'Neill (aka Honour Bright) in Dublin in 1925 was widely reported, and prompted a high-profile trial.

'The River Deben' (p. 44): *OTF* version capitalises 'darkness' and ends 'dawn; thou comest unwisht'. Pompey, the novel's narrator, explains the poem was written after 'a weekend I spent with my sister Mary at Felixstowe Ferry' (p. 113).

'Death Came to Me' (p. 46): version in *AGTWHBA* included these lines after 'handmaid of extinction'

> Had killed a better man than I had ever been
> In nineteen hundred and fourteen

These were marked for deletion in the author's copy, along with the speech marks which open lines 2 and 3 in *CP* and *AGTWHBA*. The reference to 'Mrs Hull' is an allusion to *The Shadow of the East* (1921) by bestselling novelist E. M. Hull, which begins with a Japanese woman poisoning herself.

'Feminine Charm' (p. 57): for l.2 see Bion (c.100 BC), Idyl III. Jason was crowned in Thessaly after his quest for the Golden Fleece.

'Never Again' (p. 59): for l.5 cf. Lucius Annaeus Seneca (c.4 BC–65 AD), *Epistle* 107:11, 'Ducunt volentem fata' (trans. 'fates lead the willing, the unwilling they drag').

'Little Boy Lost' (p. 60): cf. William Blake, 'The Little Boy Lost' (1789).

'Freddy' (p. 65): l.3 trans. 'from an eternal perspective'; cf. Spinoza, *Ethics* (1675). Spinoza's philosophy shapes itself around God and nature, moving away from Aristotle's grounding in practical philosophy and human experience ('sub specie humanitatis').

'This Englishwoman' (p. 70): cf. Edmund Waller, 'On A Girdle' (1645), ll.1–2.

'Lord Barrenstock' (p. 71): 'non flocci facio' (trans. 'I don't care at all'). For ll.15–16 cf. Jane Austen, *Mansfield Park* (1814), ch. 14: 'Let other pens dwell on guilt and misery [. . .] I quit such odious subjects as soon as I can'.

'Maximilian Esterhazy' (p. 73): for first line's 'stern and wild', see Sir Walter Scott, *The Lay of the Last Minstrel* (1805), VI.ii.

'What is the Time? *or* St Hugh of Lincoln' (p. 74): Smith replaced the illustration with a drawing of a boy walking a dog in *TFP*.

'Major Macroo' (p. 75): cf. Geoffrey Chaucer, 'The Clerk's Tale'.

'Private Means is Dead' (p. 77): retitled from 'Chaps' for *SP*; text follows lineation of final version prepared for *PMP*, which revises 'as you may have read' to 'as you can read'.

'Death of Mr Mounsel' (p. 79): for first line cf. Shakespeare, *Anthony and Cleopatra* (1607), IV.xv, l.41.

'Suburb' (p. 87): cf. T. S. Eliot, 'Rhapsody on a Windy Night' (1917).

'Breughel' (p. 90): in 'Syler's Green: a return journey' (1946; *MA* p. 87) Smith calls it a 'very solemn poem' inspired by 'graveyard excursions'.

'Louise' (p. 94): text follows the more heavily punctuated version of the poem prepared by Smith for *PMP*.

TENDER ONLY TO ONE (1938)

Tender Only to One was published by Jonathan Cape in December 1938, described on the cover as 'poems and drawings by Stevie Smith'. Forty-seven drawings appear in the original volume; eight were added for *SP* and *TFP* versions, with new drawings for 'Dear Muse', 'The Lads of the Village' and ' "I'll have your heart" '. She included fifteen poems in *SP* and a further twenty-one in *TFP*.

'Tender Only to One' (p. 99): cf. Robert Browning, 'Women and Roses' (1855), ll.1–3.

'O Happy Dogs of England' (p. 100): first published in *New Statesman* (30 Nov. 1935) as 'Oh! Happy Dogs!' with 'Oh' for 'O' in each instance.

'The Toll of the Roads' (p. 103): first published in *London Mercury and Bookman* (Dec. 1937) as 'Poor Tolly'.

'Eulenspiegelei' (p. 104): scatological and bawdy figure from German folklore, familiar to Smith through Gerhart Hauptmann's epic poem *Till Eulenspiegel* (1927).

'The Abominable Lake' (p. 106): first published *New Statesman* (18 Sep. 1937) with minimal punctuation; *SP* follows *TOTO* revision.

'One of Many' (p. 107): *CP* and original have 'intoned' for 'exclaimed'; Smith revised own copy of *TOTO* and for *SP*. In performance Smith sang the poem 'to a sort of dirge', UT.

'Death's Ostracism' (p. 108): follows Smith's performance revisions of 'stood' for 'trod' in l.1, 'waters' for 'water' in l.15, and 'footstep' for 'foothold' in l.21.

'Parrot' (p. 111): Noel Park is an 1880s garden suburb in London, a mile south of Palmers Green.

'I Hate this Girl' (p. 113): *TOTO* and *CP* prints title in block capitals; *TFP* normalises capitalisation.

'Infelice' (p. 114): follows Smith's later performance version, which revised 'a' to 'the' in l.1, 'presently' to 'suddenly' in l.11, 'speaking' to 'talking' in l.17, and 'he loves me' to 'he must love me' in l.22.

'The Cock and the Hen' (p. 116): punctuation follows later version prepared for *PMP*.

'Silence and Tears' (p. 177): sung in performance to the English folk song 'The Death of Poor Cock Robin'. Cf. Byron, 'When we two parted' (1806), ll.1–2. This follows Smith's later performance version, which revised 'sighed' to 'cried' in l.3, 'Pee-wee' for 'Tee-hee' in l.6, and 'had' for 'has' in l.13.

'A Father for a Fool' (p. 119): subtitle added for *SP* version, which revised original 'Here's hoping' to 'I hope they give us'; revision also in author's copy of *TOTO* and *PMP*.

'The Murderer' (p. 124): cf. Robert Browning, 'Porphyria's Lover' (1836).

'Mother, among the Dustbins' (p. 125): *TOTO* has 'what lies, what lies behind?'; revised for *SP* and *CP* and in author's copy. Punctuation follows the version prepared for the essay 'The Necessity of Not Believing' (*Gemini*, Spring 1958). In performance introductions Smith calls the mother 'a romantic revolutionary in a depressed frame of mind'.

'Le Désert de l'Amour' (p. 127): cf. François Mauriac's eponymous 1925 novel.

'Portrait (2)' (p. 128): cf. Robert Browning, 'In a Gondola' (1842), ll.63–6; original draft titled 'Schoolgirl'.

'Arabella' (p. 130): first published in *London Mercury and Bookman* (Dec. 1937) as 'White and Yellow'.

'Dear Karl' (p. 133): Karl was Smith's German boyfriend, fictionalised in *NOYP*. The poem merges the address in W. B. Yeats' 'He Wishes for the Cloths of Heaven' (1899) with section 15 of Walt Whitman's 'Song of the Open Road' from *Leaves of Grass* (1856): 'Allons! the road is before us!'.

'In Canaan's Happy Land' (p. 135): cf. John Dryden, who uses the phrase to invoke Numbers XIV:8; the first synagogue was built in Palmers Green in 1936, and here Smith ventriloquises a Jewish man trading on Sunday.

'In My Dreams' (p. 139): cf. *OTF* pp. 221–2, which includes the poem with only terminal punctuation at the end of each stanza.

'Noble and Ethereal' (p. 140): cf. Richard Curle's *Aspects of George Meredith* (1908), which imagines those who confront death by a riverside look 'noble and ethereal', p. 195.

'La Gretchen de Nos Jours (1)' (p. 147): cf. Schubert's 'Gretchen am Spinnrade' (1814) from Goethe's *Faust* (1808).

'Dear Muse' (p. 149): *TFP* substitutes the drawing for 'Mr Over' (p. 299).

'Vater Unser' (p. 152): the first two lines are a German translation of the Lord's Prayer. *CP* incorrectly notes original title as 'Vater Unser' but has 'Unser Vater'; *TOTO* has 'Unser Vater', which Smith revised to 'Vater Unser' for *SP*, although penultimate line still read 'Unser Vater'. Smith amended this in the American copy of *SP*.

'Gnädiges Fräulein' (p. 153): now archaic formal address for a German high-born woman.

'The Friend' (p. 154); see Tennyson's 'Guinevere' from *Idylls of the King* (1885), l.655.

'The Lads of the Village' (p. 156): *SP* substitutes drawing for 'Dear Little Sirmio' illustration (p. 400). *SP* revises 'sing no more' to 'sigh no more' as does author's copy of *TOTO*; *CP* has 'sing'.

'Upon a Grave' (p. 157): the source for the subtitle is unknown, although Smith may be recalling William Blake's 'I laid me down upon a bank' and 'Under the Greenwood' in Shakespeare's *As You Like It* (1600), V.ii; she played Monsieur Le Beau in a production at Palmers Green High School in 1913.

'. . . and the clouds return after the rain' (p. 160): included in *OTF*, p. 161. Cf. the hymn tune by George Crawford Hugg (1848–1907).

'Out of Time' (p. 161): *TOTO*, *TFP*, and *CP* have 'languorous' for 'ponderous'; revision from author's copy of *TOTO*.

'"I'll have your heart"' (p. 163): retitled for *SP* from 'Tu refuses à obeir à ta mère . . .!' (trans. 'you refuse to obey your mother'), a quotation from Jules Renard's novel *Poil de Carotte* (1894). *SP* omitted the second stanza:

> I do not love you, Mother
> I do not love another,
> Love passed me by
> A long time ago,
> And now I cry
> Doh ray me fah soh.

Smith used the *SP* version in poetry readings, although *CP* reinstates the final stanza. This version follows the revised text Smith prepared for the essay 'What Poems Are Made Of' (*Vogue*, 15 March 1969) and uses the original illustration: a sketchier depiction of a child on their mother's knee accompanied the poem in *SP*. Celia introduces the poem in *TH* as an expression of the animal 'kennelled close within', p. 62.

'Fallen, Fallen' (p. 166): for final two lines, cf. *Macbeth* (1606) V.v, ll.26–7: 'It is a tale / Told by an idiot, full of sound and fury / Signifying nothing'.

'Tableau de l'Inconstance des Mauvais Anges' (p. 169): cf. *Tableau de l'Inconstance des Mauvais Anges et Demons* (1613) by Pierre de l'Ancre, who led the 1609 Labourd witch-hunts. The

first line invokes the 1811 hymn of the same name by Reginald Heber, who lends his surname to a character in *TH*.

'Will Ever?' (p. 170): for ll.9–12 cf. Tennyson, 'Break, break, break' (1842).

'Ceux qui luttent . . .' (p. 171): trans. 'those who struggle are those who live' ; cf. Victor Hugo's 'Ceux qui vivent, ce sont ceux qui luttent' (1849).

'Suicide's Epitaph' (p. 172): trans. 'be punished as you have sinned, he said, looking at me in a cold and enigmatic way'.

'The Violent Hand' (p. 175): for reasons of pagination, this poem is placed at the end of *TOTO* in the *CP* reprint.

'Fuite d'Enfance' (p. 176): cf. Shakespeare's sonnet 144 and Émile Nelligan's 'La fuite de l'enfance' (1903); trans. 'unknown to them I have come to say my farewells'. Celia recites this poem in *TH*, p. 162.

MOTHER, WHAT IS MAN? (1942)

Mother, What is Man? was published by Jonathan Cape in December 1942, described on the cover as 'poems and drawings by Stevie Smith'. Eighty drawings appear in the original volume; four were added for *SP* and *TFP* versions, with new drawings for 'La Gretchen de nos Jours (2)', 'Girls', 'When the Sparrow Flies' and 'Dirge'.

'The King in Funeral Procession' (p. 182): George V's state funeral was on 28 Jan. 1936. Cf. Psalm 130. For 'loud bassoon', cf. Coleridge, 'The Rime of the Ancient Mariner' (1834), l.32.

'La Gretchen de Nos Jours (2)' (p. 184): the accompanying illustration was used as the front cover for early editions of *CP*. For *SP* Smith substitutes a marginal drawing of a woman's head.

'Murder' (p. 186): Reggie Smith married close friend Olivia Manning; Smith was a witness at their wedding in 1939 with

Louis MacNeice. Smith changed 'Reggie' to 'Filmer' for *TFP*, mindful of libel.

'Girls!' (p. 187): *CP* follows original with no apostrophe in 'don't'; Smith inserts apostrophe for *SP* and replaces illustration with drawings of a woman holding flowers, a cat, and a girl's head in profile. The *OED* quotes Smith's idiosyncratic 'balsy' as its lone example of the variant.

'Where are you going?' (p. 188): cf. Coleridge's 'Youth and Age' (1834), which recounts the 'oft and tedious taking-leave' of an old man who 'hath outstay'd his welcome'.

'Bog-Face' (p. 191): cf. William Blake, 'Infant Joy' (1789).

'The Zoo' (p. 192): *CP* follows author's own copy, which adds a grave accent on 'misused' but adds no apostrophe for 'don't'; author's proofs insert the apostrophe.

'Advice to Young Children' (p. 194): in Smith's short story 'Beside the Seaside: A Holiday with Children' (1949; *MA* p. 13), the poet-protagonist Helen recites the first stanza to her friends. Cf. Robert Graves, 'Warning to Children' (1929).

'If I lie down' (p. 196): in performance, Smith noted the child in this poem was responding to Seneca's *De Ira* 15:4, where the precipice of a cliff offers a slave liberty through death.

'Conviction (IV)' (p. 199): illustration appears in *SAMHTO* with caption 'This does not break down any barriers'.

'The Little Daughters of America' (p. 202): America declared war on Japan on 7 Dec. 1941.

'She said . . .' (p. 203): alternative titles in typescript drafts are 'The Wicked Mother' and 'Fille Infame'.

'Quand on n'a pas ce que l'on aime, il faut aimer ce que l'on a —' (p. 204): French proverb (trans. 'if you don't get the thing you love, you must love the thing you get'; cf. final couplet of Tennyson's 'Tears, Idle Tears' (1847).

'Study to Deserve Death' (p. 207): in *SP* the poem was illustrated with the drawing for 'Where are you going?' (p. 188).

'Dirge' (p. 208) was inadvertently chosen for both *SP* and *TFP*: *SP* offers an alternative illustration of a woman walking with an umbrella wearing a beret, while *TFP* reverts to the original illustration; *TIO* prints the poem twice with different illustrations.

'La Speakerine de Putney' (p. 209): cf. *King Lear* (1606) III.ii, l.1 for line 3.

'My Heart was Full' (p. 218): cf. Sir Walter Scott, *The Monastery: a Romance* (1820), which describes tears as the 'softened showers' allowing the 'seed of Heaven' to 'take root in the human breast', ch.XXX.

'Croft' (p. 218): inspired the play *Top Storey* (1987), produced by the Trestle Theatre Company.

'Rencontres Funestes' (p. 219): cf. Jean-Pierre Camus' *Les Rencontres funestes* (1644); trans. 'fatal encounters'.

'The Film Star' (p. 220): trans. for first and final lines 'give a meal to the starved'; the poem was introduced as 'Donnez à manger' in some performances.

'The Bottle of Aspirins' (p. 221): cf. Jules Barbey d'Aurevilly's short story 'Le Dessous de cartes d'une partie de whist', *Les Diaboliques* (1874), ch. III; trans. ' "It's a remedy against all ills," he added, with the morbid humour typical of those who hailed from his suicidal land.'

'The Actress' (p. 223): l.4 reads in draft: 'I earn my bread upon the boards before painted greenery'; author's note indicates this version was published in a magazine before being amended for *MWIM*.

'The Devil-my-Wife' (p. 224): 'Golden Slumbers' is a traditional English folk tune; Thomas Dekker's 'Cradle Song' in the play *Patient Grissel* (1603) provided the words for the Beatles song of the same name.

'The Broken Heart' (p. 229): 'Oh, Play to me, Gypsy' was a 1932 Karel Vacek tune popularised by Gracie Fields.

'The Magic Morning' (p. 232): punctuation follows later version Smith prepared for *PMP*; Celia in *TH* calls herself 'nervy bold and grim', p. 192, and the phrase is revised for 'Cool as a Cucumber' (p. 275).

'Après la Politique, la Haine des Bourbons' (p. 235): trans. 'after the policy, the hatred of the Bourbons'. Punctuation follows later version prepared for *PMP*.

'The Poets are Silent' (p. 236): Smith was encouraged to revise or omit this poem for *MWIM* by her editor at Cape, who worried its 'defeatist' tone would be seen as 'hindering the war effort' (28 Sept. 1942, UT).

'Old Ghosts' (p. 241): when first published in *London Mercury and Bookman*, Dec. 1937, p. 122, the epigraph from Thomas De Quincey's *Confessions of an English Opium-Eater* (1821) read: '. . . by one-half as unlimited a command over apparitions as a Roman centurion over his soldiers'. It was deleted for *MWIM*, but revised and reinstated for *SP*, although De Quincey has the opposite implication:

> I know not whether my reader is aware that many children, perhaps most, have a power of painting, as it were upon the darkness, all sorts of phantoms. In some that power is simply a mechanical affection of the eye; others have a voluntary or semi-voluntary power to dismiss or to summon them; or, as a child once said to me when I questioned him on this matter, 'I can tell them to go, and they go –, but sometimes they come when I don't tell them to come.' Whereupon I told him that he had almost as unlimited a command over apparitions as a Roman centurion over his soldiers. ('The Pains of Opium')

SSACB notes a further allusion to Shakespeare's *Henry IV* Part I III.i, ll.52–8. See also Wordsworth's 'The Affliction of Margaret' (1807): 'I look for ghosts; but none will force / Their way to me'.

'Death in the Rose Garden' (p. 242): the melody is the traditional French folk song 'Marcho dei Rei', popularised in England by Bizet's *L'Arlésienne Suite No. 1* (1872).

'Hast Du dich verirrt?' (p. 244): trans. 'have you lost your way?'. The protagonist of *TH* is asked this by Casmilus, p. 162.

'"Ceci est digne de gens sans Dieu"' (p. 247): title taken from epigram for Jules Barbey d'Aurevilly's short story, 'À un Dîner d'athées', *Les Diaboliques* (1874); trans. 'this is worthy of a godless people'.

'When the Sparrow Flies' (p. 248): reprinted in *SP* with the drawings used in *TFP* for 'Anger's Freeing Power' (p. 369).

'Voices against England in the Night' (p. 249): this follows the later version of the poem included in *TH*, which has 'braver' for 'earlier' and adds 'now' after 'songs you sing', p. 128; Celia recites the poem and suggests Britain's withdrawal from India (1945–7) is the 'answer' to it. In *SAMHTO*, the drawing appears with the caption: 'I never sleep'. Cf. Joseph Goebbels, 'Children with their Hands Chopped Off' (1939).

'"N'est-ce pas assez de ne me point haïr?"' (p. 250): cf. Alfred du Musset, 'Chanson: J'ai dit à mon cœur . . .' (1831); trans. 'is it not enough that you hate me?'

'The Failed Spirit' (p. 251): this version follows the revised punctuation Smith prepared for the essay 'What Poems Are Made Of' (*Vogue*, 15 March 1969). Cf. Thomas Gray, 'Hymn to Adversity' (1753), ll.5–8.

'The Recluse' (p. 253): follows punctuation from revised version in *PMP*.

The final illustration was titled 'Torquemada' in *CP*.

HAROLD'S LEAP (1950)

Harold's Leap was published by Chapman and Hall in December 1950, with the frontispiece noting the poems were 'illustrated

by the author'. Seventy-nine drawings appear in the original volume, where they are printed in red, and often overlay the text. Eighteen poems were chosen for *SP*, and a further fourteen for *TFP*, where drawings were removed from 'The Ambassador' alongside the marginal illustration from 'Harold's Leap'. Smith noted a number of post-publication revisions in a letter she sent to novelist Kathleen Farrell, now at UT.

'The Castle' (p. 262): the protagonist of *TH* recites the poem to her uncle, noting 'the poem is not sensible', p. 174; the *TH* version is more lightly punctuated. In *SAMHTO*, one caption reads: 'The Countess of Egremont does not wish for visitors'.

'To Dean Inge Lecturing on Origen' (p. 264): poem first published as 'Wisdom' in *The Holiday Book* (1946), p. 60, where final couplet reads: 'Oh, is it lost that good man's word? / Is it dimmed?'. See William Ralph Inge's second and third Gifford Lectures in *The Philosophy of Plotinus* (1918). Celia recites the poem in *TH*, and explains, 'I took one sentence that he said and [. . .] I made this poem'; her uncle claims Inge was quoting Tertullian, p. 146. Cf. Tertullian's *De Resurrectione Carnis* (c.AD 240), which notes popular ideas are 'commended by their simplicity', trans. Ernest Evans.

'Behind the Knight' (p. 265): introduced in performances by the Latin title 'Post Equitem Sedet Atra Cura', from Horace's *Odes* Bk. III.i, l.40. William Makepeace Thackeray makes use of the same tag in *The Newcomes* (1855) and *The Adventures of Philip* (1861–2), and Smith saw the eponymous Alfred Gilbert sculpture (1899) in the V&A.

'The Warden' (p. 266): for epigraph, see broadside ballad 'The Children's Home' (1884) written by F. E. Weatherly to the F. H. Cowen tune. Published in *SP* with drawing of young girl holding a ball.

'Harold's Leap' (p. 267): lineation and punctuation follows final version Smith prepared for *PMP*; *HL* and *CP* have 'rock' for 'place' in final line.

'Touch and Go' (p. 269): Celia recites the poem in *TH*, where her friend Tom responds by playing Beethoven's Piano Sonata no.12, p. 72; the earlier version has 'sorrow' for 'passion', though first publication in *The Holiday Book* (1946) has 'passion', p. 56.

'Thought is Superior' (p. 272): Smith revised 'proud thought' from 'pure thought' in her copies of *HL; CP* has 'pure thought'. Drafts and readings moved between 'Galileo's discovery' and 'Copernicus' discovery'; mindful that Galileo finally supported the heliocentric theories Copernicus had put forward, she revised her copy to 'the discovery'; *CP* has 'Galileo's discovery'.

'The River God of the River Mimram in Hertfordshire' (p. 273): published in *HL* and *CP* as 'The River God'; Smith amends title for *PMP* and in *SP* the additional material appears parenthetically. In performance it was introduced as 'The River God Speaks'.

'Cool as a Cucumber' (p. 275): cf. John Gay, 'A New Song of New Similes' (1732).

'The Orphan Reformed' (p. 276): cf. William Wordsworth, 'Alice Fell' (1802), ll.41–4.

'A Shooting Incident' (p. 277): cf. Matthew 4:4 for first line.

' "Oh stubborn race of Cadmus' seed . . ." ' (p. 281): cf. Sophocles, *Antigone*, ll.517–519; draft title, 'It is the bird of burial', used for early proofs (UT).

'The Ambassador' (p. 282): Smith adds subtitle in own copy and for *SP*; removed from *CP*. Cf. John Lemprière's *Classical Dictionary for Schools and Academies* (1832), which misprints 'Casmillus' for 'Casmilus'.

'Persephone' (p. 283): 'I was born good' revised from 'I had been good' in author's copy of *HL*; original version in *CP*. Drafts include final excised stanza:

> More fair than Sicilian air
> Is that frost's breath there
> More dear more dear.

'Do Take Muriel Out' (p. 285): follows performance and author's copy substitution of 'wan' for 'glum' and 'footsteps' for 'footprints'; early draft in UT has 'deceiver' for 'believer'.

'The Weak Monk' (p. 286): cf. S. T. Coleridge, 'The Mad Monk' (1800), ll.21–3, and William Blake, 'The Grey Monk' (1803), which is quoted in OTF, p. 106; follows punctuation and lineation from version Smith prepared for PMP.

'Le Singe Qui Swing' (p. 287): cf. René Fauchois' play Le Singe qui parle (1925), adapted into the silent film The Monkey Talks (1927), dir. Raoul Walsh. Smith playfully introduced the poem in performance as 'an Indian childhood memory'.

'Pad, pad' (p. 288): Smith revised penultimate line in her copy of American SP from HL and CP's 'Ah me, the power to feel exaggerated, angry and sad'; Smith offered the revised version in readings and for PMP.

'The After-thought' (p. 291): Smith revised penultimate line in her copy of American SP from HL and CP's 'What is that darling? You cannot hear me?'; in some performances, she substituted 'grace' for 'mercy'. Cf. Edgar Allen Poe's 'The Purloined Letter' (1845), where Dupin describes a parlour-room game which requires players to find large and small words on a board to illustrate the human propensity to overlook the obvious: the larger words 'escape observation by dint of being excessively obvious; and here the physical oversight is precisely analogous with the moral inapprehension by which the intellect suffers to pass unnoticed those considerations which are too obtrusively and too palpably self-evident'. Smith also invokes Katherine Craster's poem 'The Centipede's Dilemma' (1871), which gave its name to the psychological process whereby self-reflection impairs the performance of everyday activities ('the centipede syndrome'), and Titurel, the Holy Grail-keeper who lived for five hundred years. There is a more indirect allusion to Homer's Odyssey XI. ll.60–70, where the dead Elpenor explains to Odysseus that he has remained in the land of the dead as he didn't think to bring a ladder with him. The drawing appears in SAMHTO with the caption: 'Ménélas, je suis Hélène et je veux rentrer chez moi!'

'The Wanderer' (p. 292): punctuation follows later version prepared for *PMP*. Published in *SP* with drawing used for 'Farewell' in *NWBD*. Cf. Lewis Caroll, ''Tis the Voice of the Lobster', *Alice's Adventures in Wonderland* (1865), ch. X, and Isaac Watts, ''Tis the Voice of the Sluggard' (1715).

'No Categories!' (p. 293): drawing appears in *SAMHTO* with caption: 'If we have not this power what power have we?'

'The Deserter' (p. 295): Smith's performance copy revises 'admit' to 'agree', inverts line 8 from 'they say as a matter of fact', and adds 'continue to' in line 3: *CP* has 'come' for 'comes'.

'I rode with my darling . . .' (p. 296): *HL* and *CP* have 'angrily' for 'thoughtfully', which Smith revised for performances and in a letter to Kathleen Farrell, now at UT. Some performances had 'beaming' for 'burning'. For l.22 cf. Dylan Thomas' 'Do not go gentle into that good night', published two years later.

'God and Man' (p. 298): draft subtitle indicates the poem should be sung to the traditional English folk song 'Villikins and his Dinah'.

'Mr Over' (p. 299): first published in *The Holiday Book* (1946), p. 57, where final two stanzas are elided. *TFP* illustrates the poem with drawing of woman carrying funeral wreath; the drawing is used to illustrate 'My Muse' when reprinted in *TFP*.

'My Cats' (p. 300): in performance Smith glossed the second line as a reference to the North Berwick witch trials; the subtitle was added for *PMP*.

'Our Bog is Dood' (p. 302): for final stanza, see S. T. Coleridge, 'The Rime of the Ancient Mariner' (1798), ll.596–604.

'Le Revenant' (p. 306): introduced in performance as 'My Uncle' or 'Ghosts'.

'Friskers *or* Gods and Men' (p. 307): in Greek mythology, Galanthis was changed into a cat by Hera as punishment for intervening in Hera's attempt to prevent Heracles' birth.

'Cool and Plain' (p. 308): Celia in *TH* presents the poem as a diary entry written when 'London life is not so easy', p. 148.

'The Rehearsal' (p. 311): draft includes excised dedication to the singer Hedli Anderson (1907–90); Smith attended a performance of Elisabeth Lutyens' *Stevie Smith Songs* (1948) in 1949.

'Thank You' (p. 314): cf. William Wordsworth, 'Alice Fell' (1802), ll.41–4.

'The Ride' (p. 315): cf. Lord Byron, 'Childe Harold's Pilgrimage' (1812–18), ll.1639–47.

'I Am' (p. 316): cf. John Clare, 'I Am' (1848). Smith swaps l.10's 'did' and 'thought' in performance.

'From the Coptic' (p. 323): cf. Genesis 2:7. Drawing used to illustrate 'How far can you Press a Poet?' (p. 12) in *TFP*.

'In Protocreation' (p. 326): MS in UT notes it is homage to Fred Hoyle (1915–2001), the British astronomer who helped define nucleosynthesis. Cf. 'The New Age'.

'Do Not!' (p. 327): Smith revises final line in letter to Kathleen Farrell from *HL*'s 'despairing, flee strife'; original version retained for *CP*. In *SAMHTO*, the drawing appears with the caption: 'Wag, wag!'

'The Death Sentence' (p. 328): for final two lines cf. Shakespeare, *The Merchant of Venice*, IV.i, l.294.

'The Leader' (p. 332): this portrait of Hitler had been accepted for publication in *New Statesman* in 1944, but was not printed by the time of his death, so withdrawn by the author.

'Who Shot Eugenie?' (p. 334): fifth stanza quoted as a complete poem in *OTF*, p. 244.

'Voices about the Princess Anemone' (p. 338): illustration used as cover for first edition of *The Holiday* (1949).

'Deeply Morbid' (p. 340): first published in *The Holiday Book* (1946), pp. 58–9; earlier version has 'canvas' for 'pictures', 'Stays her gaze' for 'Hangs her eye', and 'athwart the spray' for 'across the spray'.

Published by André Deutsch in October 1957. Only twenty-one drawings appear in the original volume; Smith at first agreed to publish the poems without drawings, but later offered to return her advance rather than to go press without them. Five were added for *SP*, and twelve for *TFP*, although the drawing for 'In the Park' was removed, and the original drawing for 'Every Lovely Limb's a Desolation' was used to illustrate 'I Remember'. Nineteen of these poems were chosen for *SP*, and a further eleven for *TFP*. Smith selected poems for inclusion with Deutsch editor Diana Athill, drawing on comments made by Laurie Lee.

'Not Waving but Drowning' (p. 347): first published in the *Observer* (29 Aug. 1954) then revised for publication in essay 'Too Tired for Words', *Medical World* (Dec. 1956), which puts lines 3–4, 9, 11–12 in speech marks, and reduces second stanza to three lines with breaks after 'dead' and 'way'; the first two lines of this revised stanza are also in speech marks. A typed draft shows an illustration of a man being pulled from the water in place of the deliberately disjunctive female figure in published versions.

'"What is she writing? Perhaps it will be good"' (p. 350): for picture and title cf. Francisco de Goya's etchings 'It may be that is he good' (c.1818–24), 'Bad poets' (c.1818–24), and 'What is this hubbub?' (1810–14).

'The Fairy Bell' (p. 351): this follows the final version of the poem Smith prepared for *PMP*, which revises 'enchantment' to 'enjoyment', and adds an additional line break after 'hat'; the printed *PMP* version has the typo 'plying' for 'flying'.

'The New Age' (p. 353): the MS in UT notes the poem, like 'In Protocreation' (p. 326), is a homage to Fred Hoyle (1915–2001), the British astronomer who helped define nucleosynthesis; Smith quotes line 11 in her review of Douglas Hewitt's *The Returning Waters* (1954), *Frontier* (Spring 1961), pp. 41–2.

'The Blue from Heaven' (p. 354): follows revised version prepared for *PMP*, which revises tenth stanza from *NWBD*'s:

That Arthur has fallen from the grandeur
Of his power all agree

NWBD has 'powers' for 'power' in final stanza.

'A Dream of Comparison' (p. 360): cf. Milton, *Paradise Lost*, X, ll.1001–6.

'My Hat' (p. 362): the drawing was printed without the poem in *TFP*, bearing the caption 'Away, Away!'

'Fafnir and the Knights' (p. 371): in some performances Smith omitted the third stanza and substituted 'green grass' for 'long grass'. As noted in *SSAS*, Fafnir is from the Norse myth the Vosungsaga, and appears in Wagner's *Siegfried* (1876): in the opera, he is a giant changed to a dragon, and slain by Siegfried.

'Songe d'Athalie' (p. 373): cf. Jean Racine, *Athalie* (1692) II.v, ll. 29–52.

'Away, Melancholy' (p. 377): cf. George Herbert, 'The Bag' (1633); an additional comma has been added after 'God' in the fifth stanza, following Spalding's suggestion in *SSACB*, p. 223

'Dido's Farewell to Aeneas' (p. 379): cf. Virgil's *Aeneid* (29–19 BC), IV, ll.652–65.

'Childe Rolandine' (p. 380): cf. Robert Browning, 'Child Rolande to the Dark Tower Came' (1855), a poem Smith also invokes in 'A Soldier Dear to Us' (p. 605).

'The Jungle Husband' (p. 382): punctuation follows later version prepared for *PMP*, and follows Smith's preferred spelling of 'gray'. In performance, Smith noted: 'He does not like her very much, and is rather drunk.'

'"Come on, Come back"' (p. 383): poem was drafted in 1920s, and originally titled 'Incident in the Great War, 1991–7'; punctuation follows revised version prepared for *PMP*.

'I Remember' (p. 386): cf. Littleton C. Powys, *Still the Joy of It* (1956), p. 34:

[. . .] we were married in the little Roman Catholic church of
St. Mary's at Hampstead [. . .] our wedding night coincided with
the most spirited German air raid that had been experienced in
London for a long time; and the confusion was increased by a
very large fleet of our own bombers passing over London on
their way to Germany at the same time.

In interviews, Smith misremembered the poem's source as
Llewellyn Powys. The version in *NWBD* left out the couplet
beginning 'What rendered the confusion worse', which was
supplied in an erratum slip.

'God the Eater' (p. 390): cf. George Herbert, 'Love (III)' (1633).

'God the Drinker' (p. 391): cf. Goya's etching 'Porque fue
sensible' (1799) for epigraph.

'A Dream of Nourishment' (p. 395): William Blake, 'Infant
Sorrow' (1794), ll.7–8: the second stanza alludes to Book XI of
Homer's *Odyssey*, where the dead are required to drink a saucer
of blood before they can be seen by the living.

'The Airy Christ' (p. 396): in *NWBD*, Smith includes subtitle
'after reading Dr Rieu's translation of St Mark's Gospel'. Cf. *St.
Mark's Gospel: A New Translation from the Greek* (1951) trans.
Dr E. V. Rieu; text follows later version prepared for *PMP*, which
substitutes 'splendour' for 'grandeur', 'blazing' for 'burning', and
removes subtitle.

'Dear Little Sirmio' (p. 400): cf. Catullus, *Carmen* XXXI. Smith
wrote to Athill: 'I also send you a list of poems I would be willing to
leave out if necessary and I have put Laurie Lee's comments on each
in brackets [. . .] there is no "No" of his I want – except perhaps (?)
the queried "No" of "Dear Little Sirmio"' (27 Apr. 1955, UT).

'"Great Unaffected Vampires and the Moon"' (p. 401): cf. *The
Spectator* held a poetry competition in 1952 to introduce the
titular line, which is taken from Hilaire Belloc's *Caliban's Guide
to Letters* (1903). Belloc offers the line in a specimen review of
imagined poet Mr Mayhem, where the reviewer describes it as a
line 'the Anglo-Saxon race will not readily let die'.

'The Celts' (p. 402): in some performances, Smith added 'Lloyd George' after 'Old Age Pensions'; the only Welsh prime minister of Britain expanded state benefits in the 1920 National Health Insurance Act.

'The Passing Cloud' (p. 403): the Bethlehem Royal Hospital specialises in the treatment of mental illness; its former nickname gives us the word 'bedlam'.

'Loin de l'Être' (p. 405): trans. 'far from it'.

'King Hamlet's Ghost' (p. 412): cf. *Hamlet* (1602), I.i, l.45. Smith revises penultimate line from 'speak to me' in her own copy: original retained in *CP*.

'At School' (p. 413): cf. Dante, *Divina Commedia*, I.v, ll.113–38. The poem takes life in her notebook as poem about the Cold War:

> What good will it do if *we*
> stop making the atom bomb
> – it's not *we* who are going to
> drop it on *us*.
>
> The English don't want war, they've
> nothing to gain. The Russians
> *want* the world; we've
> had it.
>
> *Because of the plan we're in fear*
> *Because of the stormy weather*

In some performances Smith began l.33 with 'Hold my hand tight'.

'Can it Be?' (p. 416): *CP* omits opening speech marks.

'The Old Sweet Dove of Wiveton' (p. 417): Wiveton, in Norfolk's Glaven Valley, was one of Smith's favourite holiday destinations.

'My Heart Goes Out' (p. 422): this version follows the revised punctuation Smith prepared for the essay 'What Poems Are Made Of' (*Vogue*, 15 March 1969).

'Who is this Who Howls and Mutters?' (p. 425): cf. Goya's etching 'What is this hubbub?' (1810–14).

'Magna est Veritas' (p. 427): cf. Esdras 4.41, Latin Vulgate ('Magna est veritas et prævalet'). Smith's likely source was Sir James George Frazer's *The Golden Bough: A Study in Magic and Religion*, Bk. III, but see also Coventry Patmore's 'Magna est Veritas' (1877) and Frank Richards, *Billy Bunter's Bolt* (1956), ch. 3: 'The truth is great and shall prevail a bit'.

'In the Park' (p. 429): for first two lines, see Scottish folk ballad 'The Twa Corbies'. Typed draft used in performances substitutes 'leaped' for 'barked'. The illustration appears in *SAMHTO* with the caption: 'Thus grew up a friendship that endured to the end of their lives'.

'The Occasional Yarrow' (p. 435): cf. Wordsworth's 'Yarrow Unvisited' (1807), 'Yarrow Visited' (1815)', and 'Yarrow Revisited' (1834).

'Die Lorelei' (p. 441): cf. Heinrich Heine, 'Lorelei' (1822). The poem is a direct translation, but the final line is Smith's own.

'Farewell' (p. 442): this was also included in *Scorpion* between 'Angel Boley' and 'The Donkey', although grouped in *NWBD* for *CP*.

SELECTED POEMS (1962)

Published by Longmans in September 1962. An American edition was published by James Laughlin in 1964 with the illustration for 'Every Lovely Limb's a Desolation' on the cover; Smith's hope was that US readers would take it for a self-portrait. The original edition included 113 poems in total: sixteen new poems alongside ninety-seven from her previous five collections.

'Thoughts about the Person from Porlock' (p. 445): cf. Coleridge's preface to *Kubla Khan* (1816). Version published in *X: Quarterly Review*, Vol. 1, 1959, has additional verse after 'need not stay':

> Oh this Person from Porlock is a great interrupter
> He interrupts us forever
> People say he is a dreadful fellow
> But really he is desirable.

In performance, Smith read out the subtitle 'Thoughts About the Person from Porlock (contd.)' which follows the seventh stanza. Text follows revised version prepared for *PMP*, which substitutes 'tomorrow' for 'this evening'.

'Thoughts about the Christian Doctrine of Eternal Hell' (p. 448): version included in talk 'Some Impediments to Christian Commitment' given to the St Anne's Society, 9 Dec. 1968, includes additional material after the fourth stanza:

> Kill, kill the damned! Let them die utterly!
> Oh no, this would not be Godly.
>
> For you see in this they say his love is seen especially
> That he does not kill the damned, but keeps them alive to
> suffer perpetually,
> Our own Bishop Gore, when he said: They may perhaps
> eventually lose consciousness,
> Was not I am afraid being strictly orthodox.
>
> Who makes a God? Who shows him thus?
> It is the Christian religion does.
>
> Oh, oh, have none of it,
> Blow it away, have done with it.
>
> This God the Christians show
> Out with him, out with him, let him go.

Among Christians today it is usual
To say, The damned choose hell; this is equivocal
No creature chooses eternal pain, and was not meant
When Christ said: They went away into everlasting
 punishment.

Oh, oh, let it go,
It is abominable to believe so.

Poor Christian lov'st so much Christ's loving words
You must pretend he did not say the other words.

What sin and pain hell's doctrine hath brought
Europe is stained with the bitter draught
Oh why must Man so bitterly devise
Pain for himself? He is not wise,
But imaginative, and likes to be powerful,
And above all he likes his days to be full.

Yes, I think it was sweetness and cruelty and tedium
That made Men set up religion.

All religion, throw it away
It is our duty to throw it away.

'Was He Married?' (p. 451): in some performances, Smith added 'Yes' before 'only human beings feel this' and omitted the stanza beginning '. . . find a soft brightness'.

'Was it not curious?' (p. 454): the poem rests on Smith's misattribution of Gregory the Great's words to St Augustine, although her introduction to the poem in 1960s readings refused to confirm whether this was accidental: 'There is a poem here, which I am not quite sure is allowable, but the soft missed rhymes seduce me so much I will read it to you [. . .] I began it carelessly forgetting it was Gregory not Augustine who said *Non Angli sed Angeli*' (UT). Cf. Pierre Batifoll's *Saint Gregory the Great* (1922), trans. John L. Stoddard.

'The Frozen Lake' (p. 455): cf. Tennyson, 'Morte d'Arthur' (1833). *CP* and *SP* have no speech marks for ll.3–4 or l.11 of stanza 11. In *SP*, the poem was illustrated with the drawing that accompanies 'Not Waving but Drowning' (p. 347).

'Poor Soul, poor Girl!' (p. 458): introduced in performance as 'The Débutante'.

'From the French (1)' (p. 459): cf. Rimbaud, 'Chanson de plus haute tour' (1872). Early draft titled 'My Boat is Drunk (first verse from Rimbaud)' includes two further stanzas:

> Do I care? I do not,
> My old boat and I
> Are rather drunk
> And we roll along.

> The sea rolls too,
> My old boat is drunk,
> And so am I,
> We are older now.

'Admire Cranmer!' (p. 460): Robert Bolt's successful play *A Man for All Seasons* (1960) cast Thomas Cranmer (1489–1566) as corrupt and power-hungry. In 1955, the Church of England set up the Liturgical Commission that would result in the Alternative Service Book (1980).

'Votaries of Both Sexes Cry First to Venus' (p. 461): versions in *SP* and *CP* note the refrain should be sung to 'Angels of Jesus, Angels of light / Singing to welcome / The pilgrims of the night' [Henry T. Smart's 'Pilgrims]; the hymn 'Hark, hark, my soul! angelic songs are swelling' by Frederick William Faber (1814–63) is sung in *Hymns Ancient and Modern* to 'Pilgrims' (1868) by Henry Smart (1813–79).

'From the French (2)' (p. 463): cf. Mallarmé, 'Tristesse d'été' (1872) ll.7–8.

'I Was so Full . . .' (p. 464): Philip Larkin had reviewed *SP* enthusiastically for *New Statesman* (28 Sept. 1962), and echoes the

third stanza in the closing lines of 'Talking in Bed' from his 1964 collection *The Whitsun Weddings*:

> Nothing shows why
> At this unique distance from isolation
> It becomes still more difficult to find
> Words at once true and kind,
> Or not untrue and not unkind.

'God Speaks' (p. 466): *SP* and *CP* has 'faults' for 'flaws'; author's MS copy in UT revises to 'flaws', noting 'it was the original word but then I thought, when you *say* it, at poetry readings for instance, it sounds like "floors"'.

'Edmonton, thy cemetery . . .' (p. 467): cf. draft title 'Doubt and Belief' (UT).

'My Muse' (p. 468): cf. Baudelaire, 'La Muse malade' (1857); published in *The Bystander*, Christmas 1937, with additional middle stanza:

> O Lord incline my worldly ear to hear
> The patient mumblings of th'unearthly Muse
> For what the trivial gold, the social pause?
> These must I also lose if her I lose.
> Lord make me listen, and make her not proud.
> But speak her thoughts out plain and speak them loud.

In performance Smith sometimes omitted the first verse.

THE FROG PRINCE (1966)

Published by Longmans in December 1966. The original edition included 156 poems in total: seventy-two new poems alongside eighty-four from her previous five collections. The volume also contained three drawings with captions; these have been retained, save for a picture that replicates the illustration for 'My Hat' (p. 362).

'Exeat' (p. 481): the final line offers a translation of the title, which puns on the vernacular 'exeat' as a permission for a temporary absence from an English boarding school. Cf. Suetonius, *The Twelve Caesars* (AD 121), which reports that Tiberius once refused to grant a criminal a speedy execution with the words 'nondum tecum in gratiam redii' (trans. 'you and I are not yet friends').

'Easy' (p. 482): cf. Shakespeare, *Hamlet* (1602), III.iv, ll.178–201.

'The True Tyrant *or* The Spirit of Duty Rebuked' (p. 487): cf. Edgar Allen Poe's 'The Raven' (1845) and 'Of the Father's Love Begotten', a hymn based on the Latin poem 'Corde natus' by Aurelius Prudentius.

'Under Wrong Trees . . . *or* Freeing the Colonial Peoples' (p. 488): cf. Jean-Paul Sartre's preface to Frantz Fanon's *The Wretched of the Earth* (1961), which names European colonisers as 'zombies'; draft title was 'Splendide, Stupide and Candide' (UT).

'I had a dream . . .' (p. 489): cf. Homer's depiction of Helen in the *Iliad*, III, ll.445–61; 480–505; XXIV, ll.760–75. The poem's allusion to 'the Trojan Women' evokes Euripides' eponymous tragedy (415 BC) and Cassandra's promise that 'if war comes, there is a crown in death / For her that striveth well and perisheth / Unstained' (trans. Gilbert Murray, 1904). Poem published in *Ambit* 28 (1966) as 'A Dream' with italicised 'I' in penultimate sentence. A later draft substitutes 'ninth' for 'tenth', has line break after 'colours and spirits' and includes the following substitutions: 'Cressid lay that night, but they did not say' (l.20) and 'So there we stood / On the walls of Troy' (ll.23–4). Draft also includes following lines after 'like a good girl':

> I used to get so cross
> With everybody going. I wanted to make them cross too,
> Has it ever occurred to you, Troilus, I said, catching up with
> him one day,
> How
> Quite ordinary women
> Will use the decimal and duodecimal systems in one simple
> house-keeping sum

Adding up the pence column in twelves and to the other ones
in tens
Without giving it a second thought. He, too, went.

'Phèdre' (p. 495): cf. Marcel Proust, *Remembrance of Things Past*,
vol XI: *The Sweet Cheat Gone* (1954), trans. C. K. Scott Moncrieff
(1957), p. 60, which describes the importance of Jansenism in
Racine's depiction of Phèdre, and Jean Racine, *Phèdre* (1677), I.i.,
ll.34–6: 'all things are changed since the gods sent to these shores
the daughter of Minos and Pasiphaë' (trans. Margaret Rawlings,
1992). The significance of the line was discussed by George Steiner
in *The Death of Tragedy* (1961) and Lytton Strachey's essay
'Racine' (1922), and is mentioned as a title for 'the longest poem'
Pompey has written in *NOYP*, p. 200. Marie Bell's interpreta-
tion of Phèdre was captured in the 1968 film *Phèdre*, dir. Pierre
Jourdan. In performances Smith noted the poem 'might be called
"From the Classical Sixth at St Agatha's"'; author's performance
copies revised 'honourable simple' to 'simple honourable'.

'Everything is Swimming' (p. 498): for final line cf. Jules Barbey
d'Aurevilly's short story 'À un Dîner d'athées', *Les Diaboliques*
(1874); trans. 'she continued to laugh like a hyena'. The poem
appears as a series of captions in *SAMHTO* alongside the drawing
used for 'Northumberland House' (p. 582).

'The Persian' (p. 499): in *SAMHTO*, the poem appears as a series
of captions accompanying a drawing of a woman's head. The
first caption reads: 'I had to be careful with potatoes'.

'Monsieur Pussy-Cat, blackmailer' (p. 503): trans. 'this is the
great Monsieur Pussy-Cat [. . .] in front of the enormous fire
[. . .] indeed he knows something and blackmails his host,
another reason why [. . .] if grand and if justified, take care you
don't push the one who gives you such lovely dishes too far'. The
drawing appears in *SAMHTO* with the caption: 'C'est la vie!'

'Si peu séduisante' (p. 504): trans. 'she was only a little ten-year-
old, so very artless, who stumbled into the dining car, to find
her parents. She was in her school uniform, so very artless, and
a perfectly frightful little pair of shoes. But behind her pebble

glasses, her eyes were so full of good nature and sincerity that every other aspect of this little schoolgirl, so very artless, really only made one like her more.' The drawing appears in *SAMHTO* with the caption: 'What shall I do with my hands? But <u>what</u> ever shall I do with my hands?'

'To Carry the Child' (p. 505): l.29 amended from 'no man's blood' in author's copy; 'no man's blood' retained in *CP*, although performance introductions noted 'this poem has a misprint in it'. Various drafts delete then reinstate the final verse.

'The Last Turn of the Screw' (p. 509): cf. Henry James, 'The Turn of the Screw' (1898), Benjamin Britten's 1954 opera of the same name, and the film *The Innocents* (1961), dir. Jack Clayton. The drawing appears in *SAMHTO* with the caption: 'My little brother was delicate'. This version follows Smith's performance revision of 'make it sure' to 'make quite sure' in l.78.

'Company' (p. 513): published in *New Statesman* (25 Nov. 1963) with drawing of man taking pills, overlooked by a shrouded figure.

'Valuable' (p. 518): cf. 'Family Forum', *Daily Telegraph*, 26 April 1963, p. 12, which discusses the rise of illegitimacy in Britain. A circus panther that had escaped and injured several people was caught at a Paris school in April 1963.

'The Listener' (p. 522): Evelyn Cheesman (1881–1969) was a British entomologist and expert on New Guinea, and the first female curator of Regent's Park Zoo.

'Hymn to the Seal' (p. 523): the hymn 'Soldiers of Christ Arise!' by Charles Wesley (1707–88) is sung in *Hymns Ancient and Modern* to 'Diademata' by George Job Elvey (1816–93).

'Fish Fish' (p. 524): *CP* adds a comma to the title.

'Venus When Young Choosing Death' (p. 526): draft in UT has 'But not for friendship' in penultimate stanza.

'Pearl' (p. 530): early drafts from the 1950s offer various subtitles including 'a self-portrait in American disguise', 'a self-portrait in a dreary disguise', 'epitaph for an American Poetess committing

'suicide' and 'lines on a failed American poetess committing suicide'. In performances after the poem's publication, Smith explained she had 'made her American as I want two syllables on Pearl', downplaying the apparent reference to Sylvia Plath's suicide. The illustration is from the late 1930s, first published in *London Mercury and Bookman* (Dec. 1937) to accompany 'Swift to Depart'.

'Yes, I know' (p. 531): cf. the Leonardo da Vinci drawing once thought to be of Lucrezia Borgia (1480–1519), illegitimate daughter of Rodrigo Borgia. See also the popular historical novel *Light on Lucrezia* (1958) by Eleanor Hibbert (under the penname Jean Plaidy).

'Voice from the Tomb (1)' (p. 534): cf. Matthew 25:14–30. The poem was titled 'Here Lies . . .' in *Poetry* 105:2, Nov. 1964.

'Voice from the Tomb (2)' (p. 535): cf. the 1819 hymn by Reginald Heber is sung in *Hymns Ancient and Modern* to music by Lowell Mason (1823), though in 'A Turn Outside' Smith suggests it can also be sung as 'Jerusalem the Golden' (*MA* 335) to the tune by Alexander Ewing (1853). Celia sings 'From Greenland's icy mountains' in *TH*, p. 6. The poem was published as 'This Heart is Not Cold' in *Time and Tide* (author's undated clipping in UT).

'Voice from the Tomb (3)' (p. 536): originally titled 'On Being Neglected'.

'The Dedicated Dancing Bull and the Water Maid' (p. 537): the popular French horn player Dennis Brain and pianist Denis Matthews performed the sonata for BBC broadcast in 1946, and in concert at the Victoria and Albert Museum, 25 Jan. 1953: Brain died in 1957.

'Night Thoughts' (p. 539): cf. Edward Young's poem *The Complaint, or Night Thoughts* (1742–45).

'The Small Lady' (p. 544): variant draft has 'magic's daughter' for 'without help'.

'Animula, vagula, blandula' (p. 545): translation of the poem allegedly composed by Roman emperor Hadrian (76–138) shortly before his death.

'Friends of the River Trent' (p. 546): title taken from an article in *Angling Times* from 1953. Copies of the poem given to Kay Dick and Kathleen Farrell were inscribed: 'to remind us Literary Chaps that Others, too, have Their Troubles', and had 'body' for 'number' and omitted 'And' (l.11). See *SSACB*, p. 214.

'Is it Happy?' (p. 548): Smith's character names evoke writing contemporaries including Jürgen Thorwald (1915–2006), Barbara Pym (1913–80), and romantic novelist Jean Plaidy (1906–93); 'Lady Pym' also appears in *OTF*.

'The Grange' (p. 564): first published in *Punch*, 13 Oct. 1954, with 'bloodhound' for 'butler'. 'The Death of Nelson' was a popular patriotic tune written by John Braham, and first heard in the opera *The Americans* (1811).

'I am a girl who loves to shoot' (p. 572): *CP* runs together third and fourth stanza.

'Cœur Simple' (p. 575): first published in *The Holiday Book* (1946), p. 60.

'Nodding' (p. 576): an early draft gives last line as: 'But the thought's gone nodding'.

'v.' (p. 578): draft titles included 'Dr Nott' and 'Dr Nott is v. Nice'.

'A British Song' (p. 579): draft title was 'Bird Bath'.

'Northumberland House' (p. 582): Smith elides the 1605 Percy family house on London's Strand (demolished in 1874) with the mental hospital near Finsbury Park, which closed after World War II. A draft illustration for the poem depicts the hospital and cinema as it appeared before demolition in 1955. Cf. *TH* (p. 24), which mentions the 'fine mansion in Clapton where they have cures for these nervous disorders'.

'The Crown of Gold' (p. 584): an allegory for the troubled publication history of *The Holiday* (1949); after Cape and Duckworth rejected the novel, her German-Jewish friend Leo Kahn agreed to publish it, but financial difficulties meant he had to abandon the project. See *SSACB*, p. 191.

'Why do I . . .' (p. 587): a variant version prepared for an unpublished essay on death has 'loneliness' for 'nerviness', and 'kind Death does' for 'sweet Death does' (UT).

SCORPION AND OTHER POEMS (1972)

Published posthumously in January 1972 with an introduction by Patric Dickinson: Smith began to choose poems for the new collection but the final selection was completed by John Guest. CP reprints thirty-eight of the forty illustrations, omitting two drawings for 'Archie and Tina' which had previously accompanied 'A Dream of Comparison' and 'Nipping Pussy's Feet in Fun'. The original volume also included 'Farewell' (NWBD), where it appeared between 'Angel Boley' and 'The Donkey'.

'Scorpion' (p. 593): cf. Luke 12:20.

'Seymour and Chantelle or Un peu de vice' (p. 594): cf. 'Swishing and Swinburne', Smith's review of Jean Overton Fuller, Swinburne: A Critical Biography (1968) in The Listener, rpt. in MA 187–91. The illustration appears in SAMHTO with the caption 'I am an animal'.

'How do you see?' (p. 596): commissioned by the Guardian for Whitsun (16 May 1964); it includes the earlier 'Oh Christianity, Christianity' in full, omitting the line break after 'altered it'. Smith's reference to 'the verse in Mark' is to Mark 16:9–20, which describes Jesus' resurrection: its authorship is disputed, and Roman Catholics are not required to believe it was written by him. In an unpublished essay on the Pope written at this time, Smith noted: 'there seems to be much in the Pope's speech that suppresses truth [. . .] he should read Gibbon', UT.

'The Ass' (p. 602): version published in Ambit 28 (1966) has 'espargo' for 'esparto'; performance texts have 'tufted over with' for CP's less plausible 'tufted over the'.

'A Soldier Dear to Us' (p. 605): published in Ambit 34 (Jan. 1968) and The Honest Ulsterman (May 1968). The Ulsterman version omits: 'He was a sweet-tempered laughing man'.

[776]

'Angel Boley' (p. 610): drafts are partly in prose; the poem was prompted by the Moors Murderers, who were arrested in 1965.

'The Donkey' (p. 616): Smith prepared an alternative version of the poem without the final stanza for inclusion in a children's anthology; this was sent to Anthony Thwaite in June 1969, but never published (UT).

'The Sallow Bird' (p. 621): author's own copy revises first line of last stanza from 'Never seyd he word again'.

'The Word' (p. 624): cf. William Wordsworth, 'My heart leaps up' (1802).

'Nor We of Her to Him' (p. 625): original title 'Of any help to him' came from alternative final couplet:

> Which may be true but it is not
> Of any help to him.

See also sixth stanza of 'Who Shot Eugenie?' (p. 334).

'Oh grateful colours, bright looks!' (p. 629): in performance, Smith noted the poem was inspired by 'the idea you get in *The Iliad*, where all is grey and languid, and the poor ghosts must lap up a saucer of blood before they can speak [. . .] "Nox est perpetua una dormienda" would seem, by comparison, quite a jolly idea.' The latin tag is from Catullus 5, l.6 (trans. 'one ever-lasting night might be slept'), but the misremembered source is Homer's *Odyssey*, Bk. XI, also recalled in 'A Dream of Nourishment' (p. 395).

'O Pug!' (p. 630): cf. Marjorie Fleming (1803–11), 'Sonnet to a Monkey', which begins:

> O lively, O most charming pug,
> Thy graceful air, and heavenly mug;
> The beauties of his mind do shine,
> And every bit is shaped and fine.

The drawing appears in *SAMHTO* with the caption: 'I could eat you!', and as the illustration for 'O Happy Dogs of England' in *TFP*.

'The House of Over-Dew' (p. 637): cf. *TH*, pp. 177–81 for a prose version of the poem. Typed performance drafts have 'overdue', for as Smith explains in a 1968 radio broadcast, 'it was written so long after the event' (script in UT). Performance introductions call it 'a very long poem indeed, and flat [. . .] meant for several voices, say half a dozen, each playing in with each, as people do in conversations about friends they have in common who are not there'. The reference to Cynthia's prayer invokes Book XI of Homer's *Odyssey*, where Odysseus prays to Hades as he descends into the underworld.

'The Galloping Cat' (p. 647): draft version begins:

> He was a fairly furry cat
> But the hair had come from off
> The back of his head
> And when I asked him why, he said:

In performance introductions, Smith called the cat 'a real Tartuffe', referring to Molière's 1664 play about a pious fraud.

'Black March' (p. 653): *SABOSS* includes three untitled fragments by Smith (233); the first of these may be an early draft of the poem:

> I
> He comes to my room
> He is as tall & gray as the morning
> He stands silently
> He has a silent look
> He stands by my bed.
>
> He takes my shoulders in his hand
> His hand is as flat and gray as the morning
> Speak to me!
> He does not say a word
> I have not heard his voice

2
In the avenue of my faubourg
The white flowers shine under the green leaves
At night time.

The summer sun falls quickly
But not so quickly as your kisses fall
And the flowers
Are not so light as your eyes

3
I love you darling
The moment before it is absolutely certain that you love me
Is flying

This moment
Is like a dandelion puff before a wind that is rising.

'Grave by a Holm-Oak' (p. 655): version in *New Statesman* (21 March 1969) has 'darling' for 'Anna'.

'The Sea-widow' (p. 656): in *SAMHTO*, the drawing appears with the caption: 'What is the matter with Ireland now?'

'The Stroke' (p. 657): 'M' is Molly, Stevie's sister; in *CP*, two additional stanzas are added from the version Smith recited to Kay Dick during the interview published in *Ivy and Stevie*:

Oh, feeling of youth, you had better go
You are trapped by my age and deceased too.
Goodbye, goodbye I will send you away,
There is nothing here now to please you.
Then my feeling of youth said, 'No, I will not go;
I will comfort you with love and pain.
And also, if you like, I can procure for you a potion
That you will not take in vain.
The torpors of age could not seize the notion
To drink of the freeing grain, to measure the freeing grain.

All the same, I should not take it if I were you,
As you always can, but rather see life with me through.

It is not very long compared with geological time,
It is heaven to think of geological time.
The weight lifts . . . and this gives you a happy mind . . .'

UNCOLLECTED POEMS (1936–1970)

'Uncollected' here means not published in book form in the author's lifetime. Of the sixty-two poems here, thirty-nine were published in the posthumous MA, pp. 213–350. The additional twenty-three poems included here are:

'Casmilus'
'As falls the gravelled grouse'
From the Latin
Portrait of a Fool
Souvenir de Jacky Vandenbroeck
'The grief of an unquiet mind is a thing accursed'
Death of Cold
This Baronet
Swift to Depart
The Horror of the Midnight
The Angel
Lift Thy Sad Heart
Flounder
The Pupil
Left, Right
Ichabod
'O Silent Visitation'
Why d'You Believe?
Heartless
I walked in the graveyard . . .
Have Done, Gudrun
William the Dog
The Hound Puss

'"Casmilus"' (p. 661): printed as an epigraph in *NOYP*, p. 9.

'"As falls the gravelled grouse"' (p. 661): from *NOYP*, pp. 22–3, where Pompey introduces it as an excerpt from 'an unfinished manuscript of twenty-six pages single-spaced typewriting'. Cf. W. H. Auden, 'Consider this and in our time' (1930).

'Henry Wilberforce' (p. 661), 'From the Latin' (p. 662), 'Portrait of a Fool' (p. 662), 'Souvenir De Jacky Vandenbroeck' (p. 662), 'The grief of an unquiet mind is a thing accursed' (p. 663), 'Marriage I Think' (p. 663), 'Lulu' (p. 664), and 'Death of Cold' (p. 664): published in *Granta*, 9 June 1937, pp. 479–80.

'Via Media Via Dolorosa' (p. 664): trans. 'the middle way, the way of suffering': published in *Night and Day*, 19 Aug. 1937.

'Sigh No More' (p. 665): published in *Night and Day,* 9 Sept. 1937. Cf. Shakespeare, *Much Ado About Nothing*, III.iii, ll.47–50.

'*Salon d'Automne*' (p. 665): published in *Night and Day,* 9 Sept. 1937. The account of the annual French exhibition includes allusions to Richard Ansdell's *Stag at Bay* (1846) and Edward Poynter's *Faithful unto Death* (1865).

'Sterilization' (p. 666): published in *Night and Day*, 21 Oct. 1937. The Greek rhetorician Theopompous was known for his censorious views on the Etruscans.

'The Word' (p. 667): published in *London Mercury and Bookman* (Nov. 1937).

'Revenge' (p. 670): cf. John Dryden, *Alexander's Feast* (1697), ll.106–7, which was included in Palgrave's *Golden Treasury* (1875):

Revenge, revenge, Timotheus cries
See the Furies arise!

See also *NOYP* (p. 162): 'I came in time to view my absconded pa without indignation [. . .] and if at first "Revenge, Timotheus cried" I late shut up my old Timotheus'.

'A Portrait' (p. 673): published in *Night and Day*, 9 Dec. 1937.

'Landrecie', 'This Baronet', 'Swift to Depart', 'The Horror of the Midnight', 'The Angel', 'Revenge', 'Lift Thy Sad Heart', 'Flounder (Part of an Acrostic)', 'The Pupil', 'Portrait', 'Left, Right', 'Ichabod', 'On Coming Late to Parnassus' (pp. 668–73): published in *London Mercury and Bookman*, Dec. 1937, as a poetic sequence entitled 'I'll Have Your Heart'.

'The Horrible Man' (p. 673), 'The Octopus' (p. 674), 'As Sways' (p. 674), 'Portrait' (p. 675) and 'Two Friends' (p. 675): published in *Bystander*, Christmas 1937.

'As Sways' (p. 674): for final couplet cf. James Gates Percival's 'oak by tempest riven' in 'Judgment Day', and for 'nodding sycamores' see Frederick William Faber's 'The Lammas Shoots' (1840).

'"When I Awake"' (p. 676): from *OTF*, p. 61. Reprinted in *MA* with revised lineation.

'"O Silent Visitation"' (p. 676): from *OTF*, p. 122; in the novel, the protagonist introduces the poem by way of contrast to Titurel in Wagner's *Parsifal* (1882), who 'continues to live in the grave', p. 121.

'I Forgive You' (p. 677): from *The Holiday Book* (1946), p. 170.

'"The Midwife"' (p. 677): from *TH*, p. 191, where the protagonist explains the poem's first line was taken from a Ministry of Health poster; *MA* reprint capitalises 'midwife' on first line, and adds terminal commas for lines 2–3.

'The Royal Dane' (p. 678): from *TH*, p. 190, where the protagonist calls it 'Hamlet's father's ghost's farewell to Hamlet' sung to the tune of Arthur Sullivan's 'Of that there is no manner of doubt' from *The Gondoliers* (1889).

'O Lord!' (p. 678): published in *Nimbus* 3:2, 1955. A direct translation of Euripides, *The Bacchae* (405 BC), ll.768–76: in *NOYP*, Pompey recalls playing second messenger in the school play, and how 'the last four lines' of her speech embarrassed her abstemious schoolteacher, p. 136.

'The English' (p. 678): published in *World Review* (1955).

'Beautiful' (p. 679): published in the *Observer*, 8 Sept. 1957.

'Why d'You Believe?' (p. 679): published in the essay 'The Necessity of Not Believing' (*Gemini*, Spring 1958); *MA* reprints the essay but omits this poem. An earlier draft is titled 'In Praise of Fact (An Objection to some Neo-Medieval Tendencies on the Third Programme)' and has 'pet behaviour' for 'hard behaviour' and 'too I will allow' for 'one supposes'.

'The Vision' (p. 682): published in *Encounter*, July 1958; typed draft marked 'not keen on this one'.

'Heartless' (p. 683): published in the Poetry Book Society's *Poetry Supplement*, Christmas 1958, edited by Patric Dickinson.

'Silence' (p. 684): first published in *Time and Tide*, 6 Dec. 1958, although *MA* presents it as unpublished (p. 236). Author's own clipping in UT revises 'time' to 'age' in line 1, and 'an age' to 'a time' in line 5.

'The Old Poet' (p. 685): published in *PEN News*, Winter 1958–9; authorial note indicates the poem should be sung to 'Wrap me up in my Tarpaulin jacket' (1884) by Charles Coote.

'I walked in the graveyard . . .' (p. 685): included in 'A Turn Outside', BBC radio play broadcast 23 May 1959 and rpt. in *MA* pp. 335–59. Cf. Homer, *The Odyssey*, X, ll.1–50.

'*La Robe Chemise*' (p. 686): trans. 'flimsy and submissive', 'fresh and submissive'. The poem was published in *Spectator*, 2 Sept. 1960, but Smith worried the poem was 'a bit slight' for *SP* in a letter to Jocelyn Baines.

'From the French' (p. 687): a free translation of Arthur Rimbaud, 'Le Bateau ivre' (1871), ll.21–29; published in *TLS*, 9 Sept. 1960.

'The Holiday' (p. 687): published in the *Observer*, 10 Sept. 1961. Smith intended to collect the poem in *SP*, but sent it to Jocelyn Baines too late for it to be included.

'When One' (p. 688): early version of 'Why do I . . .' (p. 587) published with 'Dear Child of God' in *New Statesman and Nation*, 1963: early draft entitled 'Why' begins new stanza at 'Only sweet Death'.

'Miss Snooks, Poetess' (p. 689): published in *Poetry*, November 1964.

'Saint Foam and the Holy Child' (p. 689): published in *Harper's Bazaar*, Dec. 1966.

'B.B.C. Feature Programme on Prostitution' (p. 691): published in *Poetry Review*, Winter 1967.

'Pretty Baby' (p. 693): first published in *The Sunday Times* (22 Dec. 1968) as 'Sweet Baby'. Smith retitled the poem so it could be included as a new poem for *The Best Beast* (1969), forgetting she already published is as 'Pretty Baby' in *Queen*, Christmas 1968; a proof annotation now in UT notes 'same title used unfortunately – a slip'.

'Our Doggy' (p. 693) and 'My Tortoise' (p. 694): published in *Allsorts 2*, 1969.

'Have Done, Gudrun' (p. 695): published in *The Times* (9 Jan. 1970, p. 9) in response to the article 'One enormous happening, or always five inches off the ground' by German author Gudrun Tempel, *The Times* review (3 Jan. 1970), p. 1. The article diagnoses the 'deadly shock' of post-Empire Britain which now runs at 'half-speed': the article's title seemed a direct rebuke to Smith's 'foot-off-the-ground' sense of national pride.

'William the Dog' (p. 695): published in *Allsorts 3*, 1970.

'Sapphic' (p. 696): published in *Scotsman*, 28 Nov. 1970. Cf. Sappho's Fragment 3.

'The Hound Puss' (p. 697): published in *CATegories: cats according to their characters from Sphinx, Gib-Hunter, Grimalkin, Tabby to Puss* (1981) ed. Rosalie Mander, p. 25.

UNPUBLISHED POEMS (1936–1970)

'Unpublished' here means not published in Smith's lifetime, although some have been published posthumously. Poems with

approximate dates have been included chronologically: subsequent poems appear in alphabetical order by title. Twenty-four of these poems were included in *MA*, although alternative drafts have been used in some cases. Although the UT archive includes a number of additional draft poems not included here, the selection includes all poems Smith prepared for publication during her lifetime together with posthumously published poems. The additional twenty-five poems included here are:

Northumberland Park
Fussy
Porgy Georgie
Father Damien Doshing
Bed
Song in Time of War
Mrs Midnight
Professor Snooks Does His Worst with a Grecian Fragment
The Lesson
A Fiend
Le Paquebot
Voice from the Tomb
To the Brownes' Cat
To the Brownes' Hamster
Mort's Cry
Friend and Neighbour
The Publisher
Lord Henry de Bohon
The Stream with Two Faces
Soupir d'Angleterre
Death
She got up and went away
The Easter Rose
The Little Birdies
The Old Soul

'Northumberland Park' (p. 701): draft written on the typescript of *NOYP*, now in BJ.

'Fussy' (p. 701): a note in UT indicates Smith hoped to place this poem in *Picture Post*, which ran from 1938 to 1957: the paper and typewriter suggest a composition date of 1937.

'Goodnight' (p. 702): this poem was included in a 1938 letter from Smith to Naomi Mitchison, and published at the end of *CP*, p. 572. Smith removed it from *MWIM* on the advice of John Hayward; it was rejected from *The Listener* by Joe Ackerley on the grounds it would 'upset far too many of the old ladies' (2 Jan. 1940, UT).

'Porgy Georgie' (p. 702), 'Father Damien Doshing' (p. 703), 'Bed' (p. 703) and 'My Earliest Love' (p. 704) were all considered for inclusion in *TOTO* and posthumously published in 'Unpublished Stevie Smith', *Poetry Review*, 74:3 (1984), pp. 23–24: Smith considered 'My Earliest Love' as the title poem for the collection.

'The Ballet of the Twelve Dancing Princesses' (p. 705): cf. Brothers Grimm, tale 133. *MA* (p. xiv) notes the typescript for this poem is dated June 1939.

'Song in Time of War' (p. 706): the MS in UT is included with proofs for *NWBD* but marked 'very old (?)' in author's hand; the poem's subject suggests it was written as Smith revised *TH*.

'Mrs Midnight' (p. 707): the MS in UT is written on the back of a draft for 'Great Unaffected Vampires and the Moon', suggesting a composition date of 1953.

'They Killed' (p. 707): in MS in UT; in *MA* (p. xiv) editors date the poem from a holograph draft given to Kathleen Farrell.

'Professor Snooks Does His Worst with a Grecian Fragment' (p. 708): cf. Aeschylus, *Agamemnon* (458 BC) and A. E. Housman, 'Fragment of a Greek Tragedy' (1883). This poem was included with the proofs for *NWBD* and marked in author's hand 'not used', UT.

'The Lesson' (p. 709): published in *MA* (p. 222) from typed MS in UT. No date is suggested in *MA*, but the poem is marked 'No (?)' in Laurie Lee's hand, which suggests Smith was considering including it in *NWBD*.

'On the Dressing gown lent me by my Hostess the Brazilian Consul in Milan, 1958' (p. 709): written after visiting Milan with the composer Stanley Bate and his wife, the Brazilian diplomat Margarida Guedes Mogueria. See *SSACB*, p. 225.

'A Fiend' (p. 711) and 'Le Paquebot' (p. 712): sent to James Laughlin (1 March 1963) for possible inclusion in American *SP*: 'Le Paquebot' refers to the international agreement allowing letters written at sea to be delivered with stamps from the ship's country of origin.

'Voice from the Tomb' (p. 712): MS in UT; poem published in *SSACB*, p. 246.

'To the Brownes' Cat' (p. 713) and 'To the Brownes' Hamster' (p. 713): dated MS in author's hand in UT. Cf. 'O Pug!' (p. 630).

'Mort's Cry' (p. 714): dated MS in author's hand in UT.

'Friend and Neighbour' (p. 714): prepared for publication by Smith in November 1968; an unsent letter to John Guest notes the poems she has included are 'light but disagreeable' (UT). An early draft of 'Friend and Neighbour' from 1938 was titled 'First Things Last'.

'The Publisher' (p. 715): included in the same letter as 'Friend and Neighbour' (p. 714). όμισμα is 'nomisa', the ancient Greek for money; earlier draft titles included 'Mr Snooks the publisher'.

'Lord Henry de Bohon' (p. 715), 'The Stream with Two Faces' (p. 716), and 'I thank thee, Lord' (p. 716): these poems were drafted on the back of a script for a reading Smith gave in 1969, now in UT.

'Soupir d'Angleterre' (p. 717): written in response to the investiture of the Prince of Wales on 1 July 1969, and sent to Anthony Thwaite at *New Statesman* as a 'nasty poem about the Welsh' (25 July 1969, UT); see *SSACB*, p. 288. It was quoted by Martin Bax in his review of *Scorpion*, 'Three Blurbs and a Eulogy', *Ambit* no.51 (1972), p. 51.

'He preferred . . .' (p. 717), 'Like This (1)' (p. 717), 'Like This (2)' (p. 718), 'Telly-me-Do' (p. 718): this follows the MS dating in *MA* (pp. vi-vii).

'Accented' (p. 719): typed MS draft in UT; reprinted in *MA*, p. 227.

'Cars' (p. 719): typed MS in UT; fourth stanza is published in *MA* as 'No Matter Who Rides', p. 227.

'César' (p. 720): typed MS and various drafts in UT. Cf. *OTF* (p. 79): 'the only good thing about Baldur is his fondness for his dog, his dog César, his dachshund that accompanied him round and about the forests of Deutschland'.

'Childhood and Interruption' (p. 721): typed MS with drafts in UT; published in *MA* (p. 234).

'Death' (p. 722): typed MS with annotated revisions in UT.

'Mabel' (p. 723): cf. *NOYP*, where Pompey is haunted by *Alice's Adventures in Wonderland* (1865), and the fear 'she was going to be Mabel', p. 41. The phrase 'how awful to be Mabel' returns in a review, 'New Novels', the *Observer*, 14 Nov. 1954.

'"Mother Love"' (p. 723): published in *MA* (p. 217) from untitled draft in UT.

'None of the Other Birds' (p. 723): published in *MA* (p. 229) from draft in UT.

'Oh Thou Pale Intellectual Brow' (p. 724): published in *MA* (p. 239) from typed MS in UT.

'Roaming' (p. 724): cf. 'Eulenspiegelei' (p. 104). Published in *MA* (p. 233) from typed MS in UT.

'Ruory and Edith' (p. 726): published in *MA* (p. 216) as 'Ruory' from various typed MS and drafts in UT.

'She got up and went away' (p. 726): from typed MS in UT.

'The Easter Rose' (p. 727): from typed MS in UT.

'The Little Birdies' (p. 728): from typed MS in UT.

'The Old Soul' (p. 730): from typed MS in UT. Author's note indicates the poem should be sung to the folk tune 'Over the mountains', famous from the 1922 arrangement by Roger Quilter.

'The Pearl' (p. 730): published in *MA* (p. 236) from typed MS in UT.

'There is an Old Man' (p. 730): published in *MA* (p. 220) from typed MS in UT.

'Tom Snooks the Pundit' (p. 731): published in *MA* (p. 225) from typed MS in UT.

'Wife's Lament at Hereford' (p. 732): published in *MA* (p. 217) from typed MS in UT.

Index by Title

'. . . and the clouds return after the rain' 160
Abominable Lake 106
Accented 719
Actress 223
Adelaide Abner 410
Admire Cranmer! 460
Advice to Young Children 194
After-thought 291
Ah, will the Saviour. . .? 197
Airy Christ 396
Alfred the Great 8
All Things Pass 53
Alone in the Woods 23
Ambassador 282
An Agnostic 399
Analysand 51
Angel 670
Angel Boley 610
Angel Face 563
Angel of Grace 64
Anger's Freeing Power 369
Animula, vagula, blandula 545
Appetite 67
Après la Politique, la Haine des Bourbons 235
Arabella 130
Archie and Tina 632
'As falls the gravelled grouse' 661
As Sways 674
Ass 602
At School 413
Aubade 42
Autumn 189
Avondale 516
Avondall 517
Away, Melancholy 377

B.B.C. Feature Programme on Prostitution 691
Bag-Snatching in Dublin 43
Ballet of the Twelve Dancing Princesses 705
Bandol (Var) 6

Barlow 33
Be off! 212
Beautiful 679
Bed 703
Behind the Knight 265
Bereaved Swan 35
Bereavement 78
Best Beast of the Fat-Stock Show at Earls Court 479
Beware the Man 89
Bishops of the Church of England 102
Black March 653
Blood Flows Back 91
Blue from Heaven 354
Boat 110
Bog-Face 191
Bottle of Aspirins 221
Breughel 90
Brickenden, Hertfordshire 121
British Song 579
Broken Friendship 289
Broken Heart 229
But Murderous 388
Bye Baby Bother 158

Can it Be? 416
Cars 719
'Casmilus' 661
Castle 262
Cat Asks Mouse Out 406
'Ceci est digne de gens sans Dieu' 247
Celtic Fringe 330
Celts 402
César 720
Ceux qui luttent . . . 171
Childe Rolandine 380
Childhood and Interruption 721
Children of the Cross 165
Choosers 434
Christmas 255
Cock and the Hen 116
Cock-A-Doo 617
Cœur Simple 575

Come 173
Come, Death (1) 115
Come, Death (2) 658
'Come on, Come back' 383
Commuted Sentence 329
Company 513
Conventionalist 206
Conviction (I) 198
Conviction (II) 198
Conviction (III) 199
Conviction (IV) 199
Cool and Plain 308
Cool as a Cucumber 275
Correspondence between
 Mr Harrison in Newcastle
 and Mr Sholto Peach Harrison
 in Hull 36
Cousin 123
Croft 218
Crown of Bays 317
Crown of Gold 584

Darling Daughters 101
Days of Yore 529
Dear Child of God 492
Dear Female Heart 141
Dear Karl 133
Dear Little Sirmio 400
Dear Muse 149
Death 722
Death Bereaves our Common Mother
 Nature Grieves for my Dead
 Brother 41
Death Came to Me 46
Death in the Rose Garden 242
Death of Cold 664
Death of Mr Mounsel 79
Death of the Dog Belvoir 63
Death Sentence 328
Death's Ostracism 108
Death-bed of a Financier 312
Deathly Child 131
Dedicated Dancing Bull and the
 Water Maid 537
Deeply Morbid 340
Deserter 295
Devil-my-Wife 224
Dido's Farewell to Aeneas 379
Die Lorelei 441

Dirge 208
Distractions and the Human Crowd
 210
Do Not! 327
Do Take Muriel Out 285
Doctor 112
Does No Love Last? 62
Donkey 616
Dream 29
Dream of Comparison 360
Dream of Nourishment 395
Drugs Made Pauline Vague 301
'Duty was his Lodestar' 290

Easter Rose 727
Easy 482
Edmonton, thy cemetery . . . 467
Egocentric 7
Emily writes such a good letter 500
Eng. 40
Engine Drain 364
English 411
English 678
English Visitor 348
Es war einmal 27
Eulenspiegelei 104
Evangelie or The Figure of Literary
 Corruption, seeking Glory not
 Truth 432
Every Lovely Limb's a Desolation
 393
Everything is Swimming 498
Exeat 481

Face 195
Fafnir and the Knights 371
Failed Spirit 251
Fairy Bell 351
Fairy Story 562
Fallen, Fallen 166
Farewell 442
Father Damien Doshing 703
Father for a Fool 119
Feminine Charm 57
Fiend 711
Film Star 220
Fish Fish 524
Flounder 671
Flow, Flow, Flow 164

Fool 240
Forgive me, forgive me 13
Forgot! 227
Forlorn Sea 608
Francesca in Winter 618
Freddy 65
Friend 154
Friend and Neighbour 714
Friends of the River Trent 546
Friskers or Gods and Men 307
Frog Prince 471
From My Notes for a Series of
 Lectures on Murder 68
From the Coptic 323
From the County Lunatic Asylum 32
From the French 687
From the French (1) 459
From the French (2) 463
From the Greek 22
From the Italian 465
From the Latin 662
Frozen Lake 455
Fugitive's Ride 84
Fuite d'Enfance 176
Full Well I Know 337
Fussy 701

Galloping Cat 647
Ghost of Ware 343
Girls! 187
Gnädiges Fräulein 153
God and Man 298
God and the Devil 26
God Speaks 466
God the Drinker 391
God the Eater 390
Goodnight 702
Governess 222
Grange 564
Grave by a Holm-Oak 655
'Great Unaffected Vampires and the
 Moon' 401
Grief of an unquiet mind is a thing
 accursed 663

Happiness 238
Harold's Leap 267
Hast Du dich verirrt? 244
Hat 313

Have Done, Gudrun 695
He preferred . . . 717
Heartless 683
Heavenly City 215
Heber 9
Hendecasyllables 652
Henry Wilberforce 661
Her-zie 623
Hippy-Mo 650
Holiday 687
Homage to John Cowper Powys
 319
Horrible Man 673
Horror of the Midnight 669
Hostage 374
Hound of Ulster 3
Hound Puss 697
House of Mercy 476
House of Over-Dew 637
How Cruel is the Story of Eve 556
How do you see? 596
How far can you Press a Poet? 12
How Slowly Time Lengthens 142
Human Affection 181
Humane Materialist at the Burning of
 a Heretic 325
Hymn to the Seal 523

I Am 316
I am a girl who loves to shoot 572
'I could let Tom go – but what about
 the children?' 254
I do not Speak 55
I Forgive You 677
I had a dream . . . 489
I Hate this Girl 113
I Like to Play with Him 50
I love . . . 574
I Remember 386
I rode with my darling . . . 296
I thank thee, Lord 716
I walked in the graveyard . . . 685
I Was so Full . . . 464
I Wish 520
'I'll have your heart' 163
Ichabod 672
If I lie down 196
In Canaan's Happy Land 135
In My Dreams 139

In Protocreation 326
In the Night 231
In the Park 429
Infant 25
Infelice 114
Intimation of Immortality 24
Is it Happy? 548
Is it Wise? 69
It Filled my Heart with Love 398

Jew is Angry with his Friend who does not Believe in Circumcision 322
Jumbo 433
Jungle Husband 382

King Hamlet's Ghost 412
King in Funeral Procession 182

La Gretchen de Nos Jours (1) 147
La Gretchen de Nos Jours (2) 184
La Robe Chemise 686
La Speakerine de Putney 209
Lads of the Village 156
Lady 'Rogue' Singleton 216
Lady of the Well-Spring 357
Lament of a Slug-a-bed's Wife 34
Landrecie 668
Last Turn of the Screw 509
Le Désert de l'Amour 127
Le Majeur Ydow 201
Le Paquebot 712
Le Revenant 306
Le Singe Qui Swing 287
Leader 332
Left, Right 672
Lesson 709
Lift Thy Sad Heart 670
Light of Life 428
Lightly Bound 305
Like This (1) 717
Like This (2) 718
Listener 522
Little Birdies 728
Little Boy Lost 60
Little Boy Sick 174
Little Child of Brightest Face 320
Little Daughters of America 202
Loin de l'Être 405

Longing for Death because of Feebleness 421
Look! 423
Look, Look 168
Lord Barrenstock 71
Lord Henry de Bohon 715
Lord Mope 56
Lord Say-and-Seal 528
Lot's Wife 239
Louise 94
Love Me! 213
Lulu 664

Mabel 723
Magic Morning 232
Magna est Veritas 427
Magnificent Words 568
Major Macroo 75
Man I Am 228
Man is a Spirit 271
Man Saul 143
Marriage I Think 663
Maximilian Esterhazy 73
Midwife 677
Miss Snooks, Poetess 689
Monsieur Pussy-Cat, blackmailer 503
Mort's Cry 714
Mother 217
'Mother Love' 723
Mother, among the Dustbins 125
Mother's Hearse 268
Mr Over 299
Mrs Arbuthnot 567
Mrs Blow and Her Animals 626
Mrs Osmosis 83
Mrs Simpkins 10
Mrs Midnight 707
Murder 186
Murderer 124
Mutchmore and Not-So 507
My Cat Major 407
My Cats 300
My Earliest Love 704
My Hat 362
My Heart Goes Out 422
My Heart was Full 218
My Muse 468
My Soul 138
My Tortoise 694

Nature and Free Animals 37
'N'est-ce pas assez de ne me point
 haïr?' 250
Never Again 59
New Age 353
Night Thoughts 539
Night-Time in the Cemetery 19
Nipping Pussy's Feet in Fun 406
No Categories! 293
No More People 243
No Respect 48
Noble and Ethereal 140
Nodding 576
None of the Other Birds 723
Nor We of Her to Him 625
Northumberland House 582
Northumberland Park 701
Not Waving but Drowning 347
Nourish Me on an Egg 148
November 502
Now Pine-Needles 92
Numbers 31

O Happy Dogs of England 100
O Lord! 678
O Pug! 630
'O Silent Visitation' 676
Oblivion 646
Occasional Yarrow 435
Octopus 674
Oh Christianity, Christianity 484
Oh grateful colours, bright looks! 629
'Oh stubborn race of Cadmus'
 seed . . .' 281
Oh Thou Pale Intellectual Brow 724
Oh What is the Thing He Done? 426
Oh, If Only . . . 333
Old Ghosts 241
Old Poet 685
Old Soul 730
Old Sweet Dove of Wiveton 417
On Coming Late to Parnassus 673
On the Death of a German
 Philosopher 4
On the Dressing gown lent me by my
 Hostess the Brazilian Consul in
 Milan, 1958 709
On Walking Slowly After an Accident
 570

One of Many 107
Orphan Reformed 276
Our Bog is Dood 302
Our Doggy 693
Our Office Cat 321
Out of Time 161

Pad, pad 288
Papa Love Baby 5
Parents 408
Parklands 38
Parrot 111
Passing Cloud 403
Past 419
Pearl 530
Pearl 730
Persephone 283
Persian 499
Phèdre 495
Photograph 159
Piggy to Joey 541
Pleasures of Friendship 237
Poet Hin 634
Poet! 190
Poets are Silent 236
Porgy Georgie 702
Portrait 672
Portrait 673
Portrait 675
Portrait (1) 93
Portrait (2) 128
Portrait of a Fool 662
Poor Soul, poor Girl! 458
Pretty 542
Pretty Baby 693
Private Means is Dead 77
Professor Snooks Does His Worst
 with a Grecian Fragment 708
Progression 14
Proud Death with Swelling Port 136
Publisher 715
Pupil 671

Quand on n'a pas ce que l'on aime,
 il faut aimer ce que l'on a – 204
Queen and the Young Princess 359

Reason 49
Recluse 253

Recognition not Enough 450
Rencontres Funestes 219
Rehearsal 311
Religious Man 399
Repentance of Lady T 225
Revenge 670
Reversionary 132
Ride 315
River Deben 44
River God of the River Mimram in
 Hertfordshire 273
River Humber 145
Road Up 82
Roaming 724
Roman Road 261
Rothebât 167
Royal Dane 678
Ruory and Edith 726

Sad Heart 205
Sad Mother 196
Saffron 514
Saint Anthony and the Rose of Life
 367
Saint Foam and the Holy Child 689
Sallow Bird 621
Salon d'Automne 665
Sapphic 696
Satin-Clad 245
Scorpion 593
Sea-widow 656
Seymour and Chantelle or Un
 peu de vice 594
She got up and went away 726
She said. . . 203
Shooting Incident 277
Si peu séduisante 504
Siesta 120
Sigh No More 665
Silence 684
Silence and Tears 117
Singing Cat 420
Sliding Mountain 252
Small Lady 544
Smile 226
So can anger . . . 570
So to fatness come 620
Soldier Dear to Us 605
Some Are Born 588

Song in Time of War 706
Songe d'Athalie 373
Songster 20
Sorrowful Girl 437
Soupir d'Angleterre 717
Souvenir de Jacky Vandenbroeck
 662
Souvenir de Monsieur Poop 150
Spanish School 17
Starling 439
Sterilization 666
Story I Have Told 559
Stream with Two Faces 716
Stroke 657
Study to Deserve Death 207
Suburb 87
Suburban Classes 16
Suicide's Epitaph 172
Sunt Leones 54
Swift to Depart 669

Tableau de l'Inconstance des Mauvais
 Anges 169
Telly-me-Do 718
Tender Only to One 99
Tenuous and Precarious 474
Thank You 314
There is an Old Man 730
They Killed 707
This Baronet 668
This Englishwoman 70
This is Disgraceful and Abominable
 389
Thought is Superior 272
Thoughts about the Christian
 Doctrine of Eternal Hell 448
Thoughts about the Person from
 Porlock 445
To a Dead Vole 129
To a Lady in a Train 409
To an American Publisher 310
To the Brownes' Cat 713
To the Brownes' Hamster 713
To Carry the Child 505
To Dean Inge Lecturing on
 Origen 264
To School! 309
To the Dog Belvoir 58
To the Tune of the Coventry Carol 15

Toll of the Roads 103
Tom Snooks the Pundit 731
Touch and Go 269
True Tyrant *or* the Spirit of Duty
 Rebuked 487
Two Friends 675

Under Wrong Trees . . . *or* Freeing
 the Colonial Peoples 488
Unpopular, lonely and loving 246
Up and Down 21
Upon a Grave 157

v. 578
Valuable 518
Vater Unser 152
Venus When Young Choosing Death
 526
Via Media Via Dolorosa 664
Villains 201
Violent Hand 175
Virtuoso 200
Vision 682
Voice from the Tomb 712
Voice from the Tomb (1) 534
Voice from the Tomb (2) 535
Voice from the Tomb (3) 536
Voice from the Tomb (4) 536
Voice from the Tomb (5) 536
Voices about the Princess Anemone
 338
Voices against England in the Night
 249
Votaries of Both Sexes Cry First to
 Venus 461

Wanderer 292
Warden 266
Was He Married? 451

Was it not curious? 454
Watchful 551
Weak Monk 286
Wedding Photograph 494
'What is she writing? Perhaps it will
 be good' 350
What is the Time? *or* St Hugh of
 Lincoln 74
'When I Awake' 676
When One 688
When the Sparrow Flies 248
When Walking 622
When the wind . . . 580
Where are you going? 188
White Thought 230
Who is this Who Howls and
 Mutters? 425
Who Killed Lawless Lean? 80
Who Shot Eugenie? 334
Why are the Clergy . . .? 385
Why d'You Believe? 679
Why do I . . . 587
Why do you rage? 486
Widowhood *or* The Home-Coming
 of Lady Ross 532
Wife's Lament at Hereford 732
Wild Dog 214
Will Ever? 170
Will Man Ever Face Fact and not Feel
 Flat? 392
William the Dog 695
Word 624
Word 667
Wretched Woman 304

Yes, I know 531

Zoo 192

Index by First Line

A child is born, they cry, a child 255
A couple of women is one too many 240
A dark rose grew in the desert 367
A dismal bell hung in the belfry 351
A dwindling body of ageing fish 546
A mother slew her unborn babe 388
A sallow bird sat on a tree 621
A talented old gentleman painting a hedge 622
A thousand and fifty-one waves 31
A woolly dog 465
Across the bridge across the dyke 84
Adela is such a silly woman 578
Adelaide Abner is cruel 410
Admirals Curse-You and No-More 202
Admire the old man, admire him, admire him 460
All the waters of the river Deben 44
All these illegitimate babies . . . 518
All things pass 53
Aloft 218
Alone in the woods I felt 23
An antique story comes to me 441
Angel face so close above me 563
Angel most cynical 175
Archie and Tina 632
As falls the gravelled grouse 661
As sways the gentle sycamore 674
At school I always walk with Elwyn 413
Away, melancholy 377

Bandol (Var) 6
Be mine, sweet child, let not the blush departing 662
Behind the Knight sits hooded Care 265
Belvoir thy coat was not more golden than thy heart 63
Beware the man whose mouth is small 89

Brightest and best are the sons of the morning 169
Bye Baby Bother 158

Can it be, can it be 416
Carve delinquency away 666
Casmilus, whose great name I steal 661
C'est la, la, la 712
C'est un grand Monsieur Pussy-Cat 503
Ceux qui luttent ce sont ceux qui vivent 171
Children who paddle where the ocean bed shelves steeply 194
Christ died for God and me 198
Cold as no love, and wild with all negation 204
Cold as No Plea 328
Coleridge received the Person from Porlock 445
Come, wed me, Lady Singleton 216
Cool and plain 308
Cool as a cucumber calm as a mill pond sound as a bell 275
Count Flanders 235
Creature of God, thy coat 523
Crying for pleasure 461

Dark was the day for Childe Rolandine the artist 380
Darling daughters, listen to your mother 101
Darling little baby child 196
Darling little Tom and Harry 674
Deal not with me God as I have dealt with Man 312
Dear child of God 492
Dear Daughter of the Southern Cross 709
Dear Female Heart, I am sorry for you 141
Dear Karl, I send you Walt Whitman in a sixpenny book 133

Dear little Bog-Face 191
Dear little Sirmio 400
Dear Muse, the happy hours we have spent together 149
Dearest Evelyn, I often think of you 382
Death came to me and said 46
Deep in the still mysterious waters of the lake a world lies drowned 106
Deeply morbid deeply morbid was the girl who typed the letters 340
Disarmed off-guard *tendre et soumise* 686
Do not despair of man, and do not scold him 327
Do take Muriel out 285
Donnez à manger aux affamées 220
Down with creative talent 731
Drugs made Pauline vague 301
Duty was my Lobster, my Lobster was she 290

Easy in their ugly skins 482
Edmonton, thy cemetery 467
'Eh bien! Marche!', fit le Majeur Ydow 201
England, you had better go 249
Everything is swimming in a wonderful wisdom 498

Fair waved the golden corn 135
Far from his home he came, the old person 724
Far from normal far from normal far from normal I am 316
Farewell dear friends 442
Farewell for ever, well for ever fare 186
Father Damien Doshing 703
First he sat, and then he lay 693
Flow, flow, flow 164
Forgive me forgive me my heart is my own 13
Fourteen-year-old, why must you giggle and dote 206
From a friend's friend I taste friendship 208
Full well I know the flinty heart 337

Get up thou lazy lump thou log get up 34
Girls! although I am a woman 187
God and the Devil 26
God bless the lion, the British animal 706
God in Heaven, forgive my death, it lies 242
Goodbye Harry I must have you by me for a time 494

Hamster 713
Happiness is silent, or speaks equivocally for friends 238
Harold, are you asleep? 267
He blinks he sighs 182
He chases his tail 51
He flies so high 168
He is a most horrible man 673
He is quite captive to the Lady of the Well-Spring 357
He often gazes on the air 399
He preferred to be a hearthrug sage 717
He said no word of her to us 625
He says that religious thought and all our nerviness 399
He told his life story to Mrs Courtly 189
He told me he loved me 229
He stood in dream upon the brim 108
He wrote *The I and the It* 4
Henry Wilberforce as a child 661
Here lies a poet who would not write 534
Honour and magnify this man of men 8
Hop hop, thump thump 537
How cruel is the story of Eve 556
How do you see the Holy Spirit of God? 596
How far can you press a poet? 12
How fares it with you, Mrs Cooper my bride? 656
How hypocritical this dear old fellow is 691
How nice it is to slink the streets at night 87

How slowly time lengthens from a
 hated event 142
How sweet the birds of Avondale 516

I admire the Bishops of the Church of
 England 102
I always admire a beautiful woman
 311
I always remember your beautiful
 flowers 288
I am a frog 471
I am a girl who loves to shoot 572
I am becalmed in a deep sea 423
I am dying Egypt dying 79
I am Miles, I did not die 509
I am not God's little lamb 174
I am that Persephone 283
I am the self-appointed guardian of
 English literature 150
I came upon it in a dream 29
I can call up old ghosts, and they will
 come 241
I cannot imagine anything nicer 458
I can't say I enjoyed it, but the pay
 was good 223
I cry I cry 293
I died for lack of company 536
I do not ask for mercy for
 understanding for peace 55
I do not care for nature 664
I fear the ladies and gentlemen under
 the trees 219
I feel a mortal isolation 393
I feel ill. What can the matter be? 658
I fell in love with Major Spruce 14
I forgive you, Maria 677
I go to church because the Rector 714
I had a dream I was a bird 517
I had a dream I was Helen of Troy
 489
I had a dream of nourishment 395
I had a dream three walls stood up
 wherein a raven bird 369
I had a sweet bird 650
I had a sweet tortoise called Pye 694
I hate this girl 113
I have a cat: I call him Pumpkin 697
I have a friend 653
I have a happy nature 217

I have lived and followed my fate
 without flinching, followed it
 gladly 379
I have no respect for you 48
I have plunged in a poem of the sea
 687
I have two loves 176
I like to get off with people 199
I like to play with him 50
I like to see him drink the gash 391
I like to toss him up and down 300
I long for the desolate valleys 239
I longed for companionship rather
 231
I look at the bottle, when mournful I
 feel 221
I look in the glass 225
I look in the mirror 343
I love little Heber 9
I love my beautiful hat more than
 anything 313
I love the English country scene 574
I love to hear the cock crow in 617
I *love* you, Muse 719
I made Man with too many flaws.
 Yet I love him 466
I married the Earl of Egremont 262
I may be smelly and I may be old 273
I never know what to say 673
I never learnt to attract, you see 205
I only asked my friends to be friendly
 and polite 675
I raised my gun 27
I remember the Roman Emperor, one
 of the cruellest of them 481
I rode with my darling in the dark
 wood at night 296
I saw the ghostly lady fleeting 559
I shall be glad to be silent, Mother,
 and hear you speak 230
I sigh for the heavenly country 215
I stand I fall 62
I stood knee-deep in the sea 526
I thank thee O Lord for my beautiful
 bed 716
I think of the Celts as rather a
 whining lady 402
I thought as I lay on my bed one night,
 I am only a passing cloud 403

I trod a foreign path, dears 535
I used to walk quickly 570
I walked abroad in Easter Park 198
I walked in the graveyard 685
I want to be your pinkie 127
I was a beautiful plant 657
I was always a thoughtful youngster 582
I was consumed by so much hate 228
I was so full of love and joy 464
I was talking one day 64
I went into the wood one day 562
I will forgive you everything 37
I will never leave you darling 439
I wonder why Proust should have thought 495
I'll have your heart. If not by gift, my knife 163
I'm growing much fonder of Barlow 33
I'm sorry to say my dear wife is a dreamer 212
If I lie down upon my bed I must be here 196
Il était une petite fille de dix ans 504
In a shower of tears I sped my fears 160
In front of the mighty washing machine 544
In her loneliness Mabel 723
In his fur the animal rode, and in his fur he strove 398
In my dreams I am always saying goodbye and riding away 139
In protocreation 326
In the cold light of morning she was looking rather queer 153
In the dawn of a sumptuous November 502
In the flame of the flickering fire 138
In the graveyard, in the graveyard 348
In the quiet waters 371
In the wood of Wallow 602
Indolent youth 459
Is Fussy coming? 701
Is it Claudius or Clowdius? my little child Harry said 709
Is it happy for me, is it happy 548

Is it not interesting to see 448
Is it wise 69
Is she not a stupid girl? Just see 662
It is a formal and deserted garden 161
It is not difficult to kill 68
It is the bird of burial 281
It is the very bewitching hour of eight 652
It must be some disease I have 717
It seemed a curious place to rest one's body and take one's ease 82
It was a cynical babe 25
It was a dream and shouldn't I bother about a dream? 373
It was a graveyard scene. The crescent moon 401
It was a house of female habitation 476
It was a human face in my oblivion 646
It was a little captive cat 420
It was a mile of greenest grass 435
It was a slender British bird 579
It was a sweet unnatural rose 727
It was my bridal night I remember 386
It was such a pretty little donkey 616
It was the mighty Engine Drain, the Engine Drain, the Engine Drain 364
It was the War 605

Je ne peux le verstehen 671
Jumbo, Jumbo, Jumbo darling, Jumbo come to Mother 433

Kathleen ni Houlihan 330
King Arthur rode in another world 354

Lamb dead, dead lamb 41
Leave off your singing, Lord Henry de Bohon 715
Left by the ebbing tide of battle 383
Left, right 672
Let all the little poets be gathered together in classes 309
Let me know 67
Lift thy sad heart 670
Listen, all of you, listen, all of you 264

Listening one day on the radio 522
Little bird of brightest laugh 711
Little boy 3
Little Child of brightest face 320
Little children in the sunlight 669
Little Master Home-from-School 119
Little soul so sleek and smiling 545
Look, man, look 524
Lord Barrenstock and Epicene 71
Lord Say-and-Seal, Lord Say-and-Seal 528
Love me, Love me, I cried to the rocks and the trees 213

Mabel was married last week 500
Major Hawkaby Cole Macroo 75
Major is a fine cat 407
Man does not live by bread alone 277
Man is a spirit. This the poor flesh knows 271
Man is coming out of the mountains 269
Man is my darling, my love and my pain 298
Man thinks he was not born to die 679
Many of the English 411
Maria Holt 78
Marriage I Think 663
Men fear the hollow man at the top of tree 332
Miriam and Horlick spend a great deal of time putting off going to bed 702
Miss Pauncefort sang at the top of her voice 20
Miss Snooks was really awfully nice 689
Mother love is a mighty benefaction 723
Mother procure for me a golden crown 584
Mother said if I wore this hat 362
Mother, among the dustbins and the manure 125
Mother, I love you so 181
Mother, mother, let me go 359
Mr Over is dead 299
Mr Petty-Pie 675

Mrs Arbuthnot was a poet 567
Mrs Mouse 406
Mrs Osmosis 83
Mrs Simpkins never had very much to do 10
Mrs Midnight 707
Muriel, Muriel, marry me Muriel 437
My child, my child, watch how he goes 244
My dove, my doe 42
My heart goes out to my Creator in love 422
My heart is fallen in despair 289
My heart leaps up with streams of joy 624
My heart was full of softening showers 218
My life is vile 49
My little dog is called 683
My mother was a romantic girl 5
My mother was Dutch 128
My Muse sits forlorn 468
My soul within the shades of night 253
My true love breathed her latest breath 124
My Uncle from the realms of Death 306

Never again will I weep 59
Never for ever, for ever never, oh 24
No wonder 145
Noble and ethereal he sped upon his way 140
Nobody heard him, the dead man 347
Nobody hears me, nobody sees me 532
Nobody knows what I feel about Freddy 65
None of the other birds seem to like it 723
Northumberland Park Northumberland Park 701
Nourish me on an Egg, Nanny 148
Now is come the horrible mome 678
Now it is time to go for a walk 721
Now pine-needles 92
Now Vole art dead 129

O happy dogs of England 100
O love sweet love 618
O Maximilian stern and wild 73
O never girl beneath the skies of
 Italy 57
O Pug, some people do not like
 you 630
O Queen of Heaven 184
O silent visitation 676
Of all the disgraceful and abominable
 things 389
Often in her bath, ah cold 664
Oh Christianity, Christianity 484
Oh cold and ferocious are the
 children of the cross 165
Oh ho uncircumciséd Sadducee I see
 322
Oh I am a cat that likes to 647
Oh I am certain he will come again
 708
Oh I wish that there were some wing,
 some wing 520
Oh Ichabod, the glory is departed
 672
Oh Lion in a peculiar guise 261
Oh Lord have mercy on my soul 172
Oh Mr Pussy-Cat 406
Oh my darling Goosey-Gander 487
Oh there hasn't been much change
 564
Oh thou intellectual brow – 724
Oh what can be happening pray what
 are they at? 307
Oh what is the terrible thing he has
 done 426
Oh where are ye going ye human
 faces 188
Oh where is the word 667
Oh would that I were a reliable spirit
 careering around 421
Oh, Lamb of God I am 714
Old age is unbecoming, so they say
 712
Ormerod was deeply troubled 210
On a black horse 689
One thousand and one naked ladies
 665
Our Bog is dood, our Bog is dood 302
Our Office cat is a happy cat 321

Our Princess married 608
Out driving one day in the Merc 719
Outside the house 287
Over-dew 637

Parents who can barely afford it 408
Passing at my pleasure's pace 243
People who are always praising the
 past 419
Piggy to Joey 541
Poet, thou art dead and damned 190
Poor human race that must 620
Poor noble Ghost that comes from
 place of pain 412
Porgy Georgie 702
Private Means is dead 77
Profit and Batten 201
Proud Death with swelling port
 comes ruffling by 136
Pull my arm back, Seymour 594
Put out that Light 428

Rapunzel Rapunzel let down your
 hair 291
Rather a fishy thing to do – 671
Revenge, Timotheus cries, and in that
 shout 670
Riding slowly along the banks of a
 canal 315
Rise from your bed of languor 513
Rothebât, Rothebât, the days that are
 gone 167
Ruory loved the aged Edith 726

Satin-clad, with many a pearl 245
Shall I tell you the signs of a New
 Age coming? 353
She got up and went away 726
She is not Indian, she's ill 409
She said as she tumbled the baby in
 203
She was not always so unkind I swear
 93
She went to bed 120
Sholto Peach Harrison you are no
 son of mine 36
Shut me not alive away 329
Sigh no more ladies nor gentleman at
 all 665

Sin recognised – but that – may keep us humble 450
Since what you want, not what you ought 254
Sir 695
Sisley 43
Sitting alone of a summer's evening 121
Some are born to peace and joy 588
Stand off, Mother, let me go! 250
Standing alone on a fence in a spasm 123
Study to deserve Death, they only may 207
Stupid and self-satisfied 672
Such evidence I have of indifference 536
Sweet baby, pretty baby, I bless thee 693
Swift 669

Telly me do 718
Tender only to one 99
Tenuous and Precarious 474
The ages blaspheme 90
The angel that rebellion raised 166
The angels wept to see poor Tolly dead 103
The animal that most loved Hans 720
The beast 732
The Best Beast of the Show 479
The big family 507
The blood flows back behind my eyes 91
The boat that took my love away 110
The boating party 232
The City Dog goes to the drinking trough 214
The Cock of the North 116
The cross begot me on the stone 197
The deathly child is very gay 131
The English are our friends of course 678
The foolish poet wonders 634
The funeral paths are hung with snow 19
The gas fire 499
The grass is green 629

The greatest love? 718
The grief of an unquiet mind is a thing accursed 663
The intellectual Englishman shrank away from the bedside 333
The lads of the village, we read in the lay 156
The Lion dishonoured bids death come 132
The lion sits within his cage 192
The lions who ate the Christians on the sand of the arena 54
The little birdies 728
The love of a mother for her child 268
The man Saul 143
The midwife guards the mother's health 677
The milky love of this bland child 222
The monk sat in his den 286
The mune ha gien her loicht an' gan 696
The nearly right 15
The nervous face of my dear wife 224
The nettle and the bog-wort grew 716
The old sick green parrot 111
The orphan is looking for parents 276
The painters of Spain 17
The pale face stretches across the centuries 531
The parrot 80
The people say that spiritism is a joke and a swizz 32
The pleasures of friendship are exquisite 237
The portrait of my mother 200
The rocks and trees in silence stood 392
The schoolgirls dance on the cold grass 705
The shadow was so black 199
The stricken Belvoir raised a paw and said 58
The tears of the widow of the military man 117
The terrors of the scenery 252
The time is passing now 687
The wood was rather old and dark 60

The world is come upon me, I used to keep it a long way off 295
Then cried the American poet where she lay supine 530
There is a face I know too well 195
There is a fearful solitude 227
There is a god in whom I do not believe 390
There is an old man 730
There is far too much of the suburban classes 16
There was a careful Wykehamist 715
There was a dog called Clanworthy 626
There was a wicked woman called Malady Festing 608
There was an old poet lay dying 685
There were thoughts that came to Phil 539
There's a great many things I'd rather not be than dead 722
There's no new spirit abroad 236
There's so much to be said on either side 664
These before the worlds in congress 682
These hands so well articulated 247
These magnificent words that I read today 568
They do not come separately 570
They gave him a crown of bays and dressed him up 317
They killed a poet by neglect 707
They photographed me young upon a tiger skin 159
They played in the beautiful garden 266
This Baronet is very funny 668
This Englishwoman is so refined 70
This god then, O lord whoever he is do receive into the city 678
This heap of ashes was a learned girl 209
This is my bed 703
This is my earliest love, sweet Death 704
This night shall thy soul be required of thee 593
This old man is sly and wise 319

Thought is superior to dress and circumstance 272
Three angels came to the red red clay 323
Through the Parklands, through the Parklands 38
Tizdal my beautiful cat 576
To a mere 455
To be so cold and yet not old 104
To carry the child into adult life 505
To many men strange fates are given 21
To those who are isolate 251
'Twas the voice of the sweet dove 417
Twas the voice of the Wanderer, I heard her exclaim 292
Two ladies walked on the soft green grass 360

Under wrong trees 488
Underneath the broad hat is the face of the Ambassador 282
Underneath the ice 514
Underneath the speckled leaves 670
Underneath the tangled tree 338
Unpopular, lonely and loving 246
Up and down the streets they go 21
Upon a grave 157
Upon his loneliness and pain 673

Vater Unser 152
Venez vite 173
Very *louche* is this dog, very *louche* 662

Walking one day in the park in winter 429
Walking swiftly with the dreadful duchess 114
Wan 35
Was he married, did he try 451
Was it not curious of Aúgustin 454
We had ridden three days Eugenie and I 334
We have given the Welsh a most *awfully* 717
We have no father and no mother 314
We needs must love the highest when we see it 154

We shall never be one mummy only
463

Weep not my pretty boy, grieve not
my girl 730

What care I if good God be 7

What has happened to the young
men of Eng.? 40

What is she writing? Perhaps it will
be good 350

What is the time, my limber lad 74

What pleased him more 529

What shall I say to the gentlemen,
mother 668

What shall we say of this curious
young man? 56

What's wrong with you-zie? 623

When all was young the Race began
730

When ancient girl is garbed in spite
226

When I awake 676

When one torments another without
cease 688

When shall that fuel fed fire grown
fatter 325

When the sparrow flies to the delicate
branch 248

When the wind is in the East 580

When Watchful came to me he said
551

Where is the sky hurrying to 575

White and yellow were the flowers
130

Who is this that comes in grandeur,
coming from the burning East?
396

Who is this that howls and mutters?
425

Who shall we send to fetch him away
434

Why are the clergy of the Church of
England 385

Why d'you believe that God is cruel
679

Why do I think of Death as a friend?
587

Why do people abuse so much our
busy age? 684

Why do you rage so much against
Christ, against Him 486

Why dost thou dally, Death, and
tarry on the way? 115

Why is the child so pale 94

Why is the word pretty so
underrated? 542

Wicked and corrupt 432

Will ever the stormy seas and the
surges deep 170

William the Dog 695

With my looks I am bound to look
simple or fast I would rather look
simple 427

Would he might come 147

Wretched woman that thou art
304

You are not looking at all well, my
dear 112

You are only one of many 107

You beastly child, I wish you had
miscarried 305

You can't look out of the window
713

You don't look at all well, quite loin
de l'être in fact 405

You hang at dawn, they said 374

You lie there, Anna 655

You never heard of me, I dare 536

You say I must write *another* book?
But I've just written this one 310